WOMEN OF THE FRENCH REVOLUTION

MADAME DU BARRY
From the painting by Madame Vigée-le-Brun.

WOMEN OF THE FRENCH REVOLUTION

By

R. McNAIR WILSON

With 16 Illustrations

KENNIKAT PRESS
Port Washington, N. Y./London

WOMEN OF THE FRENCH REVOLUTION

First published in 1936
Reissued in 1970 by Kennikat Press
Library of Congress Catalog Card No: 72-110928
SBN 8046-0910-1

Manufactured by Taylor Publishing Company   Dallas, Texas

TO

MY DEAR

DORIS MAY

PREFACE

I DO not think that any earlier attempt has been made to tell, in historical sequence, the story of the Women of the French Revolution. My excuse for the present volume is that the lives of these women can scarcely be understood apart from their setting in time, since there is all the difference in the world between the height and the aftermath of a storm.

The bibliography upon which this account is based is of so extensive a character that it has seemed better not to attempt a listing of it. There are, on the one hand, the original sources, and on the other the histories and the biographies. To the number of these I have added lives of Germaine de Staël, of Thérèse Tallien, of Letizia Buonaparte, of the Empress Josephine and of Marie Walewska. Full bibliographies are appended to these studies.

R. McNair Wilson.

London: *Nov.: 1935.*

CONTENTS

Book I

THE BEAUTIES

CHAPTER   PAGE

I. THE KING IS SHORT OF MONEY . . . 19

II. THE KING MARRIES MONEY 24

III. THE CRUSADER 29

IV. CINDERELLA 35

V. THE PRINCESS 43

VI. SUZANNE 46

VII. THE GOVERNESS 54

VIII. GERMAINE 59

IX. THE QUEEN WAS IN THE PARLOUR . . . 67

X. SOPHIE'S MAN 72

XI. AN IMMORAL MAN 82

XII. THE BAKER'S WIFE 90

Book II

THE BLUE STOCKINGS

XIII. " GOLD MINE " 99

XIV. MANON 108

XV. A WOMAN AT BAY 124

XVI. " THE ANGEL OF THE ASSASSINATION " . . 136

XVII. PASSING OF A PURITAN 143

XVIII. THÉRÈSE 149

XIX. THE WOMAN-HATER 160

XX. FAIRY PRINCESS 166

Book III

THE BLOOD-SUCKERS

CHAPTER   PAGE

XXI.   QUEEN BEE 171

XXII.   JOSEPHINE 182

XXIII.   WIFE AND MOTHER 210

XXIV.   DISCIPLINE OF DAMES 223

XXV.   ESTHER 233

XXVI.   DIVORCE 254

XXVII.   WOMAN HAS THE LAST WORD 263

CONCLUSION

XXVIII.   CURTAIN 282

LIST OF ILLUSTRATIONS

MADAME DU BARRY . . . . . . *Frontispiece*

FACING PAGE

MADAME DE POMPADOUR 32

MARIE ANTOINETTE 48

NECKER 64

MIRABEAU 84

SOPHIE DE MONNIER 100

MADAME DE STAËL 112

MADAME ROLAND 128

MAXIMILIAN ROBESPIERRE 144

MADAME TALLIEN 162

JOSEPH FOUCHÉ 176

NAPOLEON AS A YOUNG GENERAL 192

PAUL BARRAS 212

JOSEPHINE 228

THE COUNTESS WALEWSKA 244

MARIE LOUISE 260

INTRODUCTION

THE French Revolution was an experiment, not in politics only but also in human relationships, beliefs and impulses. Its mainspring was the idea that man is the creation of his own reason. Its demand was for freedom, political and intellectual, so that Reason might complete, speedily, the number of her elect. Women, from the first, were sceptical and unenthusiastic.

" The men," wrote Napoleon before the Revolution had begun, " are all in love with Liberty ; they are no longer interested in the women who are jealous."

He was speaking for himself, a callow and embittered lad ; but there was truth nevertheless in his accusation. It is part of the sanity of woman that she has ever rejected the brain as a substitute for the womb and has remained, permanently, unassured that creation in any form can proceed apart from herself and the love of her.

But there are exceptions to this rule—women with men's minds, intellectual women, witty women, restless women, lewd women, greedy women. These welcomed the Revolution with passion of joy, constituted themselves goddesses of Reason and priestesses of Liberty and so came, at a bound, from distrust and contempt to worship. They were Sibyls, Egerias, sooth-sayers, occultists, witches, feminists, full of magic of word and gesture, gadabouts, harlots, vampires. Or they affected a monstrous chastity, which, feeding upon itself, became perversion in sheer incapacity of surrender.

It was no accident that most of these women were connected by blood or marriage with the new class of financiers and bankers who were coming quickly to power by reason of their wealth. There is, has always been and always will be, close association between feminism and rationalism on the one hand and rationalism and money-lending on the other—that is to say between the idea that man made himself and the self-made man. For, inherent in the idea of self-creation is the idea of the survival of the fittest, of self-preservation, of the " law of the jungle," that ogre-like force of circumstances which, as is now commonly believed, transformed fishes into birds, birds into beasts and beasts into men, creating, in its march, fabulous shapes of mermaids and centaurs, and were-wolves, the obscene and melancholy company of the de-natured.

The financiers, long before the Revolution began, had obtained possession, by one means or another, of the bulk of the money in Europe. But their hold upon their wealth was precarious so long as a powerful Church, which forbade money-lending, exerted influence over men's minds and while great Kings retained the right to protect their people from robbers. While, therefore, the Revolution was an experiment in philosophy, it was also a battle to the death between monarchy and money-power.

The women of the Revolution, that is to say the women who became famous during the Revolution, were largely the Amazons of this war. They fought for financial dictatorship with all the weapons which nature had given them, being assured, as they fought, that they were the champions of enlightenment and the foes of superstition and tyranny—that is to say of Christianity and Kingship.

But from first to last as has been suggested these women of the Revolution were opposed by the women of France, the wives and the mothers. The Revolution, even at its height, was a minority movement, and if its authors succeeded, for a time, in convincing large numbers of people, conviction was never robust. There was always Womanhood and Wifehood and Motherhood to oppose it, those eternal witnesses of the truth that creation is by ecstasy and not by reason, by persuasion and not by force, and that the first law of nature is self-sacrifice in passion, and not self-preservation. This is the truth which no philosophy has been able to eradicate from the minds of men. Consequently though the money-lenders and their priestesses triumphed over Church and State and became the Masters of all, men and women have not ceased to look forward to a day of deliverance. That day being now very near at hand, the story of the women possesses a contemporary as well as an historic interest.

BOOK I

THE BEAUTIES

CHAPTER I

THE KING IS SHORT OF MONEY

EARLY in the seventeenth century a small group of men in Amsterdam and London cornered the world's supply of gold. Every government in Europe, consequently, was forced to borrow gold from these men on their own terms.

One government, however, the proudest and strongest of them all, resented the humiliating necessity, and determined to put an end to it. France, under her greatest King, Louis XIV, went to war to break the gold corner, and succeeded so well that for a time the coffers at Versailles were bulging with the precious metal. But war breeds hate. Because the French attacks had been delivered against Austria and Holland, and, later, England, what was essentially a struggle for national freedom began to wear the complexion of a bid for universal power.

The King of England, Charles II, knew better because he, too, was struggling, as his father Charles I had struggled, against the authors of the corner in gold. Charles II kept in close touch with King Louis XIV, helped him, and was helped by him. But the gay and patriotic King of England died while the struggle was still going on, and his brother, James II, who succeeded him, proved unequal to the task he had inherited. James was driven out of the country ; the throne of England passed to his daughter Mary and her husband William, Prince of Orange, who had made himself, already, the champion of the gold corner and its authors. Louis XIV saw England changed, overnight, from friend to enemy. England became the head of the coalition against

France. When John Churchill came to the command of the allied forces, Louis' power was broken.

The old King was bankrupt as well as broken because the wars had drained away all his resources. He was forced, therefore, to humble his pride and ask for loans from the Dutch bankers on the security of his revenues. When he died the Parisians, who were suffering by reason of the increasing burden of taxes, hooted his body as it was carried to the Royal mausoleum at Saint-Denis.

The new King, Louis XV, was a child of five. The people of Paris cheered when he drove among them in a coat of violet velvet, seated on his governess's knees. But cheers change nothing. Louis XV had inherited Louis XIV's burden—namely, the necessity of borrowing gold from the Dutch bankers. He inherited in addition the debts piled up by his kinsman, the Duke of Orleans, who reigned as Regent during his minority. Philippe d'Orléans was on good terms with the Dutch bankers and their partners in Paris. France slipped pleasantly through his gay fingers in exchange for the means of enjoying himself. When the young King began to reign almost everything he possessed was already in pawn.

He was an exceptionally handsome young man to whom women lost their hearts very easily. But he was shy. His ministers had married him at fifteen to a princess of Poland; he had, apparently, fallen in love with her. Paris observed the happy couple gratefully. So virtuous a king, it was prophesied, would not delay to rid the country of the harpies who were devouring all her resources. Ten children, two boys and eight girls, were born in quick succession. The King developed a passion for hunting, and the Parisian prophets began to shake their heads. The King, they said, was too much married.

There was great and sincere rejoicing, therefore, when it became known that Louis had fallen in love for the second time. He was not yet thirty; it was predicted with confidence that Mme de Mailly would inspire him with that soldierly spirit by which alone the bondage of debt could be broken. A writer here and there ventured so far as to hint that such was the hope of France. But, no. This eldest of the de Nesle sisters lacked apparently the qualities of her illustrious ancestors.

Nothing happened. The King, after a short time, transferred his favour to Mme de Vintimille, the second of the sisters, but she died in childbed and left him so desolate that he returned to Mme de Mailly. That did not last long. The youngest of the de Nesle sisters, Mme de Lauragnais, quickly replaced the eldest sister, and was, in her turn, as quickly replaced by another sister, the Marquise de la Tournelle.

This astonishing devotion to a single family gave Versailles and Paris plenty to talk about. Nobody hoped any longer for the change of character which was so much to be desired ; on the contrary, there was convincing witness of the King's lack of boldness, of his shyness and diffidence. But Mme de la Tournelle was not like her sisters. She took Louis in hand and made him realize that he must become Master in his own house. She made a soldier of him and sent him into Flanders to wage a new war for money and freedom.

That campaign was splendidly successful. The young King won the love of his army and became its idol. He became at the same time the idol of Paris and all France. He won -victories just as his ally, Frederick the Great, was winning them. Austria and England and the money-lenders in Amsterdam became seriously alarmed. Was the gold corner going to be broken after all by this dashing and reckless young man ? Mme de la Tournelle, now Duchess of Châteauroux, joined him at the front. They rode together through the camps and received together the congratulations and blessings of France. The name of Marie-Anne de Mailly-Nesle was inscribed upon the hearts of all patriots. When the Austrians attacked in Alsace, she accompanied the King to Metz.

Suddenly glory was transmuted to fear. Louis fell ill and became unconscious. The doctors gave him up and the Bishop of Soissons arrived to administer the last sacraments. He could not perform that holy office, he said, while Mme de Chateauroux remained with the King. Marie-Anne was ordered to go back to Versailles. Along with her went the rumour that she was the cause of the King's illness and that her excesses had destroyed his constitution. Love of her died in every heart, and angry mobs attended her carriage at every posting-place. She was hooted and stoned and barely escaped with her life. The Queen travelled to Metz. France went into mourning.

Then the King recovered. He returned to Paris a conqueror and the city went mad with joy, calling him *Bien Aimé*, and saviour. Marie-Anne was recalled, instantly, to her lover's side. Titles and honours were heaped upon her and the Bishop of Soissons lost his post as Royal chaplain. A month or two later she died declaring, with her last breath, that she had been poisoned.

The foundation of Louis' character, so laboriously builded by this girl who, when she died, was only twenty-seven, began immediately to crumble. The King passed from despair to diffidence. He resolved, suddenly, to go back to his armies and took his young son, the Dauphin, with him. He was just in time to play a part in the Battle of Fontenoy when his Marshal Saxe won the most spectacular victory in the history of Old France—the only victory France had won against England. Next year Louis was present at the taking of Brussels, Antwerp, Mons, Charleroi and Namur. Saxe won the victories of Raucoux and Lawfeld.

Austria was humbled, Holland was conquered. Even England had suffered severely. But the object of the campaign had not been attained. The corner remained, the gold, as the armies advanced, had been removed from Amsterdam to London. Louis had spent 120,000,000 francs and could scarcely obtain a penny. He needed ready money. There was no way of obtaining it except a war with England or a loan.

This was the weakness which the outside world did not see.

It was the weakness which, since Marie-Anne's death, had troubled the King more and more. He had defeated armies and taken rich cities ; he had not obtained money. On the contrary, he had been forced, month after month, to spend like water what money he possessed. Worse still, he had been forced to borrow from the bankers in Paris who, as he understood, were in close touch with the bankers in Amsterdam and London.

That necessity of borrowing is the key to many mysteries, notably to the mystery of the choice of a successor to Marie-Anne. The Parisian bankers, who alone could supply the means of victory, were anxious, above everything, to obtain a footing for themselves and their wives in French society. They wanted to break down the barriers which excluded them from Versailles. As the King's demands for money grew more insistent the idea formed in their minds of asking for the official position of *maîtresse déclarée* for one of their own womenfolk.

CHAPTER II

THE KING MARRIES MONEY

THE Parisian bankers had already chosen their candidate for the King's favour. She was Jeanne Antoinette Poisson, a girl whose beauty had earned for her, in her teens, the nickname of " *morceau du roi.*" Jeanne had been baptized as the legitimate daughter of François Poisson, an officer in the household of the Duke of Orleans, and of his wife, Madeleine de la Motte, but had been adopted, while very young, by a financier named Le Normant de Tournehem, who gave her an exceedingly good education, and then when she was twenty, married her to his nephew, Le Normant d'Etioles. This young man was also a banker. He was very rich and his wife became, immediately, a leader of middle-class society in Paris.

She was as clever and as talented as she was beautiful. Moreover she possessed a capacity for discussing political questions which attracted to her side the men who, at that time, were making ready to undermine the foundations of European society. These men agreed with her that it was monstrous that her beauty and her wit could not secure for her entry to the King's palace. Was a banker's blood not as good as the blood of a beggarly noble? After all, King and nobles were eager enough to borrow the bankers' money.

Mme d'Etioles was fully instructed about the object of the King's war in Flanders. She knew all about the corner in gold and realized fully that the power of her husband and his friends was based upon that corner. They were the masters because nobody could obtain large supplies of money except by borrowing from them. She was ready, consequently, to play her part in supporting the corner and defeating the attempt of the King to break it.

Personal ambition, undoubtedly, played a large part in determining this attitude. But Jeanne's ambition was not solely personal. She represented a class which, everywhere in Europe, was chafing at the restraints imposed upon it by feudal custom and struggling to have these restraints abolished. She was militant, calculating, resourceful, and she possessed a crusading spirit which was anything but narrowly selfish. The idea of forcing her way into the circle of the Court and making herself mistress there was no impulse of a vainglorious girl. It was rather the plan of a woman who knew that the means of accomplishing her end lay ready to her hand and who was furnished, in advance, with a plan of campaign. Jeanne meant to conquer King Louis. She was persuaded that King Louis had no option but to allow himself to be conquered, seeing that his need of money was so great. She was determined that her conquest, once made, should place the King, irrevocably, in the hands of her people.

Soon after Mme de Châteauroux's death the city of Paris gave a ball in honour of the Dauphin. Jeanne, as queen of the financial world, was presented to the King, who was still mourning his loss. Louis showed her marked attention. A few months later she abandoned her home and her husband and went to live at Versailles as *maîtresse déclarée*.

The King had married money, breaking thereby all the traditions of his house and office. Jeanne, now to be called Marquise de Pompadour, had broken down the stoutest barriers in the world and flung open the palace gates to the new nobility of money. Louis professed himself ravished ; but the melancholy which had fallen upon him when Marie-Anne died was not relieved.

There is, perhaps, an instinct of Kings which warns its possessor of impending catastrophe. Louis would have been a

much less clever man than he was had he not seen in his new
favourite a portent and a shadow. This woman of the city with
her agile wits and her clear brain was different, entirely, from
the women who, until now, had surrounded him—the Queen
and Mme de Mailly and Marie-Anne. They were his womenfolk ; she belonged to the lives of other men. They held him in
veneration ; she had no knowledge, apparently, of the meaning
of that word. In Versailles, as in Paris, she was determined to
make and hold her position by virtue of her own personality, so
that it was necessary to remember, sometimes, that her position
depended upon his favour. What could he do ? A King who
must borrow is a King in exile, and the hand that gives is above
the hand that takes. He listened to her advice that he should
make peace without demanding harsh terms of his beaten
enemies and, to the astonishment of the world, acted upon it.
He gave up Belgium, two Dutch provinces with Berg-op-Zoom
and Maestricht, Genoa and Madras. The English restored to
him the little island of Cap Breton. His enemies rubbed their
eyes as they signed the incredible treaty of Aix-la-Chapelle.

But the philosophers who thronged the bankers' drawing-
rooms in Paris, and who were all Mme de Pompadour's friends,
expressed a lively approval.

" The King looks upon Victory," said Duclos, in a speech to
the Academy, " as a misfortune for mankind, and in the title
of hero he sees only the cruel necessity of being a hero in truth."

The war had cost the lives of 100,000 men and France was full
of wounded and disabled soldiers. The King had to borrow
once more in order to succour these men and had to pledge,
further, his credit and that of France in order to borrow. He
was sinking deeper into the mire and could see no way of
extricating himself. His melancholy, like that of all hopeless
debtors, became a settled habit so that a craving for gaiety
began to devour him. Mme de Pompadour knew how to
feed that craving and how, by feeding it, to ruin what was left
of his character. She ceased to be his mistress and became,

instead, his procuress. While he amused himself by hunting young women or stags, she gathered up the reins of government.

What did Louis care ? He knew what was past and he saw what was coming. No man was more completely convinced than he that all hope of breaking the corner in gold might now be abandoned. Those who wanted money for any purpose would, in future, have to borrow it from what was, in fact, an international syndicate. Consequently, the King of France, like all the other Kings in Europe, was a prisoner within his own kingdom. He could initiate nothing and effect nothing. The reason for his existence had vanished. A stupid man might have tried to make the best of this position ; but Louis was not stupid. On the contrary, he was as clear-sighted as he was proud. He knew that, sooner or later, the power which had overcome and replaced the power of Kings would cast down their thrones into the gutter if the Kings refused to play a lackey's part. Why, in such circumstances, play any part at all ? If one could not be King one could philander and hunt. " After me, the deluge."

The King sat idling in the room where the Pompadour worked. She read the despatches, the reports, the secret memoranda, annotating them in her firm hand. She received the ministers and ambassadors, even the generals and admirals. She ruled the Court and set the fashions for France and Europe. Every hour was quick with her enthusiasm so that none observed the weariness on the Royal features or the smile, half-melancholy, half-cynical, on the Royal lips.

Had those lips spoken they might have told that a new kind of woman was being fashioned to fit the new kind of world that was coming. Woman multiplied in vanity, in restlessness, in appetites, in wit, in capacity. In love, too, and the excitements of lovers. Woman let loose from her history and her traditions, from custom and habit, from womanhood even. But having zeal like a Crusader and the lively sense of mission and object to rescue her from harlotry. The old orders were no match for this prodigy. Mme de Pompadour played the philosophers, with Voltaire at their head, against the Jesuits, the Queen and the Dauphin. She played the magistracy and the *salons* against the Court, the Austrian party among the ministers against the Prussian party, and against them all, on occasion, Majesty himself. Against the King she played the power of the purse.

CHAPTER III

THE CRUSADER

MME DE POMPADOUR spent money in a way which made Europe dizzy. Even virtue grew ashamed of her homespuns in the presence of this glory, to which a thousand artists of every complexion made daily contribution. Palaces were rebuilt; gardens replanned; furniture remodelled. Frocks and millinery cast away their childhood. Food, and even wine, were born again.

The King paid, having first borrowed the money from Mme de Pompadour's friends in Paris and Amsterdam and London. Noblemen's wives and daughters demanded finer feathers and their husbands and fathers were compelled to find more money. They, too, borrowed from Mme de Pompadour's friends. The rage for luxury spread to Paris and to every provincial town. Everybody borrowed from Mme de Pompadour's friends.

Seeing that these friends owned all the ready money in Europe, that was inevitable. Lands, castles, houses, gold and silver plate, jewels—all were pledged to the counting-houses in exchange for credit. And still the butterflies at Versailles and in Paris were unsatisfied. Under the Pompadour's sway fashions changed so quickly that it was necessary to spend without reckoning in order to keep pace with them. Mme de Pompadour's friends saw the old nobility of France being shepherded to bankruptcy by laughing girls. As hope ebbed away, gaiety grew more reckless. The *tempo* of life quickened.

The interest of life too. When people are deep in debt they

tend to feel that something is going to happen. The women, who were ruining their husbands in order to keep in Mme de Pompadour's fashions, began to chatter about revolution. They began to listen to philosophers who assured them that the old world, their world, was dead. Mme de Pompadour was surrounded by philosophers, and even the King talked to them. The fact that the philosophers entertained uncanonical views about love which made husbands and priests very angry was an added attraction. One could no longer afford to be frumpish, even in personal relations. The necessity of wringing as much money as possible out of one's estates in order to pay the interest on loans was regrettable ; but it was not found to be an obstacle to discussions about the Rights of Man and the Social Contract. Versailles became something of a debating society, with the Pompadour in the chair.

She kept sleepless vigil when the butterflies were abed. The spirit which had carried her to power burned, always, with a more intense flame. Her people were eating up those courtiers. Every day held its conquest, another great name humbled, a fresh slice of immemorial France pledged to the counting-houses, a new haul of gold or jewels. Her thin lips were compressed. No more campaigns in Flanders against the Masters of Europe.

" If I were King," the Dauphin told his mother, " I would make such an example of that woman as would terrify for a century any having designs against a King's honour."

She knew better. Whoever was King would be compelled to borrow from her friends, if only for the purpose of making war upon them. Kingship was impotent ; soon it would be wholly discredited.

So also thought Frederick the Great, King of Prussia. Frederick, since the glorious days when, as France's ally, he had saved his people and established his throne, had been watching affairs at Versailles with anxiety. The King of Prussia had no illusions about Mme de Pompadour. He knew her for what she was, a cold, hard almost spinsterish agent of the new aristocracy of debt, who cherished in her heart hatred, amounting to fanaticism, against the old aristocracy of service. Mme de Pompadour was *bourgeois* to the bone, a woman on the make not from greed or vanity solely but because " the make " is the appointed end of every good *bourgeois*. With passionate sincerity, as Frederick of Prussia perceived, she was engaged in delivering King Louis and his Court into the hands of the Philistines, satisfying in that work the needs of her own embittered spirit. The woman for all her splendour was Puritan and Stoic, a Greek come to the judgment of disintegrating Christendom.

Frederick knew the type. Especially he understood the lack of humour, even of human feeling, which always characterises it. He began to write and broadcast ditties about the " little fish " who was swimming so gaily in the Royal pond at Versailles. As he very well understood the reference to the Pompadour's surname, Poisson, was likely to occasion her mortification and burning anger. He was not mistaken. The "*poissonades,*" as Paris called them, aroused all the violence of the woman's hatred against nobility, producing an apoplexy of rage and despair.

Mme de Pompadour was ruling France now, with the help of the duc de Choiseul and his masculine sister the duchesse de Grammont, because the work of debauching the King had been pursued so successfully that he had ceased to interfere. She let it be known that King Frederick had wounded her to the quick and that she would not rest until she was revenged on him. The news was carried to Vienna where Maria Theresa was smarting still under the chastisement which Frederick had administered to her forces in the recent war. Maria Theresa caused the Pompadour to be informed that she, the Empress, understood and sympathized. Instantly the idea of a Franco-Austrian alliance against Frederick began to form in Mme de Pompadour's mind.

It says much for the skill of Maria Theresa that this idea soon became the dominant note of French statecraft. The Empress, at Vienna, was a pious and sentimental woman with a long head, a sharp eye and an exceedingly greedy appetite. Astonishingly unscrupulous where her own interests were concerned, she had managed to play the part of respectable widow before Europe and thus to win sympathy against Frederick. Mme de Pompadour easily convinced herself that this was an example of womanhood being victimized by male aggression, and thus united the Austrian quarrel with Frederick to her own personal quarrel. Nor was the fact that the merchants of debt wanted a war between France and Prussia any obstacle to this union. Mme de Pompadour never acted without the advice and approval of her own people.

The truth was that King Frederick was become too powerful for the taste of the London and Amsterdam money-lenders. Frederick disliked money-lenders and refused, so far as possible, to borrow from them. It was necessary to get him into debt and thus into a state where he could be controlled. There is nothing like a war for achieving this purpose. In addition, the moment had come for the transfer of the French Empire, India and Canada, to British possession. As the new financial centre, London needed a free hand in every part of the world.

To Frederick's surprise, therefore, the "*poissonades*" drove France into the arms of her hereditary enemy, Austria, and led, very quickly, to a declaration of war by France and Austria against himself. The Seven Years' War began. Almost immediately England became Frederick's ally. While the great Prussian soldier was defeating and destroying the French and Austrian armies, the British Navy made itself mistress of the Seas. Canada, most of India and numberless smaller French possessions passed into English hands. The British Empire was created.

When the war ended France and Prussia and Austria were loaded with debt ; London, on the contrary, had become the

MADAME DE POMPADOUR

world's creditor, as well as the owner of most of the world. In face of that tremendous fact the defeat of the French was matter of as little importance as the victory of Frederick. The King of Prussia retired, in bitterness, from his triumphs and opened negotiations with Maria Theresa and the Empress Catherine of Russia for the partition of Poland—as a means of recouping some of the losses. Mme de Pompadour was abandoned among the ruins of the Bourbon Empire.

And not of the Bourbon Empire alone. The European system of Louis XIV had been wrecked. France, formerly the friend of Prussia against Austria, was now isolated. The German peoples were drawing together. That fierce and capable woman, the Empress Catherine of Russia, was ranging herself behind the Teutons, while England, mistress of all the seas, remained implacably hostile to her neighbour on the other side of the Channel. A mountainous debt to Amsterdam and Geneva and Genoa weighed upon King Louis, who, by losing India and Canada, had lost the means of paying it.

In such circumstances kings must submit to the demands of bankers, no matter how ruinous these demands may be. What King Louis' creditors demanded of him was that he should greatly increase taxation, while, at the same time, cutting down expenses. He obeyed and became involved, at once, in furious quarrels with his nobles, who refused to pay him an additional farthing. Thus, to defeat and loss of empire was added revolt within the Kingdom itself.

Mme de Pompadour had completed her work. She was grown thin and had a persistent cough which her doctors warned her was a sign that her lungs were affected. But she would not listen to her doctors. Her skinny hands clutched at the reins ; the fever of her crusade burned with ever more intense flame, as though ruin was not enough. In ecstasy of bitterness she likened herself to Christ, proclaiming a martyrdom without end. Her disease-ridden body wasted away. In the middle of her labours of government, suddenly she was stricken down.

Louis commanded that she should confess herself and receive the last sacrament. A priest was brought to her bedroom. As he was going away she bade him " wait a moment " in order that she might go with him. It was the last flicker of her dauntless spirit. Her body was taken from Versailles that same evening. The King watched the funeral from a window of the palace. There were tears in his eyes, but his sole comment was the remark :

" Madame has a cold day for her journey."

CHAPTER IV

CINDERELLA

MME DE POMPADOUR left, as her legacy to France, the betrothal of the King's grand-nephew to the Archduchess Marie Antoinette of Austria, daughter of the Empress Maria Theresa. The young man was Louis' heir, for death had already removed the King's son and grandson. The Austrian girl, in consequence, would be Queen.

Louis was not enthusiastic, for the betrothal had taken place during the Seven Years' War, before the time of great disaster. But he was the last man to go back on a bargain of that sort. Let France have her Austrian Queen. He turned wearily to the business of Kingship as a bankrupt to his ruined affairs. Nothing, so far as he could see, could now make any difference.

That mood lasted until a successor to Mme de Pompadour was found in a girl named Jeanne Bécu. Jeanne was the illegitimate daughter of a cook. She had been sent as a child to a convent by a certain Dumonceaux, a financier, in whose kitchen her mother worked, who was attracted by her beauty. Later she had been saleswoman in a fashionable dressmaking shop in Paris, where she had met a drunken and wholly disreputable fellow, Count Jean du Barry. She had been du Barry's mistress for some four years, during which time he had lived upon her immoral earnings. Her lovers included the duc de Ligne, General Dumouriez, the Duke of Berwick and the duc de Richelieu. Her meeting with the King in the park at Versailles had followed.

It was an accidental meeting. But Louis was so greatly

attracted that he sent for the girl. When she came to him her gaiety and good humour thawed immediately the frost of gloom in which, for long, he had been held prisoner. Louis, like most active-minded men, possessed no weapons of the spirit against frustration. It was Jeanne Bécu's achievement that, with a laugh, she convinced him of the continuing excellence of life. The King was invited, tempted even, to descend the stairs to those kitchen regions where, if everything counts, nothing matters and where misfortune and frustration are discounted with a shrug. Louis had married money and knew the ineffable boredom of the daughters of usury. The spirit, which Mme de Pompadour had quenched, flamed up suddenly in the genial presence of this child of the gutter, whose values were red blood and hunger and action. Jeanne Bécu was bidden to Versailles after she had been married, discreetly, to the brother of her former " protector," the Count William du Barry. Louis gave her the house of an earlier favourite, a delicious little villa hidden and yet close at hand.

But Jeanne did not wish to be hidden. She wished to be Cinderella at the ball, the envy of all the ugly sisters. Native wit began to oppose itself to Royal scruples. The girl looked about for allies and found the party which had suffered under Mme de Pompadour—the party which, from the beginning, had been opposed to the money-lenders and financiers in Paris. This party included the Jesuits. Its leader was the duc de Richelieu. Jeanne became its staunch supporter.

Thus she became, in a sense, the mainstay of Clericalism and Royalism against that rich and arrogant middle class of which Mme de Pompadour had been the support. The gutter, as often before in history, was come to the rescue of the throne. Jeanne bade the King awake out of his torpor and play a man's part. She persuaded him to get rid of the Pompadour's people, de Choiseul and the others, and gather about him men who would fight for what remained of the Royal authority. She succeeded, even, in awakening a flicker of hope. Louis began to reign once more and his people, always responsive to leadership, called him again their " well-beloved."

He recognized the service which had been rendered him and rewarded it. Jeanne was presented at Court to the delight of the Parisians and the confusion of the new-rich. The bankers and their friends felt themselves grossly insulted by the honour paid to a cook's daughter; nor was the insult made more easy to endure by the knowledge that the cook's daughter had succeeded to the power and prestige of the Pompadour. Louis, it may be, understood these feelings because, from the beginning, monarchy has relied upon the common people rather than upon wealth or power. The King was ever the people's man. As for Jeanne, she was wild with delight. Unlike Mme de Pompadour, who had been awkward and stiff at her presentation, she displayed, on that great occasion, a lively grace which won the admiration of her enemies. She actually kept the King and his Court waiting; but when she came, with hair powdered and cheeks glowing, a figure of youth and loveliness, there was forgiveness.

No more secrecy after this. Jeanne was an official now of the Court, with her own suite in the palace, and with the right to play her part in the nation's affairs. The nation, far from resenting it, glowed with satisfaction. Never was a girl so justly entitled by her beauty to be a King's mistress. Where is the people, after all, which does not exalt beauty above blood or money? The nobles and the bankers had had their turn; it was the turn now of the common folk. And this common folk had given to Majesty the loveliest lady of all his galaxy. That was admitted by all. The people were proud of Jeanne.

Pride grew when the girl displayed qualities of common-sense as well as qualities of vigour and activity. Jeanne, unlike the Pompadour, held the King's office in respect. She believed, as all her folk believed, that France needed a King and that, in the King's weakness, the people was humiliated. She had the gutter's profound suspicion of wealth—the gutter's contempt too. None in France realized more clearly than she that France had been betrayed and ruined ; and if the means of betrayal lay beyond her knowledge, the fact sufficed. She gave Louis her strength of body and spirit for use against enemies who were hers as well as his.

The King was sixty years of age and his debaucheries had not lightened the burden of his years. Nevertheless, he fell in love with this girl sincerely and even passionately. She became, very soon, wholly indispensable to him, so that he could scarcely endure to be separated from her. In her presence his strength seemed to return to him so that he thought and acted as if he was still master in his kingdom. Commands went forth from Versailles to all the provinces of France and bodies which had been accustomed to flout the Royal power learned, anew, to respect it. Chief among these was the so-called *parlement* of Paris. This assembly, which had enjoyed great liberty of action under Mme de Pompadour, was bitterly hostile to the du Barry. When, at her urging, the King dismissed the duc de Choiseul, the Pompadour's favourite, the *parlement* refused to meet and thus brought a large volume of business to a standstill. Louis replied by dissolving the *parlement* and then, at once, through his new Minister Maupeou, turned upon all the other *parlements* in France and brought them to submission.

These *parlements*, though ancient institutions, were now largely controlled by the new rich, the men who had cornered the world's money and their associates, the Parisian bankers and financiers. The whole body of organized wealth ranged itself instantly against the King and his mistress. And since a large part of the nobility, as has been said, was already in debt to these money-lenders, noblemen were not lacking to support the cause of the *parlements*. Noblemen paid no taxes ; but if the King succeeded in making himself master that privilege would be abolished.

An opposition which included blood and money on this lavish scale might very well have daunted stout hearts. But it did not daunt Mme du Barry. She knew, instinctively, that in this quarrel the King had the people on his side—that great mass of men and women who were being compelled, by high prices and heavy taxes, to pay the interest on the loans made to the nobles. The girl from the gutter was doubtless wholly ignorant of finance and politics, but her common-sense assured her. Louis would have France behind him, she believed, if he broke the nobles' power and compelled them to shoulder their share of the national burden. It was the indispensable first step towards the control of wealth because, unless he could find new taxpayers, the King could not hope to escape from the money-lenders' clutches.

As it happened these convictions were shared by Voltaire, who was watching Mme du Barry and her favourite Maupeou, with an astonishment which he did not hide and who declared that Maupeou had " restored to the King the whole of France." Voltaire was not sure that he liked the restoration because his instincts were republican—his tribute is the more impressive on that account.

Louis played his new part with a zest which suggested that he really believed he could overcome his difficulties. But that was tribute to Jeanne du Barry rather than sincere conviction. Like Charles II of England, Louis XV understood enough about what is now called " high finance " to realize that practically no hope existed of escaping out of its clutches. The men who had succeeded in seizing the world's stock of gold and who had held that stock against all the armies of Louis XIV, were secure behind the British Fleet. Thanks to Mme de Pompadour and her Seven Years' War, they were in possession of nearly all the sources of Colonial produce. Nor had England herself dared to dispute their virtual ownership of her resources. The British Government was as deeply in their debt as the French Government.

In these circumstances it would be necessary to salvation to begin the Seven Years' War over again. That was impossible.

The only means of relief, therefore, was to organize the kingdom in such a way that it would become self-supporting.

Louis realized much more clearly than either his Minister or his mistress how difficult a task such organization must be. He knew that, in any prolonged struggle with the nobility, he would have against him the whole power of money, seeing that taxes paid to the King would be interest on loans taken from the money-lenders. The nobles, too, would try to pass on such burdens as he imposed on them to their tenants and would thus rouse the anger of farmers and craftsmen who, probably, would come to believe that their troubles originated with the King. Thus the people might be alienated from the Throne by the very measures taken to secure their welfare.

That, with these ideas clearly in mind, this ageing and cynical monarch acted resolutely, is testimony to his mistress's influence. The King, who had said, and who still in his heart of hearts believed, that the " deluge " must follow his reign, behaved now as though opposition existed only to be crushed. There was a clean sweep of the rebellious nobles ; the philosophers and their books were banished ; Versailles became once more the King's house. Preparations to impose taxation on the whole of the nobility were pushed forward.

So sudden and so vigorous was the assault that even money adopted a conciliatory tone. If the King became self-supporting, that is to say if he was able to meet his expenses out of his income, his power would, undoubtedly, be increased. In such circumstances, his dependence on money-lenders would come to an end. The Parisian bankers reduced the rates of interest which they were accustomed to charge and professed a lively satisfaction—which they were far from feeling—at the new turn of events. Foreign Courts, too, grew respectful once more. Maria Theresa actually condescended to flatter little Jeanne Bécu, while the Poles, writhing under Russian and Prussian and Austrian heels, appealed to her to save them.

But there was one woman in the world who would have no

dealings with the du Barry—namely, the wife of the Dauphin, Marie Antoinette of Austria. Never were mother and daughter less like one another than Maria Theresa and the girl who, when King Louis died, would be Queen of France. The mother was suave and diplomatic, under her façade of matron and moralist; the daughter proved unbending, generous, honest. Marie Antoinette had come to Versailles in rather difficult circumstances. For the Pompadour, who had arranged her marriage with the Dauphin, was dead and the policy of which her marriage had been a part, was covered with shame. The price of this Austrian princess had been the whole French Colonial Empire, including India. She was a pretty girl, but scarcely, in French eyes, worth that price. France was not unduly elated by her coming to Versailles.

Nor was Versailles specially eager to receive her. Louis was in the act of embarking on his new policy—which was a complete reversal of Mme de Pompadour's policy. The little Austrian came, like the uneasy ghost of a past which everyone was anxious to bury. Even the charm of French manners could not completely obliterate the fact that she was a bad bargain which nothing but an exalted sense of honour could have saved from repudiation.

The girl reacted instinctively and strongly. She wrote to her mother that she found the King charming but that she could not endure the favourite on any terms. And she made her early friends among the enemies of the du Barry, among, that is to say, the opponents of the new Kingship. These, after all, were the people who still, some of them at any rate, professed to believe in the Austrian policy.

But Marie Antoinette, as the friend of liberals, philosophers and money-lenders, was a figure of pathos. Every instinct of her being was opposed to all such people and she contrived to endure them only by giving herself, immediately, to a gaiety which was as reckless as it was innocent. The little Dauphine was gay because she was unhappy. Versailles, with its profligacy, had shocked her ; the realization that she was the skeleton at the feast in Versailles had shocked her ; Jeanne du Barry shocked her, but so also did the opinions of Jeanne du Barry's enemies. And over and above all these distresses was the personal distress of her relations with her young husband. The Dauphin suffered from a congenital defect which made him impotent, until that defect was cured by a surgical operation—a matter of years.

CHAPTER V

THE PRINCESS

MARIE ANTOINETTE'S wild gaiety, her flirtations with liberalism and finance and her choice of friends among those noblemen who were most anxious to defeat the King, made an unfavourable impression. Nobody took her seriously, but many looked forward with anxiety to the day when she and her timid and uneasy husband would ascend the throne.

King Louis was among this number. He exerted himself to make the Austrian girl feel at home and so to remove the occasion of her opposition; and he made use of the Austrian Ambassador to urge upon her a greater circumspection in the choice of friends. Letters of admonition from Maria Theresa reached Versailles in great numbers. Marie Antoinette was urged by her mother to pay the utmost respect to the King and to display a friendly spirit towards the du Barry. She was bidden, also, to remember her simple and pious upbringing and to renounce her butterfly existence.

The girl wrote dutiful replies and plunged deeper into gaiety. She was hurt, wounded, affronted. She spent money like water and gathered about her a Court of Spendthrifts more reckless than herself. These were nobles whom the King was trying to deprive of their privileges. Marie Antoinette became the defender of rebels and a focus of disaffection, and drew her husband, whose deficiency had robbed him of authority, into her circle. These two were called liberal and enlightened by men and women whose sole concern it was to avoid contributing anything to the national expenditure.

43

The effect upon Marie Antoinette's character was disastrous, because her conduct and her instincts were divorced. She was an able woman with a strong mind which approved of everything that the King and his mistress were doing and which repudiated utterly the sentimental opinions of their opponents. Instinct, therefore, had to be suppressed; and imperiousness lost its wisdom and grew stubborn. A great queen was debased to a partisan of the greedy and implacable enemies of monarchy. Nor did the mischief stop with the woman. Her husband, too, became involved in it. The Dauphin fell into the error of supposing that the royal authority ought not to be exercised against a nobility which was, apparently, deeply imbued with liberal principles. This Dauphin was a gentle soul, brave and honest and eager above all things for the welfare of France ; he was to learn that a King's first business consists in protecting the sheep from the wolves.

It is a tragedy of history, certainly, that Marie Antoinette and Jeanne du Barry never became friends. Had they done so, the resolute policy of the mistress would have discovered in the Queen an exponent of genius. Marie Antoinette, fortified by her instincts, would have co-operated with her husband in abolishing privilege and imposing service upon the whole body of the nobles. The nobility might thus have been compelled to serve and been prevented from passing on their burdens to the people. In consequence, the King might have become financially independent and thus have been able to offer some sort of resistance to the money-lenders. Even the sceptical Louis XV had begun to believe, however half-heartedly, in the possibility of such an outcome. And, in his case, belief reposed solely upon Jeanne. What the girl from the gutter had accomplished doubtfully in the case of a worn-out debauchée, might have been accomplished splendidly by a daughter of the Hapsburgs as Queen of France and wife of a generous-hearted and courageous young King.

Louis XV realized the possibility ; so did Jeanne du Barry.

The mistress, indeed, humiliated herself again and again to establish friendly relations with the princess. Every agency of influence, including that of the King's frumpish daughters, was canvassed. The Austrian Ambassador and his Empress renewed their solicitations. But Marie Antoinette was ice. To her mother she replied that " the woman " revolted her, to the King's daughters that she refused to insult them. They were ungrateful for this courtesy and gave her the name of ill-omen, " Austrichienne," which was to follow her to her life's end. The very utmost which she could be persuaded to accord was a chill recognition of the favourite when they happened to meet one another.

And so it lasted until Louis, with his work still unaccomplished, was stricken down by smallpox. The King, on realizing the nature of his illness, gave himself up immediately for lost. He craved the office of Holy Church and bade Jeanne du Barry farewell. She was escorted from Versailles the same evening. Next morning the King asked for her and was told what had happened.

" What," he cried, " she has gone already ! "

It was not Jeanne's fault. She had nursed her friend with great devotion, well knowing the nature of his disease ; and she had pleaded with tears to be allowed to go on nursing him. But her enemies, and the King's enemies, would brook no delay. The King, they urged, must not die in his mistress' arms.

Paris heard the news and parties of sightseers began to arrive at Versailles. They picnicked in the park, where vendors of wine and food did a brisk trade. When evening fell a candle was lighted in the window of the King's bedroom to show that he was still alive. Thousands of eyes held that flickering flame in constant view. The flame was extinguished. An usher came out into the ante-room and spoke the usual formula :

" *Le roi est mort : Vive le roi !* "

Marie Antoinette was Queen of France.

CHAPTER VI

SUZANNE

ONCE again the Parisians hooted a dead King's funeral—
which took place in this instance by night—and welcomed his successor with rapture. On the morrow
of his accession Louis XVI and his Austrian wife were the most
popular figures in Europe.

They were popular, however, with different groups for
different reasons. The mass of the people loved them because
Louis XV had won the mass of the people by his campaign
against the nobles and the bankers, and it was believed that
Louis XVI would carry on the work. The nobles and bankers,
on the other hand, felt good hope that their days of tribulation
were ended. They had the Queen on their side.

Marie Antoinette, as they had already discovered, preferred
those who agreed with her and flattered her to those who gave
her advice. Care was taken to surround her with friends who
understood her weaknesses and knew how to exploit them.
The taste for excitement, which she had acquired in the first
days of her married life, was defended as a sign of a vivid and
eager personality, and the Queen was encouraged in every
possible way to gratify her whims without, for a moment,
counting the cost. Was not the French Monarchy the richest
in Europe ?

The King offered no objection. Louis remained deeply in
love with his wife. His difficulties as a husband had been
resolved, but the shadow cast by them remained so that he had
become incapable of exerting authority. This weakness, added

to a shy and nervous disposition, made him in almost everything his wife's slave. Had Marie Antoinette loved him that would not have mattered; but her heart, as her letters show, had been given to another—namely, Count Fersen, a Swede. She remained strictly and even rigidly faithful to Louis; but she had no deep sympathy with him. Nor did the births of her children bring about any change.

Louis, on the other hand, found himself, from the first moment of his reign, in the same grave financial difficulties which had beset his predecessor. He had to get money somehow if disaster was to be avoided; he must, therefore, follow in the footsteps of Louis XV and Mme du Barry. That was, emphatically, the view of his minister, Turgot, a man of uncouth manners, but of exceptional ability and honesty. The position as Turgot saw it was simple : the fact that the nobles were privileged to pay no taxes made it necessary to impose the whole burden of taxation on the peasantry and the poor. Such a system, which had been instituted when noblemen were compelled to keep and arm troops or ships for the King's service, was ruinous at a time when the King kept his own army and navy and paid for them out of his own income.

" You must force the nobles to pay taxes," Turgot urged, " because if they do not pay, you will either have to sacrifice the defences of the country or beg the money-lenders to supply you with funds. And if you go to the money-lenders, they, and not you, will reign in France."

It was the old difficulty expressed once more in forcible language. The King made it known that he would persist in the old policy. He would not borrow. He would cut down expenses at Versailles and he would force every nobleman to pay his due share of the national expenditure.

He knew, of course, that these plans would be opposed by the nobles and the higher clergy; but it is doubtful if he realized how violent the opposition was destined to become. Nor did he expect to meet opposition upon his own hearth. When, therefore, the Queen took sides against him, he was plunged into a most lively distress. He tried to explain, to argue, to remonstrate ; but he failed to make any impression.

Marie Antoinette's point was that for the sake of objects which she did not pretend to understand, her gay Court of Versailles was to be changed into a nunnery. What, did the King propose to cut down the allowances which she made to her friends ? Gabrielle de Polignac, for example ? Did he suggest that the Queen of France should not continue to be the best customer of the great Parisian houses ? If money was scarce, why not borrow ? All the bankers of the world were ready, eager, to lend to the King of France.

These questions were not solely of the Queen's making. Everyone who felt himself endangered by the King's economy campaign rushed to Marie Antoinette. The cleverest brains at Court were busy inventing objections and difficulties wherewith to supply Marie Antoinette's need to temper Louis' zeal. The King was bidden to consider the serious position in which he must find himself if his nobles revolted against his authority. He was urged, again, as a good Christian, to think twice before he laid his hands on any of the privileges of the Church. The people could not be trusted. If authority was weakened in any way, disaster must follow. And so on.

Louis listened and hardened his heart. He wrote to Turgot promising support and saying : " It is only you and I, my dear Turgot, who truly love the people." There was a bad harvest. Turgot sent large quantities of wheat into the famine areas and so defeated the attempts of the grain merchants to obtain famine prices in these districts. This action aroused the anger of a Swiss banker named Jacques Necker whose business it was to lend money to the grain merchants. Necker, who had made a huge fortune in a very few years and was looked upon, in consequence, as a wizard of finance, attacked Turgot bitterly in pamphlets and articles in newspapers (several of which he

MARIE ANTOINETTE

owned), and was immediately hailed by the Queen's friends at Versailles as a genius.

Jacques Necker was no genius. But he was a type of the international money-lender who, at this period, was coming to the front almost everywhere by reason of the corner in gold. He was a big oily man with a subservient wife and an adoring daughter. A very pious man, who wrote books on religion; a learned man with a bodyguard of philosophers and artists and musicians—to say nothing of journalists and actors and pamphleteers. Mme Necker acted as whipper-in of this ill-assorted pack.

She was a prim, but not frigid woman, named before her marriage Suzanne Curchod, the daughter of a Swiss pastor. Simplicity and gentleness were combined in her nature with natural ability far above the average so that at eighteen she was one of the most learned women in Europe. But not a blue stocking. There was something soft and kittenish about Suzanne which no amount of learning could extinguish. It was this quality which made slaves of many young men, including Gibbon, who would have married her if his father had not absolutely forbidden him. Suzanne suffered a great humiliation because of young Gibbon and grew a little harder; but when Necker met her, he was as much impressed as everyone else by her modesty and gentleness. He jilted a widow to whom he was engaged and married her immediately.

Suzanne came to Paris as the wife of one of its richest citizens —possibly of its richest citizen. Necker lived in the style of a great nobleman; he was surrounded by a Court which, for brains and talents, threw the King's Court into darkness. Suzanne became terribly homesick. Her husband filled the house with philosophers, among them Diderot and Suard, who knew how to flatter a pretty woman, and little by little the Swiss girl's loneliness was banished. Little by little Suzanne learned the secrets of philosophy and finance and began to understand that she had been called by Destiny to play a leading part in one of the great dramas of history. Gentleness did not desert her but she became excited and impatient.

The secrets she had learned related to the corner in money. Jacques pointed out to her that, thanks to this corner, the King of France was forced to borrow from himself and others like him and that consequently he, and not King Louis, was the real master. The only danger which threatened the banker was the policy of Turgot because, if the Church and the nobles could be forced to pay taxes, the King would no longer require to borrow. Happily there was the Queen.

Suzanne possessed a mind almost exactly like that of her husband. It was a mind fertile in invention so that no action of its possessor lacked, at any time, justification upon the highest grounds of morality. The girl from Switzerland did not see her husband as an unscrupulous money-lender; she saw him as a saviour of a tottering state and the appointed instrument of Providence for the regeneration of the French people. And so the downfall of King Louis' plans and the ruin of King Louis' Minister, Turgot, seemed to her an urgent necessity. She was able, in consequence, to support her Jacques in his efforts to set the Church and the nobles against the throne and even in his plottings to encourage the Queen in her resistance to her husband. These, as she assured herself, were the melancholy means to a glorious end. Nor did she find occasion of qualm in the attacks being launched, anonymously, upon the extravagance of the Queen and the riotous gaiety of Versailles. It was necessary, as she had been assured, to tell the people the truth.

Suzanne might perhaps have doubted her husband if he had not taken care to supply her with a religious basis of thought and observation. The object of human existence, Jacques maintained, was the pursuit of perfection. All men and all women possessed the quality of perfectibility, which was a moral as well as an intellectual quality. Consequently the greatest crime that any Government could commit was the crime of standing still. Men were marching towards liberty and right; but they needed leaders. It had pleased God to appoint these leaders and to endow them with fabulous wealth, wherewith to control the extravagance and warlike propensities of Kings.

Suzanne believed all this, partly because she held Jacques in great reverence and partly because the ideas he professed were in the air. A fellow Swiss, Jean Jacques Rousseau, had declared that there was a " social contract " for the perfecting of men and his book was become the testament of the new age. The philosophers, too, assured her that men were born with rights which could only be exercised when kings and queens and priests had been brought into subjection.

Suzanne was not a Swiss and a Calvinist for nothing. She understood clearly that nothing but the power of money was strong enough to overthrow the Old Order. Consequently, her husband's business of money-lender seemed to her a God-appointed calling, and all his plans and plottings necessary moves in the battle for liberty and righteousness.

She threw herself with enthusiasm into the work of helping him and her *salon* became soon a centre of propaganda where journalists and pamphleteers received their orders and were supplied with copy. Jacques owned several newspapers and these were used daily to inform the Parisians about " perfectibility " and the rights of man, as well as about the extravagance of the Queen and the tyranny of the King and Turgot.

Louis, meanwhile, was proving himself more of a man than Marie Antoinette had expected. He insisted upon " cuts " at Court and reduced many of the pensions which his wife and his brothers had secured for their friends. He also reduced the cost of government. It looked for a moment as if he might succeed in his plan; so much so that Turgot began to prepare for the great attack on the privileges of the nobles.

The moment was critical for Jacques Necker and his Suzanne.

Jacques mobilized his forces and, with Suzanne's active help, " exposed " what he described as the Royal plot against the safety and security of France. It was easy to convince people that, in the general clean-up, their particular interests would suffer ; when the suggestion was added that the new taxes had been made necessary by Royal extravagance, anger began to flame out against the throne. So well did the banker and his wife perform their work of agitation that very soon the whole of France was aroused. Parties which had nothing in common except their fear of loss became, for the moment, allies against Turgot and his master—the list included the King's brothers, the Queen, the whole body of the higher clergy and nobles, the *parlements*, the trade guilds and innumerable small corporations throughout the country. It included also the philosophers and writers, the actors and artists and all those who professed the doctrines of Rousseau and believed in the march towards perfection.

A hurricane, in consequence, broke over the King's head. Louis found himself alone in his kingdom, for even his own ministers deserted him. But he stood fast nevertheless by Turgot, who continued to assure him that the choice lay between action and virtual abdication to Necker and his fellow money-lenders.

Turgot prepared a budget in which he showed that the talk about the King's extravagance was calculated falsehood to hide the fact that national income and national expenditure could not be made to balance, however greatly the expenses of the Court were cut down, and that in consequence those who now escaped taxation must put their hands in their pockets.

This budget, had its contents become widely known, would have put an end to the assertions of Jacques Necker. Unhappily what actually occurred was that the banker published abroad statements to the effect that Turgot was no financier and that his budget was a clumsy and amateurish job. Jacques asserted that the King's income was sufficient—ample indeed—for all his needs and that what was required was not an attack on existing rights but a stern cutting down of Royal expenditure.

There was the cue for the journalists. Suzanne's splendid drawing-rooms buzzed with excited throngs of ambitious and greedy young men who asked nothing better than to enjoy her hospitality and plead her husband's cause. The news went out over France that King and Queen were devouring the nation's substance. Thus, many of the people, for whom Louis was braving this storm, were turned against him.

Even so, he might have persisted in his course, had not a new element, in the shape of the American War of Independence, been imported into the dispute. Louis wanted to help George Washington because he saw in the American rebellion against England a way of recovering some of the Empire which Louis XV and Mme de Pompadour had lost. But he could not at one and the same time fit out an expedition and wage a civil war against his own nobles. Moreover, if he went to war with England he would be compelled to borrow money.

Turgot begged the King not to go to war but to concentrate on home affairs. But Jacques and Suzanne told the French about the struggle of the American people against the King of England and worked up so blazing an enthusiasm that, even if he had wished to keep out of it, the King of France could scarcely have avoided taking part in the war.

Louis broke, therefore, with Turgot and abandoned, temporarily as he assured his minister, the campaign against the nobles. Necker was installed in Turgot's place, that the necessary loans for the war might be supplied.

CHAPTER VII

THE GOVERNESS

AND so Suzanne Curchod came to Court at Versailles. She came as the occupant of a position more powerful, in many respects, than that of the Queen. The courtiers, alive to reality, nicknamed her instantly "the Governess."

That name and the appearance of the banker's wife exerted upon Marie Antoinette an effect of a sudden and even violent kind. In an instant, as it seemed, the Queen came to knowledge and understanding. This banker's wife with her gentleness and her air of superior virtue did not impose upon the daughter of the Hapsburgs as she had imposed on the philosophers. Marie Antoinette began by hating and then grew afraid. She submitted humbly to the demands of Jacques that expenditure must be cut down as a condition of lending and that each loan must be secured both as regards interest and sinking fund. Louis, who was accustomed to violent opposition when he proposed any economy, was surprised and delighted.

But the Queen hid her feelings in her heart. She knew now that her gaiety was likely to cost her dear and asked only that Suzanne might be gone as soon as possible from Versailles. A mouse in the presence of a cat could scarcely have felt more uneasy. There is an intuition of women where other women are concerned which is nearly infallible. Marie Antoinette knew that her " extravagance " had not been greater than that of other Queens of France—in fact it had been quite modest by comparison with the expenditure of the Pompadour; she knew, too, that a brilliant Court was necessary to France, but there was alive in her mind the conviction that the banker's wife had come to measure queenship by the standards of the pastor's house in Switzerland and by the still more grudging standards of the counting-house. Suzanne had come to observe and to condemn.

Suzanne's letters prove it :

" I am sensible," she wrote, " of the rewards—the unique mark of esteem which the King has bestowed on M. Necker, the conviction that he fully deserves it, the delight of the whole people, which had chosen him (as leader) long before the Court chose him, the struttings of these marionettes that we call men —all this pleases and interests me."

She wrote to a friend who had asked a favour :

" The custom here (at Versailles) of canvassing for positions, and especially the custom of getting women to do the canvassing, has caused us (Jacques and herself) to take a very necessary decision : I will ask nothing for anybody."

She expressed pious horror in numberless letters, all of which were designed to serve as propaganda. Thanks to her tireless pen and air of wounded virtue—reinforced by the paid scribes of her husband—Marie Antoinette and her friends were presented naked to the world as figures of profligacy.

Thus, a Queen who had quenched in gaiety the home-sickness of a young girl, the sense of being unwanted and the frustration of a difficult marriage—which gaiety, at the worst, represented a drop in the bucket of governmental expenses—was held up to her people and to the world as a heartless and selfish vampire. Nor did the King escape. Scarcely a schoolboy to-day who has not heard of the weakness and stupidity of Louis XVI of France. When it is borne in mind that King and Queen were the victims of a man and woman who, a few years before, had been penniless but who commanded now greater wealth than that possessed by the Throne itself, a clearer view becomes possible. Necker was a member of the international gang which was holding the world to ransom. His weapon was poverty inflicted amid plenty by the simple process of taking away money and so preventing people from exchanging their goods. One can do that if one has cornered the world's supply of gold and forced all one's neighbours to become borrowers. And in addition one can read these unhappy people lectures upon their profligacy while they are engaged in a deadly scramble for such small quantities of the means of exchange as one may have left in their hands.

As she grew more accustomed to the life of the Court, Suzanne's disapproval increased. She wrote letters to Geneva about senseless luxury and vice and vain conversations. These were designed to show how severe was the struggle in which Jacques was engaged. Nevertheless, as she insisted, Jacques was managing to " balance the budget." He was proving that the King's income was ample for all reasonable, and even some unreasonable needs.

The truth, unhappily, was that Jacques, the King's treasurer, was balancing the budget by borrowing at very high rates of interest—from Jacques the banker. Neither Louis nor Marie Antoinette realized this at first, because Jacques Necker was a most accomplished liar. King and Queen were told that such borrowings as were taking place were for the purpose of meeting the cost of the American War. Both supposed, therefore, that they were lucky to have found so excellent a treasurer. The terrible fact, that they had been getting steadily into the debt of Necker and his fellow bankers to the tune of about £170,000,000, remained hidden from them during several years.

Jacques, in other words, was completing the work begun by Mme de Pompadour. With Suzanne's help he was hurrying the King and Queen of France into hopeless bankruptcy so that he and his gang of financiers, as their creditors, might possess complete power over them. It was Suzanne's part to be gentle and pious and disapproving, while the unsuspecting victims were being lured into the trap with assurance that they had plenty of money, provided only that reasonable caution was exercised. Both King and Queen did, in fact, exercise caution. The Royal establishments were further reduced and all kinds of petty savings instituted and the Queen, with the King's approval, refused to buy the famous diamond necklace which a group of Parisian jewellers brought to Versailles.

These trumpery economies were advertised from day to day in the banker's chief newspaper, the *Courier de l'Europe*, in such a manner as to suggest that royalty was being taught some valuable lessons. Meanwhile, profound silence held the secret of the loans, rising million by million, in the very dark background.

These loans were the proof that the King's income was not sufficient for the needs of government. In four short years they had grown to a size which made it impossible that the King could ever repay them. Louis and Marie Antoinette were doomed whether they succeeded in making the nobles pay taxes or did not succeed. Nothing now could save them from becoming the puppets of Necker.

It says much for the intuition of Marie Antoinette that she had recognized an enemy in Suzanne at their first meeting. Nor is it easy to blame the King and Queen for believing what the banker told them. It is human to be easily persuaded about what one wants to believe, and Necker came to Versailles with the reputation of a wizard of finance. Could Bourbon and Hapsburg conceivably have guessed that this Swiss of the counting-house and his dowdy, frumpish wife were the apostles of a new order of society, implacably determined to humble their throne in the dust, greedy of power and without scruple in its pursuit?

Disillusion came when Jacques published a statement of the King's accounts which was palpably false. This document, called, insolently, *Compte Rendu*, aroused a hurricane of protest in well-informed quarters and an even greater hurricane of praise among the uninitiated. But it had the effect of opening the eyes of both King and Queen. They learned to their horror that Necker had fastened upon their shoulders a load of debt which was so heavy as to be unbearable. Nor had this money been used to pay for the war ; on Necker's own showing only about £80,000,000 out of the £170,000,000 which he had raised had been devoted to that purpose. No, the money had been spent chiefly in defraying the costs of a government which had shown itself niggardly in Versailles, but singularly open-handed in most of the provinces of France. Necker had been buying popularity for himself by a reckless prodigality and, at the same time, lining his own pockets with the interest charges on that money.

How ridiculous poor Marie Antoinette's economies looked in face of this mountain of debt, builded, day and night, by the insatiable Jacques and his Suzanne. These two had put the Crown of France in their pockets. They had bought honour and glory for themselves with the King's money, and the King owed them and their friends most of the money with which the purchase had been made. History holds no record of any other swindle at once so barefaced and so pious.

CHAPTER VIII

GERMAINE

MARIE ANTOINETTE and her husband became united in face of this dire calamity. What were they to do? If the King got rid of Necker, Paris would suppose that Versailles had rebelled against the honest banker's economies. If Necker remained, more and more millions would be added to the burden of debt.

King and Queen need not be blamed if they hesitated in face of this choice. Necker's dismissal, as they now understood, would be the signal for an outburst in the capital, perhaps for outbursts all over France. The churchmen and nobles who didn't want to pay taxes would rouse up the people against the throne; had not M. Necker said and proved that the King's income was more than adequate to meet his expenses? There would, too, be a sudden and terrible drying up of the supply of money—the banker would see to that. Every creditor would present his bill and demand payment and the King's treasury was empty. Where were they going to find £170,000,000? Who would lend a penny if the banker was no longer at Court to guarantee the money? The war with England was still going on. How could they hope to wage war without money?

Jacques and Suzanne had counted on this line of reasoning to secure them in their positions at Court. They did not believe that either King or Queen would dare to get rid of them. The evident reluctance of the unhappy victims of their cunning convinced them, therefore, that they had nothing to fear. But Louis and Marie Antoinette possessed courage and honour.

They took counsel with old and tried friends, one of whom, Vergennes, the Foreign Minister, wrote to the King :

" A battle is in progress between France and her interests and M. Necker and his interests. . . . His pamphlet, *Account Rendered*, is nothing but a bid for popularity. . . . It will take your Majesty a long time to heal the wound which has been inflicted upon the dignity of the throne. . . ."

Marie Antoinette hesitated longer than the King, for she had inherited her mother's gift of statesmanship. Louis made up her mind for her. He would play the King's part, no matter what that might cost him. He dismissed the Neckers and banished them to their estate of Saint-Ouen.

Instantly the hurricane which had been foreseen began to blow. France took Jacques and Suzanne and their young daughter, Germaine, to its heart. The Parisians plucked leaves from the trees in the Tuileries Gardens and wore them as badges, because green was the colour of the banker's livery. The banker's newspapers were filled with praises and lamentations and also with veiled threats. Where, now, was the money to come from ? Churchmen and nobles, who saw themselves being forced to pay, began to organize against the Court. There were articles about fashions and millinery, the object of which was to suggest that there was no limit to the extravagance of Versailles. On the exchanges French funds fell disastrously and the price of bread in Paris began to rise. Hungry men and women joined their curses to the chorus of hate.

And, meanwhile, at the palace, creditors began to press their claims with new energy. Among these came a great Parisian jeweller, asking payment for a diamond necklace which had been supplied to the Queen. His demand was presented to King Louis who received it with amazement.

" I refused, with the Queen's consent, to buy this necklace," he said.

The Queen was sent for. She declared that she had not bought the necklace. The jeweller insisted that he had delivered it to her Majesty's order. King and Queen ordered a searching inquiry. It was discovered that a woman calling herself a countess had stolen the necklace by means of a clever trick. She had found a girl named Olivia who bore a strong likeness to the Queen, and had persuaded her to impersonate Her Majesty. The necklace had been delivered to this girl, and by her handed over to the thieves.

The culprits were arrested and brought to trial in Paris, and the case occasioned a frenzy of excitement. It became obvious that persons in high positions were implicated, if not as parties to the swindle, at least as dupes. Rumour and malice did the rest, so that although the Queen's innocence of all connexion with the matter was established beyond doubt, a heavy burden of suspicion remained. One knew, from the treatment meted out to M. Necker and his family, the kind of things that went on at the King's Court.

Marie Antoinette faced a second time the hostility of the French. But it was no longer the passive dislike of a nation smarting under defeat which she had to support, but active disapproval. Her pride and her experience came to her rescue. She grew in dignity, and that quality of fineness, which had never been wanting to her nature, was increased. Louis XVI found a friend and helper in his adversity upon whom, more and more, he was to lean in the days to come. The King was not a clever man in the sense in which Louis XV had been clever. But he saw his problem now clearly and simply and recognized his duty. He must return to the policy of Mme du Barry and of Turgot and compel the whole of the privileged class to pay taxes, even though these taxes could not deliver him from his burden of debt.

Easier resolved than accomplished in the embittered atmosphere of the year 1781. For the first time for more than a century the King of France met with blank refusal from his nobles, who did not even trouble to hide their determination to fight to the last against any attack on their privileges. The nobles gathered round Jacques and Suzanne; the King and Queen became more and more isolated beings in a hostile world. Marie Antoinette began to feel real devotion towards her husband; Suzanne's devotion to Jacques glowed at white heat.

" The retiral of M. Necker," she wrote to a friend, " has taken place to the accompaniment of the regrets and stupefaction of all France and we ourselves, try as we may, cannot even yet understand how an administration, the success of which had ever matched the purity of its aims, has been abandoned. We are at Saint-Ouen, but are by no means suffering an ordinary eclipse. On the contrary, we have been followed not only by noblemen whom we believe to be specially attached to us, but also by a great crowd of ordinary citizens of all classes. . . . M. Necker has been bathed in their tears and covered with their praises and benedictions. . . .

" The weaknesses of great men are a gift which kindly Nature bestows upon their wives. . . . One must have faults and weaknesses in order to feel the joys, the needs and the consolations which a loving heart can offer. . . ."

In fact, in Jacques' case, there were two loving hearts, that of his daughter as well as that of his wife. Little Germaine was growing up and was becoming so idolatrous of her father that she and her mother were already jealous of one another. She was an ugly little girl with prominent teeth and a coarse, rather yellow skin; but she had fine black eyes and a plentiful supply of black hair. She was, too, very quick witted and an excellent talker. Jacques loved her almost as much as she loved him. His dismissal had filled her with fury and she spent all her days making plans for his restoration to power.

There was no need to trouble. The fearful debt which her father had created and fastened on the shoulders of the King was doing its work. The interest on the debt had to be found in addition to the ordinary expenses of government and the extraordinary expenses of the war with England. The King was beaten. He could not find the money. In consequence, when

America achieved her independence, he had to patch up an unsatisfactory peace with England and allow English manufactured goods free entry into France. He had got nothing out of the war except debt, for all the glory went to General Lafayette, who was a friend of Necker's. The banker's newspapers informed the public that General Lafayette and his brave Frenchmen had been making war on a King in order to deliver his subjects from his tyranny. Everyone understood. The best excuse which Paris could now find for Louis XVI was that he was a weak man with a very bad wife.

The virtues of Suzanne, indeed, became in these newspapers, a heavenly background against which the profligacy and extravagance of Marie Antoinette could be displayed. Paris heard daily about Mme Necker's hospital in the parish of Saint-Sulpice:

" The smallest and the saddest parish of Paris, but the parish where Mme Necker's spirit is at work."

The same papers told the story of Royal balls and the latest extravagances in hair-dressing. Suzanne's hatred of the Queen mounted far above the Queen's hatred of Suzanne : even so, it was nothing to little Germaine's hatred. When Necker, in order the better to attack the King and Queen, betook himself to his native Switzerland, to a house named Coppet on the Lake of Geneva, which he had just bought for £120,000, his daughter's bitterness overflowed :

" A fine sort of retirement for my father," she wrote in her diary, " a desert in a republic after having served a King ! What a position for a proud heart ! How splendid it would be if he were sent for and begged to take the reins of the French Government again ! Then he could accept or refuse at his own good pleasure ! "

So thought Jacques and so thought Suzanne. But Marie Antoinette was determined that this calamity should never occur. She had persuaded the King to accept as Finance Minister a friend of her own, Calonne, and was exerting all her influence to support him. Calonne has been described as fool and knave, but in truth, as has been said, the task he had undertaken was an impossible one. The burden of Jacques' debt was too heavy. Calonne, in consequence, played for time. King and Queen lived, literally, from hand to mouth. The Queen tried hard to economize, even in small domestic matters, while the King made such cuts in personal expenditure as seemed to be possible.

But the " deluge " was upon them. When the demands for money became insupportable, Calonne tried to squeeze more money from the existing tax-payers. Charles I in England had tried to do the same thing. The effect was as disastrous in France as it had been in England. People refused to pay, and in order to resist the King, joined forces with the Church and nobles. Jacques had been awaiting this day. He came hurrying back from Geneva with his wife and daughter and renewed his campaign of abuse against Marie Antoinette.

" What did I tell you ? " was the keynote of this propaganda. King and Queen, but especially Marie Antoinette, became objects of public suspicion ; no new money could be collected and Calonne was forced to go to the Paris *parlement* and demand the tax on land which Louis XV had hoped to collect. In his speech to this body Calonne told the truth about Jacques and called the banker, roundly, a liar.

So horrible a blasphemy against their idol threw Suzanne and Germaine into paroxysms of rage. Suzanne had had a nervous breakdown, caused by Germaine's refusal to marry William Pitt, the younger, and was beginning to retire into invalidism. But Germaine, newly married to the Baron de Staël-Holstein, the Swedish Ambassador, was full of fight. She urged her father to reply to Calonne and Jacques produced a long justification of himself. He sent this to the King, who forbade him to publish it. But the banker defied the King.

" One evening," Mme de Staël recounts, " in the winter of 1 37, two days after the reply to M. de Calonne had appeared, a message came for my father. We were entertaining some friends

NECKER

A bust by Houdon.

in the drawing-room. He left the room. A moment later he sent first for my mother and then for me. The lieutenant of Police, M. de Noir, had just delivered a *lettre de cachet* in which my father was ordered to leave Paris and not again approach nearer to it than 120 miles. I can't describe the effect which the news produced upon me. My father's exile seemed to me an unexampled act of despotism; I felt for him the more acutely because I knew so well how noble and disinterested were all his feelings."

Germaine, in the short period since her marriage, had already completely subjected her Swedish husband, Eric Magnus, who was a gambler and good fellow, with a great need of ready money. Eric Magnus was mobilized instantly to rescue Jacques and forced to use his position as Ambassador to this end. Meanwhile Germaine herself drove off at full gallop to Versailles, and as an ambassador's wife, demanded audience of the Queen. Marie Antoinette had already received her officially and shown her consideration when, on making her third curtsey, she had put her foot through her skirt, but there had been no question of politics or finance on that occasion. It was different now. The Queen's distrust of Suzanne, " the governess," was multiplied in the presence of Suzanne's daughter with her domineering manner and flashing eyes. Marie Antoinette said that she could do nothing. Germaine then asked, directly, if she would try to influence the King on behalf of her father. The Queen refused. Germaine drove back to Paris, to the Embassy, and told her husband that she had been insulted. She demanded that poor Eric Magnus should show his resentment. He was an old and close friend of Marie Antoinette; nevertheless, he obeyed his wife.

The control of Necker's newspapers now passed to his daughter, who salted the attacks on the Queen with her wit and her venom. So much so that the portrait which many historians present of Marie Antoinette, even at this present hour, is that painted by Mme de Staël. Not a word about the loan of

£170,000,000 to Treasurer Jacques from Jacques the banker
and his friends. Not a word about the failure to use that loan
as a means of paying the War Debt. Not a word about the
unscrupulous use made of it to buy personal popularity for
the Necker family. Not a word about the false statement of the
King's accounts that had been published broadcast over France
and Europe. Nothing but lists of the Queen's dresses and
entertainments and angry attacks on the suggestion that rich
men should pay anything towards the cost of government.
M. Necker, it was stated, had imposed no taxes. The reason
why—namely, that he had lived on loans from himself to himself—was not stated. Marie Antoinette replied to these assaults
by suggesting to Germaine that, even for an Ambassador's wife,
she lived in too lavish a manner, and that, in hard times, such
display was apt to create a bad impression.

This was the truth.

" I live," wrote the daughter of Necker, " in a whirlwind of
pleasures and duties which fill up all my time, whether I like it
or not."

Her dinner parties became famous as the most extravagant
ever seen in Paris, and her coaches and liveries outshone those
of the King and Queen and the greatest of the nobles. Her
salon, too, attracted the cleverest and most ambitious among the
nobles and financiers, the journalists and pamphleteers, the artists
and actors. Here was the whole apparatus of the new Liberalism, its religion, its politics, its finance and the " atmosphere "
which was calculated to sustain it. Germaine presided over all.
She represented the power and splendour of the new money ;
the woman who is stronger than armies and whose passions
demand all the riches of the earth for their gratification. She
was Suzanne carried a generation forward in development as if
the chieftain had become the enthroned monarch.

CHAPTER IX

THE QUEEN WAS IN THE PARLOUR

THE more astute among Germaine's courtiers recognized her power. They perceived that she was stronger than Royalty—not in herself or of herself, not even because she was her father's daughter, but because she was part of that unseen force which, by capturing money, had conquered the world. To her and her friends would belong, henceforth, all that excellent patronage which, formerly, only Kings had dispensed. For those who served her there would be wealth and honour ; her enemies would fall.

There is the explanation of the behaviour of Talleyrand and of Louis de Narbonne.

Talleyrand was Bishop of Autun ; Narbonne was an illegitimate son of Louis XV who had been brought up with Louis XVI. Both made violent love to Germaine, to the lively indignation of her husband. Both professed themselves ravished by her wit and her intelligence. They were able, unscrupulous men, consumed by ambition but without substantial wealth, determined, at all costs, to back the winner in the struggle which, as they realized, was going on under the surface of social life. Both knew enough about the true state of affairs to feel convinced that Necker's debt had ruined the King and Queen. At best France must become a constitutional monarchy like England. They desired to be associated with the wielders of power rather than with gilded figureheads.

Both had taken pains to study the great banker and his

women-folk and had measured the immensity of Jacques'
vanity. To flatter a woman it is necessary to make love to her.
They made love without ceasing, marrying money, like Louis
XV, *à main gauche*. Germaine was easily persuaded, so easily
indeed that she began to treat her husband with the utmost
contempt and to convince herself that he was wholly unworthy
of her. She had taken to writing novels. In one of these,
Adélaïde et Théodore, an old man's bride writes to her aunt on
the day following her wedding :

" They have done for my future : the ecstasy of love is for
ever denied me ; henceforward, because I can know neither
joy nor sorrow, I must remain indifferent to everything."

Germaine did not remain indifferent to anything. She was a
bundle of nerves, but, like many nervous women, as strong as
the proverbial horse. Her active mind dominated her lovers
and indeed everyone who came into contact with her. She
took up the task which Suzanne had relinquished and became
not only her father's helper but his business manager also.
Everyone was pressed into the work of advertising him—his
virtues, his genius, his glory, his worth. The Swedish
Embassy became Necker's Committee Room.

Life there, too, had an English rather than a Swedish or
French flavour. The money-lender's daughter, like the money-
lender himself and like all money-lenders, was necessarily in
close touch with London, where the world's stock of gold was
hidden away and whence by one means or another, all the loans
upon which all the world was nourished came forth. London
was the centre for debt : those who lived by debt lived with one
eye directed towards Lombard Street. In consequence, they
aped English customs, adopted English manners and persuaded themselves that they had acquired the English point of
view. They demanded a Constitutional Monarchy in France,
with a House of Lords and a House of Commons, and continued to declare that the French King's absolute power was the
cause of all the trouble. Had not M. Necker said so ? And

had not M. Necker shown that the King's income was enough for the King's needs ? A parliament which could be controlled from the counting-house was the object in view. Having saddled France with £170,000,000 of debt it was necessary, now, to put in the bailiffs in the shape of obedient and greedy politicians. The attacks on King and Queen were, therefore, only another move in the game which had been opened by Mme de Pompadour and played so successfully by Jacques and Suzanne. Louis XVI and Marie Antoinette could have bought off all these attacks, had they been willing to place themselves unreservedly in Necker's hands. All the nobles and all the churchmen who burned incense before Necker's daughter—and the list was long and illustrious—were of one mind : the King must adopt the " English system." He must reign but not govern.

Louis XVI, let it be repeated, has been presented to history as a fool. Marie Antoinette as a heartless and greedy spendthrift. But the fact is that King and Queen deliberately refused to adopt a course which must have made their throne as safe as the throne of England. One cannot have it both ways. If Louis was a fool who cared only for hunting and making locks, then the position of a King who is a mere figure-head was exactly the position he would have desired to fill. If Marie Antoinette cared only for pleasure and the spending of money, then the terms offered by Necker and his gang must have been attractive in the highest degree. For the lords of finance would have rewarded a King and Queen of France who had shown themselves accommodating with anything they cared to ask.

Why, then, did this " dull and stupid " man and his selfish wife reject the glittering prizes of the bankers, to offer, instead, such resistance as they were able to offer ? Why did a King who cared nothing for his great office—who scarcely understood the meaning of that office—choose to fill it when it had become a fierce trial of courage and resourcefulness and refuse to take the bribes of leisure and influence and wealth which, daily, were pressed upon him ? Historians have not, as a rule, troubled to answer such questions, possibly because few historians know anything about money.

The truth, as proclaimed by their actions, is that Louis and Marie Antoinette believed themselves to be responsible to Heaven for the discharge of their office and were prepared, in consequence, to do their duty. They knew that Necker was a smug rogue who had practised upon them and upon France a dirty financial swindle. They were able, therefore, to measure the worth of Germaine de Staël's propaganda. Were such as she fit or worthy to manage the affairs of France ? Both King and Queen were deeply religious. The Queen, as has been said, had given her heart to Count Fersen, but this friendship was maintained without blemish because Marie Antoinette's spirit was strong and faithful. The discipline which she had exerted upon herself had transformed her character so that, as troubles gathered, she put away easily her gaiety and assumed a dignity which, always native to her instincts, had sometimes been forgotten. She drew closer, too, from day to day to her husband and gave him at last the sympathy and support which he had always craved.

When, therefore, Calonne failed to move the nobles, King and Queen resolved to make another attempt. The choice of men capable of acting as treasurer was now become exceedingly limited because most of those who understood finance had joined themselves to Necker and his daughter. The King appointed Lomenie de Brienne, Archbishop of Toulouse and later Cardinal Archbishop of Sens, possibly in the hope that he might be able to persuade his fellow churchmen. But Brienne was a broken reed with no capacity other than his power to flatter. He told Louis that he shared the view that an absolute monarchy was necessary to France and expounded this opinion to the *parlement* of Paris and the assembly of Notables. But he fared no better than Calonne. The King was beaten ; but he would not acknowledge defeat. He called Marie Antoinette into consultation and, a few days later, dismissed the Assembly of Notables, banished the *parlement* of Paris to Troyes and placed several of its members under arrest. On November 9, 1787, he proclaimed to his subjects that the Crown in France possessed absolute power and that this power would be used forthwith to collect from nobles and churchmen their share of the national burden in the form of a tax on land. Battle was joined between Versailles and the Swedish Embassy, between the daughter of the Cæsars and the money-lender's daughter.

CHAPTER X

SOPHIE'S MAN

FROM the time of the discovery of Necker's debt, Marie Antoinette exerted a dominating influence at Versailles, partly because she was abler than her husband, and possessed of a stronger will, partly because Louis loved and trusted her as a friend who would never, in any circumstances, sacrifice his France to personal gain. If it is not quite true that the decisions taken by the King were the Queen's decisions, it is true that had she not approved of them, they would have been set aside.

Marie Antoinette had begun, let it be repeated, by opposing her husband. She had played her part in the dismissal of Turgot and she had put her trust in Necker, though never in Suzanne. These errors have received their full meed of censure. But in fact this Austrian girl, brought up in the austere simplicity of her mother's Court at Vienna, where money was scarce and frugality the rule, had been taught from her childhood that the riches of the Court of France were the wonder of the world. She had come and seen all the prodigality of Louis XV and easily convinced herself that what she had been told was true. Economy in those circumstances was scarcely to be endured. Was the daughter of Maria Theresa to pinch and save where a cook's daughter had been allowed to spend without limit ? A shock of knowledge was necessary in order to dispel the illusion. It had been administered. From that hour Marie Antoinette was warrior as well as Queen.

Nor was Madame de Staël's influence over her father less than the Queen's influence over the King. Necker, like most cunning men, was timid in action. If, under the influence of his greed and his vanity, he could be bold, he was liable, when action had produced reaction, to run away. Figures in books rather than the hearts and minds of men were his study and when man grew threatening he knew of no weapons with which to subdue them. In consequence, his daughter's resolute nature became a necessity to him. He loved Germaine as deeply as he was capable of loving anybody on earth and her love of him, which was as unreasoning as it was boundless, removed all doubts from his mind. Everything, even Suzanne's influence, was subordinated to the strength of mind and clarity of vision of this paragon among daughters who, " possessing the wisdom of the centuries," remained " a child in nature." Jacques shed tears when he thought about Germaine. He had bestowed upon her the pet-name of Minette and his joy of her was so unrestrained and so foolish that Suzanne, by reason of it, lost the savour of life, feeling, apparently, that she too was expected to worship. She did worship.

" Was it not, indeed, a singular spectacle," wrote de Feletz, " to see the family together; M. Necker always admiring Mme. Necker; Mme Necker prostrated before M. Necker; M. Necker enchanted by Mme de Staël; Mme de Staël in ecstasies before M. Necker and every one of them unrelaxing in their efforts to implant their transports in the souls of others ? "

It was Germaine, therefore, rather than her father, who met the challenge which, by imposing the tax on land, Louis XVI had uttered. And that challenge was the Queen's rather than the King's. The two women faced one another across the woods and the river which separate Versailles from Paris. Germaine resolved that the land tax should not be paid. Her weapons were her father's newspapers, her *salon* and the misery which her father's debt was already causing throughout France. From these and by these sprang the feverish interest in the Rights of Man which, everywhere, was replacing the older, more philosophic attitude, of the period of military eclipse. Suzanne had been the patron of the philosophers. Germaine led the hosts of Rousseau. She demanded the right to freedom and the right to love—every kind of right including that of not paying any taxes if one happened to be a nobleman.

Against these big battalions with their unlimited resources of wealth and wit, Marie Antoinette possessed only the prestige of the Throne, sadly tarnished, but still powerful. The battle was decided in a few weeks. Nobody paid the King's tax and he was literally starved out. With empty coffers and a bankrupt credit it is impossible to wage war upon anybody. In bitter humiliation King and Queen recalled the exiled *parlement* (which the Parisians, who had to pay taxes themselves, received with bouquets) and despatched messengers to Necker, asking him to return to his place in the King's Treasury.

Jacques was writing a book about religion when Germaine arrived to tell him the news. He shook his head sadly, saying that he feared it was now too late. But Germaine let herself go :

" While driving through the Bois de Boulogne that night," she recounted, " on my way to Versailles, I was in horrible fear of being attacked by robbers ; for I felt that the happiness which my father's restoration to power was giving me was bound to be offset by some cruel blow. I presented myself to the Queen according to custom on St. Louis' Day. The Archbishop of Sens (Brienne) had been dismissed that morning and his niece had come at the same time as myself to take leave of Marie Antoinette. The Queen made it clear, by her manner of receiving us, that she much preferred the Minister who was quitting office to the Minister who was entering upon it. The courtiers, however, behaved differently ; never before had so many people wanted to conduct me to my carriage."

She was tingling with joy and excitement. She had been writing her *Lettres sur Jean-Jacques Rousseau* ; she now added a summons to the dead prophet to come forth from the tomb :

" Arise, O Rousseau," this summons ran, " arise from your

ashes ! And may your life-giving prophecies inspire the man (Jacques) who, in his quest of perfection, has put away all evil, the man whom France has recognized as her guiding Spirit, the man who sees only his duty towards France in her enthusiasm for him, the man to whom all must give their help and support."

Germaine believed all this. Like her father she had acquired the power to cheat and swindle with a warm sense of virtue. The secret of this power lies in self-love. Those whose affections are set upon themselves or upon their own families, to the exclusion of all other persons or causes, necessarily look upon actions which benefit themselves or their families as good actions and actions which injure themselves or their families as bad actions. Being wholly self-centered, they are incapable of any other judgement. Their moral law is, therefore, identical with their inclinations, and they can, without any sense of shame, justify flagrant misbehaviour and even glorify it.

It is no accident which associates this attitude of mind with money-lending in all its protean forms, because the money-lender is always the enemy of Society and would, therefore, always be unhappy if he shared the ordinary feelings of men and women. In fact he shares none of these feelings. He is possessed, on the contrary, as Necker and his daughter were possessed, of an overwhelming sense of his importance and merit. If society blames him it is society which has gone astray ; if he is exposed to danger, then civilization itself is being destroyed.

In the case of women, the prototype of the money-lender is the harlot, a fact observed and recorded by, among others, King Solomon. When, therefore, Germaine demanded as many lovers as the world could supply, she did so in good faith, with a clear conscience, and her resentment against her husband for opposing her was a genuine resentment. Eric Magnus did not stand, in her eyes, as a badly treated husband, but as a greedy tyrant preferring claims against her which were both selfish and damnable.

" Happy that being," she wrote virtuously, " who has never

had to respond in relations not springing from the heart ; who has never had to submit except gladly out of love."

One need not blame Germaine. She was wholly sincere, as wholly sincere as her father. The blame and the tragedy lie elsewhere in the fatal accident which allowed such people to gain control of money and, with it, the lives of millions of men and women. For that control meant, inevitably, the downfall of the civilization of Europe and the erection, in its place, of a different kind of civilization, based upon debt and fashioned according to the ideas or necessities of the most selfish among the children of men ; a civilization in which everything had its price and where, in consequence, money value in the form of classes and class distinctions replaced rank, the value whose measure is service.

Germaine had a philosophy, but no religion, for religion is based on the truth that the impulse to serve others, of its nature essentially ecstatic, is the fountain of all creation, whether material or spiritual. Philosophy substitutes for ecstacy a process of intellect, and thus assumes a passionless creation. It is true that Necker's daughter would have denied, vigorously, that she was passionless. But since her passion was centred upon herself, she had no impulse to serve others. She was the victim, indeed, of a continuing frustration which, since it belonged to her own spirit, was without cure. An unhappy woman, raging in bitterness against a world made for happiness. Thirsty for the water she was not able to drink.

Germaine's hatred of Marie Antoinette belonged to this region of spiritual conflict. The Queen did possess the impulse to serve others. She possessed religion and was prepared to make sacrifice. Consequently she was rebuke and even shame to the banker's daughter, who choked always in her presence. Germaine felt the Queen's disapproval and, according to the necessity of her nature, reacted against it by accusing the Queen —of profligacy, of heartlessness, of tyranny, even of treachery to France.

In this atmosphere of hate Necker began his second Ministry. He found only a few thousand francs in the King's coffers, but the loans bounded up in value by some thirty per cent on the day on which he took office. He had King and Queen completely at his mercy and he treated them like dishonest bankrupts. An assembly of the nation, he declared, must be called at once so that the loans—the debt he had himself created—might be paid off, or at any rate put upon a sound footing. The Churchmen and Nobles when they heard about this plan took fright at once because they realized that an assembly of the nation would try to make them pay. They appealed to their dear friend M. Necker to change his mind. And suddenly they saw facing them not the unctuous author of *Compte Rendu*, but the money-lender who is going to have interest payments on his loans if the world must be destroyed in the process. They recoiled from that terrifying spectacle. When, a few days later, they dared to threaten resistance, the banker's newspapers opened an attack upon them which brought howling mobs to their hotels. " Why," Necker's scribes asked, " should these drones in the hive not pay taxes like other people ? "

Resistance wilted and died. King Louis summoned the States General of the nation to meet him at Versailles ; Necker prepared a list of the loans made by himself and his friends and drew up plans for meeting the interest payments. These provided for a monarchy on the English pattern, with himself as Prime Minister. He and Germaine were about to step into the shoes of King and Queen and rule France according to their good pleasure. Germaine called this plan " liberty."

But if King and Queen had been conquered, there remained men and women in France who were still capable of fight. Chief among them was Mirabeau. He was a nobleman who, in his early youth, had been the victim of a half-crazy father. Young Gabriel de Mirabeau had not been born with teeth in his head for nothing. He defied his father who, in return, used his influence with the Government to have him placed under detention in various fortresses.[1]   Gabriel had married, but his wife was unfaithful to him.   He forgave her, but she refused to share his misfortunes.   Then he fell in love with Sophie de Monnier, the seventeen-year-old wife of a sexagenarian.

Gabriel, as lover, was terrific.   His wife, even when he first married her, had scarcely ruffled the surface of his feelings; but Sophie unloosed the hurricane.   She was a gentle soul, timid and rather retiring, but with great and deep capacity of affection.   Ruin and disaster engulfed both the lovers almost from the beginning.   They ran away to Holland.   They defied the world.   Gabriel earned a few shillings a day translating foreign books.   Sophie, with motherhood in sight, wrapped him in love.   The man, who was a rake by nature, with ice in his proud heart, tasted ecstasy so lively that, in great joy, he proclaimed ambition and honour and fatherland—all that his rank held valuable—well lost for Sophie's sake.

And he meant it.   Gabriel de Mirabeau possessed a knowledge of values which was unflinching.   He had not willed to throw away his career, his comfort and his honour, but had, on the contrary, put up a stout fight within himself against Sophie. As man of the world, he had desired, above everything, to disentangle himself, to be rid of the young woman, to leave her under her aged husband's roof.   Nor would Sophie have raised a finger to call him had he told her that he wished to be free. But his heart would hear none of this world's wisdom.   He knew himself undone, disarmed of caution, the servant not of desire (women were always at his disposal), but of a need like the need of light and air.   Knew, too, with cool understanding, that the passion might burn itself out one day, when all life's prizes had been sacrificed because of it.

It was great calamity of ambition, but it was a spiritual re-birth.   Gabriel knew that he had come into a realm in the

[1] This was done by many fathers at the time, usually to get their sons out of scrapes, seeing that no legal action could be taken against a prisoner:

existence of which, hitherto, he had disbelieved, and that the sweetness of the place had given him ecstatic joy though his coming had been at the expense of his own and other people's serenity and welfare. He knew, further, that he had sacrificed himself in the true meaning of that word, seeing that he was an ambitious man, of great natural power of leadership and deeply interested in public affairs.

Sophie knew it all, too. But she knew, in addition, that she had served well her Gabriel by raising him from the dead of his selfishness and arrogance and libertinage. Perhaps she realized that he would go back again, someday, to the old ways; but not as he had come. Because of her, Gabriel would never be the same man again, whether he was called good or bad. He had given himself. It is a gift, however made, which sets the giver, for all time, apart from those who have not made it.

Their respective families tracked the lovers down, had them arrested, and separated them. Sophie was consigned to what was little better than a house of correction; her child, a daughter, was born there. Gabriel was imprisoned in the fortress of Vincennes, in the dungeons. They managed to write to one another, but did not meet for four years. Then Gabriel, who had been released, lived again with his "spouse" during five days. A fresh threat of imprisonment separated them once more, but, in any case, Gabriel's passion had cooled. He remained the man that Sophie had made him, and in that sense belonged to her for ever. But this man, prisoner newly released from his dungeon, was full of such violence of energy that gentleness could hold him no longer. Sophie, fearful lest he should be imprisoned again, bade him go, with clear knowledge in her heart that he would never return.

" People think," she wrote to him afterwards, " that you and I cannot live without one another; alas! my spouse, they were wrong."

Her child had died. She went to live in a convent and gathered round her there a small circle of friends, men and women. One of these men was stricken with consumption ; she nursed him, and in the end became fond enough of him to promise to become his wife—for her husband was dead.

Gabriel rushed into public affairs and private intrigues. A madness of action seized upon him as if he must atone to himself for the long years he had spent in prison. His great head, with its mop of riotous hair, became familiar in Paris, upper world and underworld. But none, man nor woman, knew him. He was locked, barred, bolted like his prisons. Man in armour for all his agility of speech and flash of humour. Sophie's Man hidden, as she was hidden.

Seven years passed. The King had summoned the States General. He, Gabriel, would sit in that assembly and help remake France. He had visited England and Germany and been by turns pamphleteer, diplomatist and, as ever, the lover of women. That first fierce joy of liberation had passed. He was older, more sober, more cynical, when his father refused support to enable him to sit as a noble, he asked for election as a commoner. Two different constituencies, one of them Marseilles, elected him because the fame of his eloquence had gone out over France. The common people believed that, at long last, they had found their man.

Gabriel understood the common people, and he hated the system which had torn him from Sophie and made his " marriage " to her a shame to be punished in dungeons. He came to Versailles roaring his indignation against absolutism and both Louis XVI and Marie Antoinette saw in him an enemy. The Queen felt for him the same kind of disgust as she had felt for Mme du Barry. But neither King nor Queen was afraid of him. That was left to Necker and his daughter.

Mme de Staël saw him at the opening of the States General by the King and the sight made her gasp :

" It was hard," she wrote years afterwards, " not to keep gazing at him once you had begun to gaze. His tremendous head of hair marked him out from all the others so that you felt that, like Samson, his strength dwelt in it. Its very grossness lent something to the expression of his face and his whole being conveyed the idea of power, irregular perhaps but such as ought to be possessed by a tribune of the people. His name, and his alone, was famous then among the six hundred members of the Commons."

Gabriel de Mirabeau had never supposed that Necker was the saviour of France. He knew the banker's game and had exposed it already in speeches and pamphlets. They met. Mirabeau bristled in Necker's presence. Sophie's Man knew the Swiss then for what he was—calculating, cunning, greedy, without loyalty, incapable of giving himself to any cause. Nor was Gabriel's feeling towards Germaine kinder. Those who have loved truly acquire a power of testing the sincerity of others.

And so the Parliament that was to have made the banker King, made Gabriel King instead. It was Gabriel, not Jacques Necker, who withstood the officers of King Louis when they ordered the Commons to sit apart from the Clergy and the Nobles. And it was Gabriel, in those hot summer days of the year 1789, who dominated the National Assembly—as the Parliament called itself—and became in consequence the Master of France.

One night, as he sat in the Assembly, a note was handed to him. It announced that Sophie had committed suicide because the man she had been about to marry had died. The blood ebbed out of his face. He rose and went blindly from the hall. The Assembly did not see him again for more than a week.

CHAPTER XI

MIRABEAU, as has been said, had already made it his business to find out why France was so hopelessly sunk in debt. He made it his business now to tell the Assembly what he had found. Night after night he made the flesh of his fellow-members creep with talk about the " hideous bankruptcy " that had overwhelmed them.

Contact with Necker had abated his liberalism. He was no longer angry with the King and Queen. On the contrary, he offered to advise and help them. The banker and the banker's daughter exerted their utmost efforts to keep him out of the palace. Necker was playing his old game. At any sign of Royal opposition he threatened to resign : that threat brought out angry mobs of his creatures who went shouting about the streets.

Neither King nor Queen was intimidated by these demonstrations. But the banker contrived nevertheless to persuade them that a show of military force was necessary to the maintenance of order. Some regiments were ordered to Versailles and Paris. The regiments which went to Paris were commanded by one of Necker's associates, Besenval. Mirabeau gasped with dismay. Did the Swiss mean to bring them all to heel with bayonets ? Or was he trying to alienate the nation from the King ? He sprang up in the Assembly and in a speech which deeply moved that body cried to the King :

" Sire, we conjure you in the name of the Fatherland, in the name of your goodness and your glory, send back your soldiers

to the outposts from which your advisers have brought them.
. . . Your Majesty does not need them. . . . Sire, you are among
your children, let their love protect you."

But it was too late. Warned and enlightened about Necker's
subterranean activities the King dismissed him a second time and
ordered him to leave France. Jacques, with Suzanne, took the
road to Brussels ; Germaine followed some hours later with Eric
Magnus. Next morning the news reached Paris and battalions of
the banker's supporters began to spread it through the city. The
King, they insisted, was about to fill the streets with soldiers.
He was about to punish unmercifully those who had dared to
criticize him. Had he not already sent into exile the only man
who had dared to tell him the truth ?

The soldiers were there to confirm the story. Panic seized
upon the inhabitants. There was a rush to the Hôtel de Ville
where already General Lafayette, the hero of America, was
installed. Lafayette had been one of Necker's closest friends ;
he was a liberal and therefore, no doubt, marked out for destruction. The Parisians rallied round him. Once more they plucked
leaves from the trees in the gardens to make " Necker Cockades."
Someone suggested an attack on the state prison known as the
Bastille. Off they all rushed in a madness of fear and hate. The
soldiers remained in their camp. The impregnable fortress
opened its doors. Bloody heads were carried through the
streets on pikes ; affording excuse to Lafayette and his friends
for the formation, there and then, of a National Guard.

Everything had been arranged and everything had gone
according to plan—the panic, the inaction of the King's troops,
the surrender of the King's prison, the formation of a Citizen
army to oppose the Royal army. Louis and Marie Antoinette,
who knew nothing about what was happening in Paris, were
shown to the people as monsters thirsty for the blood of
Frenchmen. To the horror of the debt was added the greater
horror of massacre. King and Assembly heard the news late
at night. Louis came down, at once, to his Parliament, which

received him in frozen silence. He returned to the palace and sent messengers to recall Necker from his exile.

The Swiss was at Basle with his wife and daughter. He met there one of the Queen's friends, Gabrielle de Polignac, who was fleeing with her husband out of France. Before the King's messenger arrived he knew that he had succeeded. Paris belonged to him. The Assembly was cowed.

That was a great night for the Swiss family. None of them got any sleep because couriers kept arriving every hour—from the King, from the Assembly, from Paris—beseeching the banker to come back. He, he alone, could save the fatherland. His eyes filled with gentle tears, and he was still lachrymose next morning when his big *berline* rolled out across the frontier. Suzanne and Germaine, too, were weeping. There were deputations at every village.

" Respect property, my friends," the banker counselled his idolators, " honour your priests and nobles, love your King."

Germaine's heart nearly burst. She tells how the horses were taken from the carriage and how the carriage itself was filled with flowers. But she passes quickly over an incident which drove most of the satisfaction from her father's face—namely, an encounter, near Paris, with Besenval, the general who had been in command of the King's troops stationed in the capital. Besenval was under arrest and was being hurried off to prison to answer for his behaviour. Would he tell what he knew ? Necker tried to secure his release there and then, but even he was unable to achieve that. He continued his journey with gnawing anxiety in his heart. Next day, when he made a triumphal entry into Paris with his wife and daughter, he could think of nothing except the danger which threatened him. He replied to the frenzied welcome of the Parisians with a demand for a universal pardon of past offences. He mentioned specifically the name of Besenval.

" M. Necker," wrote Germaine, " came out on the balcony and proclaimed in a loud voice holy words of peace between

MIRABEAU

Frenchmen of all parties. The entire multitude was transported. From that moment I saw no more. I fainted with joy."

Necker's request was granted and M. de Besenval retired discreetly from the scene. The banker returned to Versailles to enter upon his Kingdom. He found King and Queen in deep bewilderment. Louis had gone, in person, to Paris a few days before and with great courage had faced there the men whose treachery was undermining his throne. As proof that he had willed nothing against the city he had pardoned offenders, sanctioned the formation of the National Guard and pinned upon his own coat the tricolour cockade which Lafayette had compounded from the red and blue of the City of Paris and the white of the Bourbons.

Marie Antoinette would have none of that tricolour and plucked it from the King's coat when he returned. But Louis ordered his guard to wear it and the Queen was compelled to acquiesce.

Necker now began to appoint the members of the House of Lords which he meant to set up, and Germaine entertained them in her huge house, rue du Bac. Most of them were nobles of old family ; some had become bemused by the doctrines of Rousseau and were busy upon the problem how liberty could be combined with equality—a problem that still awaits solution ; others were frank adventurers, worshippers of the rising sun, ready to espouse any philosophy so long as there was money in it. Among the former was Germaine's lover, the gentle Mathieu de Montmorency, among the latter her lovers, Louis de Narbonne and Talleyrand. She wore them all, indiscriminately, and she possessed such power of dominance that none of them dared to object. She attracted them too, for all three had a feminine streak to which her strength made appeal. All three were men of exceptional ability ; her wit, unfailing and excellent, rejoiced them like wine. The immense treasure of which she disposed and the patronage of the crown that seemed to be about to fall into her father's hands were added advantages.

Moreover, her *salons* were always gay with pretty women. Many of these were wives and daughters of the great, but there was a sprinkling of less illustrious beauty emerged from the counting houses. Among the latter, conspicuous for her childish loveliness, Thérèse, Marquise de Fontenay, daughter of Cabarras, the King of Spain's banker. Thérèse was still in her teens, but informed about all the miseries of marriage to a drunken ne'er-do-weel. She had been beaten by her husband and, again and again, subjected by him to the greatest insults. She was finished with him ; she was hungry for life.

But behind her big, dark eyes and under the masses of her black hair, fine as Germaine's was coarse, was a brain cool and calculating. This girl served her father just as Germaine served Necker. She understood money and debt and knew very well about the game that was being played out in the King's house and in the Assembly. Cabarras, she was resolved, should have his share of the booty once it had been taken. Her house in the country at Fontenay-aux-Roses was often full of members of the Assembly—among them a lawyer from Arras named Maximilian Robespierre and a Parisian barrister called Jacques Danton. It was known already to those who were in touch with the inner circle of finance which of the deputies could be bribed and which could not. Robespierre was numbered among the latter. Thérèse did not like Germaine much, because Providence had not supplied the girl from Spain with a quick wit ; Germaine did not like Thérèse at all, because Thérèse was so beautiful that men lost their hearts in her presence.

The Neckers held court, indeed, like sovereigns. That shrewd observer, the American, Gouverneur Morris, who visited them, wrote :

" He (Necker) has the look and manner of the counting-house, and being dressed in embroidered velvet he contrasts strongly with his habiliments. His bow, his address, say ' I am the man.' If he really is a very great man I am deceived. . . . In the *salon* we find Mme de Staël. She seems to be a woman of sense and somewhat masculine in her character, but has very much the appearance of a chambermaid."

Nor was Gouverneur Morris much impressed by the play of wit, which was the conspicuous feature of Germaine's *salon*, and which was, intentionally, incomprehensible to the uninitiated, who were expected to gaze in envious wonder and be impressed with their own insignificance.

" I feel very stupid in this group," wrote Morris viciously. " A conversation too brilliant for me. . . . The few observations I make have more of justice than splendour and therefore cannot amuse. . . . She (Germaine) is a woman of wonderful wit and above vulgar prejudices of every kind. Her house is a kind of Temple of Apollo."

He visited the Neckers frequently after that and observed how the banker's greatness was making him intolerant of criticism of any kind, so that he could not endure to hear his opinions called in question.

" Our conversation," he wrote in his diary, " is loud. He (Necker) makes it so purposely. At this point Mme de Staël, with the good-natured intention of avoiding ill-humour, desires me to send her father to sit next to her. I tell her, smiling, that it is dangerous to send away M. Necker, and that those who tried it once had sufficient cause to repent of it. This little observation brings back good-humour, and he (Necker) seems inclined to talk further with me. But I take no further notice of him, and after chatting a little with different people, I take my leave."

All this company shared in the execration of Mirabeau. Indeed, the chief subject of talk was the man who, having defied society with Sophie, was now avenging himself.

" Mirabeau," wrote Germaine viciously, " was banned from decent society, and his dearest wish was to get back there. He was ready to burn down civilization in order to open the doors of Paris. Like all immoral men he saw his own interest first ; his foresight was limited by his egoism."

The truth was that Mirabeau had, once more, dethroned Necker from his position as the idol of the Assembly. Mirabeau, as has been said, knew the money game and kept on exposing it. He would ask to whom all the debts incurred by Jacques, the £170,000,000, were owing? And the answer was Jacques. He would point out that money-lenders thrive only when other people are poor and that consequently national poverty is as necessary to the banking fraternity as disease to doctors.

"This hero," he cried one day, when speaking of Necker, "has hobbled to fortune on the twin crutches of famine and debt."

Germaine and Thérèse heard some of these great speeches because Mirabeau drew "decent society" to him like a magnet.

"He had a damnable way," Germaine wrote afterwards, "of praising M. Necker. 'I don't approve of his plans,' he would say, 'but since the Nation, in its wisdom, has hailed him as our dictator, we must accept with faith.' M. Necker's friends realized with what cunning Mirabeau sought to snatch his popularity away from him, in thus exaggerating it. For nations are like people; they love less when they are told too often how much they love . . . I was quite near Mirabeau one day when he brought down the house and although I had no illusions about his aims, he captivated me for two whole hours. Nothing could be more impressive than his voice ; and if the gestures and the biting words he used did not spring straight from his heart, they held at least a living force the effect of which was tremendous."

Necker and Germaine began to lose their nerve. Nobody would pay taxes now and the Government was bankrupt. The money-lenders in Holland and London refused to make any more advances : Necker began to see that the loans he had contracted might not be paid. He made a desperate effort to float a new loan and put his own name down for some £60,000, but the plan miscarried. Meanwhile, his activities as the chief financier of the wheat trade were being watched in Paris by hungry men and women, including Robespierre, Danton and

Marat. Marat, who was a doctor, conducted a newspaper of his own and openly charged Necker in its columns with stealing the people's bread. Mirabeau, at Versailles, charged the banker daily with stealing the King's money.

Germaine passed from rage and fear to terror. Something must be done to put a stop to these attacks and to restore her father to popularity. She addressed herself to her lover the Bishop. Why should not the Nation seize the Church lands and so obtain the means of paying its debts? Talleyrand liked the idea. One day, in his cool, well-bred tones, he proposed to the assembled deputies that Mother Church should be despoiled.

They jumped at the bait. Few of them, probably, realized with what cunning it had been made ready for them. If they did not know, Germaine and her father knew that the King and Queen would refuse to consent to such a seizure. Louis had wished to tax the Church lands; he was determined to save them from spoliation.

When his views became known, the ugly charges against Necker found a new target. What, did the King and Queen place the welfare of the Church above that of the people? These Church lands would buy bread for Paris; was Paris to starve? Nicknames of terrible import were bestowed on Louis and Marie Antoinette—namely, "the baker" and "the baker's wife." Bring the King to Paris declared one of the newspapers and the price of bread will fall.

Necker, as has been said, was in virtual control of the wheat trade, and therefore able to secure such a fall in the price of bread when it suited him. Necker wanted the Church lands in order to obtain money for himself and his friends. Necker wanted to bring the King from Versailles to Paris because the Assembly would have to follow the King. In Paris, agitated daily by the banker's newspapers and paid agitators, Mirabeau's influence would be much less potent than in the quiet atmosphere of Versailles.

CHAPTER XII

THE BAKER'S WIFE

GERMAINE began to talk to her bodyguard of nobles about the remoteness of Versailles. Her friend, General Lafayette, said that it might be necessary to march the new National Guard out there in order to direct the minds of the Assembly to the people's needs. And always the terrible nicknames—"Baker" and "Baker's Wife," continued to be howled, like curses, from the gutters of Paris after the King and Queen.

They had their own personal sorrow in these autumn days because, earlier in the year, they had lost the elder of their two sons. That shadow lay still upon their lives. Marie Antoinette had no more gaiety. Both she and her husband began to see that the way they had chosen must soon become a *via dolorosa* unless they submitted to all the demands of the banker, including the seizure of the Church lands. They resolved on the contrary to resist. When they learned that it was proposed to force them to go to Paris, Marie Antoinette appealed to the officers of the King's Bodyguard to protect her husband and her children. She distributed white cockades to them and they tore Lafayette's tri-colour cockades from their coats. The song of Royalty:

" O Richard, O mon roi "

broke defiantly from their lips.

But it was useless. Spies carried the news to Paris and Germaine's intelligence department spread it, instantly, through the city. Everything was in readiness. Two days later, on

October 5, 1789, a large body of women, most of whom were harlots, collected early in the morning, near the river. They were all in possession of bottles of wine and some were already drunk. They kept shouting for bread and demanding that " the Baker, the Baker's wife and the Baker's brat," should give it to them. They began to march towards Versailles. After they had been allowed a good start on their journey Lafayette called up his National Guard and set off, slowly, in pursuit, saying that he was going to protect the Royal Family. He did not arrive until after the drunken women and their attendant mob had reached the palace.

Germaine, however, got to Versailles in plenty of time, " going by a way that was little used on which I met nobody." She found her father and mother there and learned that : " The King had ordered his carriages but the townspeople had refused to let them pass," and, further, that the Flanders Regiment, having been ordered to clear a way for the carriages, had mutinied—a sufficient refutation of the statement that the march of the women from Paris was wholly unexpected by anybody. Necker, having secured that the King should not escape, offered to accompany him whever he might choose to go, but advised him to go to Paris.

As night fell the women, nearly all drunk now, arrived at the palace. They howled " Bread, bread, bread," in horrible chorus. Men from the gutters of Paris, who had accompanied them, demanded blood and heads. While they were shouting and threatening, Lafayette appeared with his National Guard. He did not attempt to clear the great courtyard but merely posted guards round the building. He advised that everyone should go home to bed. During the night the drunken mob, which had spent its time dancing and carousing, broke into the palace. A gang of roughs reached the Queen's bedroom and had she not possessed a private way into the King's apartments, would have murdered her. Many of the King's Bodyguard were massacred before Lafayette's guard came to the rescue.

The day of October 6 came up, smiling, over the woods. It discovered the mob still drinking and dancing and threatening in the King's courtyard. Lafayette's guard, the same which had been recruited on the day of Necker's dismissal, was in command. The mob shouted for the King and his family.

"The Queen," wrote Germaine long afterwards when Louis XVI's brother reigned in France, "entered the room where we were. Her hair was in disorder, her face was pale, but she looked so dignified that everyone was impressed. The mob called for her to come out on the balcony. The whole court below was crammed with men armed with guns. We saw from her expression what she feared but she went forward unhesitatingly, with her two children, who served as a protection. This spectacle of Queen and Mother softened the hearts of the mob and stilled its fury. The very people who had, perhaps, wanted to kill her during the night, now exalted her name to the skies. When she left the balcony she went up to my mother and said to her, with choking sobs : ' They want to force the King and me to go to Paris with the heads of our bodyguard carried in front of us on poles.'

" That was what happened. Thus were the King and Queen brought to their Capital. We (Germaine and her father and mother) returned to Paris by another way that took us far from the terrible spectacle. Our way led us through the Bois de Boulogne. It was a lovely afternoon with scarcely a leaf stirring. The sunlight filled the whole land with glory, mocking our distress. . . .

" The King went to the Hôtel de Ville where the Queen displayed an extraordinary self-possession. The King said to the Mayor :

" ' I come with pleasure to live in my good City of Paris.'

" The Queen added : ' And with confidence.'

" Next day the Queen received the Diplomatic Corps and the Court. Every time she tried to speak, sobs choked her ; we couldn't answer her. What a sight was this old palace of the

Tuileries, abandoned by its august owners during more than a century. . . . As nobody had foreseen the coming of the Royal family, very few of the rooms were fit for occupation and the Queen had had to have camp beds got ready for her children in the room where she received us. She excused them, saying : " ' You know that I didn't expect to come here.' "

Louis and Marie Antoinette were now Necker's prisoners in the gloomy Parisian palace from which Louis XIV had escaped so long before. The Assembly, as the banker had foreseen, soon followed them to Paris and became, in its turn, a prisoner. Even Mirabeau found himself overawed by the mob with which Necker, Lafayette and their associate, the Duke of Orleans, the King's cousin, filled the galleries of the Riding School where the sittings were heard.

Time now to divide up the spoil of Holy Church. Necker proposed that the Church lands should be made over to him as security for a new loan wherewith the earlier loans might be paid off and the immediate needs of the Treasury met. That proposal brought Mirabeau to his feet, bellowing and threatening. Who was this banker, he demanded, that he should be made fat with the wealth of France ? The roots of all their troubles were Necker's loans ; what madness to add one more to the number of them. " Land is Money," Mirabeau shouted ; he urged that if Necker was to have the land he ought to be made to pay for it outright.

The members of the Assembly were badly instructed about money and did not understand either the bankers' demands or Mirabeau's objection to them. What they did understand was that Necker could raise money whereas they could not raise it. If Necker refused to buy the Church lands outright, therefore, there was no option, so far as they could see, but to agree to his terms and offer the lands as security for a loan.

Necker, therefore, got his way. He took possession, on behalf of his bank, of some of the richest land in France. In exchange he issued to the Government bank notes, payable, if the holder so wished, in gold or silver. Only Mirabeau, among all the deputies, realized that Necker did not possess enough gold or silver to cover the notes, supposing that people became suspicious of them and tried to cash them. Mirabeau, in other words, knew the inner secret of finance—namely, that it is possible to lend the same piece of gold or silver several times over, so long as people believe that every note is " backed," in the vault of the bank, by its equivalent in the form of the precious metals. That belief prevents holders of notes from cashing them.

Mirabeau resolved to break Necker by advising as many people as possible to cash Necker's notes for gold or silver. He accomplished his purpose so successfully that a " run " upon Necker's bank took place. It was then quickly revealed that the banker could not meet his liabilities. Overnight the idol of the people, the breaker of thrones, the master of Kings was hurled from power. All men saw the " wizard of finance " in his true colours as a shabby trickster who had been pretending to lend what he did not, in fact, possess. Jacques packed and, with Suzanne, bolted out of France. His carriage was held up at Arcis-sur-Aube where he was placed under arrest. But the Assembly let him go. He crossed the Swiss frontier under a shower of brickbats. Only fourteen months had elapsed since his triumphal journey from Basle to Versailles.

Suzanne was far from well and the shock of this home-coming to Switzerland nearly killed her.

" La Fontaine," she wrote, " made use of tigers and lions so as not to shock men and women, now we shall have to write about men and women so as not to shock tigers and lions. Forgive me, the barbarous treatment we suffered at Aix haunts me day and night. My health is shattered."

Germaine, as it happened, had just been brought to bed with a son. From her bed, in a trembling hand, she wrote to the President of the Assembly demanding safe conduct for her parents, about whose arrest she had been advised. Her letter was a challenge as well as a prayer; she was still Swedish ambassadress, and she was still a member of that company of money-lenders who had their hands upon the world's gold. Mirabeau had shown, doubtless, that the credit system cannot withstand a " run " ; but where was Mirabeau going to obtain money ? Not a banker in Europe would lend a farthing now to the French Government.

Germaine did not know her Mirabeau. That great man came to the Assembly and asked, simply, why the French Government should not become its own banker. We have the land, he argued, therefore we can create the money. Necker—as we now know—created the money without having the gold. He went on to urge that if people knew that they could cash the Government's notes for pieces of land, they would be satisfied with these notes.

And so it was. The Government issued millions of notes, called " Assignats," each of which was " backed " by a piece of the Church land. Those notes had not been borrowed and so there was no interest to pay upon them. It was as if the penniless and distracted Government had stumbled, suddenly, upon a gold mine of almost inexhaustible richness. Mirabeau got into touch with the King and actually saw the Queen, secretly, for a few minutes. He told them that their troubles were at an end because, now, any quantity of money was available. He urged them to leave Paris and its mobs and go into the country and he promised, if they did, that France would be restored to peace and prosperity.

His argument was this : all our troubles are due to the fact that a small body of people have got possession of the gold stock of Europe. We have had to borrow from these people, and Necker, while he was your treasurer, piled debt upon debt until, at last, there was no hope of ever getting out of his clutches. But now we have found a new source of money and a new backing for money—namely, land. Instead of basing our money on gold and silver we are going to base it on land.

And you, as King, possess the land. Consequently we are as rich as we can possibly wish to be.

It was true as Europe was soon to discover. Mirabeau had found a " gold mine " ; he, not Necker, was the real wizard of finance. But neither King nor Queen could bring themselves to believe it. They could not believe it even when they saw Mirabeau's assignats being accepted eagerly in every market as good and honest money.

And so they hesitated. And while they hesitated Mirabeau, whose health had broken at the news of Sophie's death, sickened and died.

BOOK II

THE BLUE STOCKINGS

CHAPTER XIII

" GOLD MINE "

MIRABEAU'S land-money sent a shiver of fear through the hearts of those who owned the world's gold. What was to become of them and their power if France, and after France the other nations of Europe, found out how to create their own money and so how to dispense with the use of the precious metals.

The owners of gold, as has been seen, had fought their way to world mastery by playing off one nation against another. They prepared again for battle. Unless and until the land-money was destroyed their victory was in pawn.

The Revolution, in other words, was given a new direction. Until now the object had been to get the King into debt and so to control and devour France. Mirabeau's magic had brought that plan to ruin. The new object was to obtain control of the land-money in order to destroy it.

The King and Queen unhappily did not understand what was afoot. Marie Antoinette, in her affliction, was displaying a noble courage but her heart was heavy with fear for her children. Only one desire possessed her—namely, to escape out of France. That was Louis' wish too. The King seems to have felt that if he remained in Paris he would be made the tool of whichever party happened to be in power. He could not reconcile such a position with his conscience.

Count Fersen, Marie Antoinette's friend, provided a carriage and arranged for relays of horses. On a June night of the year 1791 the Royal Family slipped out of the Tuileries palace on

foot and hurried through the darkness to the waiting vehicle.
By morning they were out on the high road which leads across
France to Alsace.

Spirits rose as the good miles were left behind. As the
frontier drew near, caution was relaxed. The coach came to
Varennes and drew up at the post-house. It was then discovered
that a mistake had been made, because no fresh horses were
available. The King, in his anxiety, put his head out of the
window. The post-master recognized him.

After some delay the carriage resumed its journey. Suddenly,
from the trees which bound the road horsemen appeared. A
challenge rang out. The brakes ground on the wheels . . .

A few days later the Royal Family was brought back to Paris
in a carriage, the blinds of which were drawn. A silent crowd
welcomed the sovereigns whom it was not permitted to look
upon. In the Assembly the Vicomte de Beauharnais, who was
President during that gloomy week, urged the members to
refrain from demonstration.

Alexandre de Beauharnais was a handsome man, very learned,
a philosopher and a prig. A shadow of resentment lay upon his
features because it had been his misfortune to make an unhappy
marriage and to emerge from his marriage ridiculously. He
might have forgiven his Rose her infidelities; he could not
forgive her for having made a fool of him.

There was something to be said for Alexandre. While he was
still a boy his father, the old Marquis, had separated from his
mother, in order to live with a Mme Renaudin whom he had
met while on naval duty at Martinique. Mme Renaudin
belonged to the noble family of Tascher-la-Pagerie and her two
brothers, the elder of whom, Baron Tascher, wore the Cross of
St. Louis, were engaged in growing sugar. Mme Renaudin
had arranged his, Alexandre's, marriage to her niece Rose
Tascher-la-Pagerie and had given him no peace until he had
consented to fall in with her wishes. When Rose began to
quarrel with her husband's studious habits and to spend his

SOPHIE DE MONNIER

money as if it was water, Mme Renaudin had taken her side against him and, in addition, had alienated his father's sympathies.

The end, after that, had come quickly because Alexandre was incapable of compromise. Rose had borne him a son but he had felt no joy of the child and gone off, alone, to Italy. In his absence, or so he declared, Rose had found a lover. A daughter was born ; Alexandre repudiated it and opened proceedings for divorce. While these were pending he went to Martinique. ostensibly to play a part in the American War of Liberation, really to find out ugly facts about his wife's girlhood. He go, his divorce but the Court decided that the daughter was hist Rose went to live with his father and Mme Renaudin at Fontainebleau. Later, when even her aunt had tired of her, she returned to Martinique with her two children.

She was still in Martinique when the Revolution began. Alexandre was alone in the world, with his philosophy and his politics and his good opinion of himself. A man whom no woman could influence except by appeal to his vanity. An able man and a capable soldier, whom, years before, Marie Antoinette had called her *beau danseur* in the careless days of Versailles.

Not that Alexandre de Beauharnais had ever been received officially at Court. That had been refused on the ground that his family was not entitled to the honour ; but the real ground of refusal was the behaviour of his father and the fact that Rose was Mme Renaudin's niece. Alexandre had not forgiven the Royal Family for rejecting him ; he had not forgiven his father ; he refused to forgive his wife. Nor could he forgive a world which, as he guessed, spared him little of its sympathy. Unforgiveness was stamped upon his face ; it lay, a canker, in his heart. The noble words and ideas which flowed from his lips came out of a spirit frozen by selfishness, incapable of renunciation. The contrast with Mirabeau is sharp and decisive. Sophie's man and Rose's man belonged to different worlds. Nor could Sophie, with all her passion of love, have made anything of Alexandre.

Mirabeau had found a gold mine for the King and bidden him possess it. Alexandre, as President of the Assembly, took the King prisoner and seized the gold mine in order to hand it over to the money-lenders. No sooner were Louis and Marie Antoinette shut up again in their old palace than Necker's friends began to come hurrying back to Paris. Germaine de Staël arrived from Coppet, where, during many months, she had been hiding from the wrath of her father's customers.

Germaine was entirely without shame about the part which her father had played. The idea that it was disgraceful to default in payment had not so much as entered her head, though, day after day, she and her companions complained about the King's default. The King was a dishonest bankrupt, so they said ; Necker, on the contrary, was victim of circumstances. That, also, was Necker's view. The powers of self-deception possessed by this Swiss were unlimited. In that respect, however, he was in the tradition of financiers, all of whom, in all ages, have worn self-righteousness like a garment even while busy with the most questionable transactions. Father and daughter had been accustomed, during her stay in Switzerland, to commiserate with one another on the black ingratitude of human nature :

" As we walked together, my father and I," she wrote, " under the great trees of Coppet, trees which seemed to me to be friendly witnesses of his noble thoughts, he asked me once if I believed that the whole French people shared the vulgar suspicions of which he had been the victim during his journey from Paris to Switzerland.

" ' It seems to me,' he said, ' that there were some districts in which, until the very end, the purity of my aims and my devotion to France were recognized.'

" He had scarcely asked me this question before he brushed it aside as if afraid of being too much moved by my reply.

" ' Say no more ! ' he exclaimed. ' God can read my heart. That's enough.'

" I didn't dare to reassure him at that moment, because I saw
how deeply he was moved."

This was written long after Necker's death, when Germaine
had constituted herself his apologist in order, also, to apologize
for herself. The account contained the admission that :

" M. Necker regretted bitterly that popularity which, without
a moment's hesitation, he had sacrificed to his sense of duty.
People have blamed him for attaching so much value to it.
Unhappy those statesmen who have no need of the support of
public opinion ! Courtiers or oppressors, they are ready to win
by intrigue or terror what men of generous mind seek not, except
as the expression of the regard of their fellows."

Necker, meanwhile, was engaged in defending himself. He
wrote to the Assembly :

" I know that I shall be blamed for my stubborn devotion to
the principles of Justice, and the attempt will be made to
discount these principles by calling them snobbery. I know my
own principles better than you (the members of the Assembly)
know them. The first on whose behalf my feelings of affection
were kindled were yourselves, when you had neither cohesion
nor power. You were the first people for whom I fought.
Then, when I was distressed at the contempt with which you
were being treated, when I proclaimed the respect that was due
to you, when I displayed a ceaseless anxiety about the people's
lot, I was held up to the same kind of scorn which you yourselves
now heap on me. You say that I was ready, at the time when
you abandoned me, to transfer my allegiance to others ; that I
lusted after power. I cannot thus flatter myself. Your enemies
and mine have interposed between us a barrier which I will
never try to break down. Your enemies and mine will hate me
for ever because they have loaded their own sins upon my
shoulders. It was not I who encouraged them to hope that they
might, one day, be able to enjoy undiminished, their ancient
privileges. It was not I who stiffened their resistance when the
time had come for them to treat with fortune.

" Ah, if they were not now being sorely oppressed, if they were not steeped in misfortune, how many reproaches could I not heap upon them ! The next time I venture to put in a word for them in the matter of their rights or possessions, they won't suppose, I hope, that I am trying to get rights or possessions back for them. I have no desire, to-day, to associate with them or with any other person. Let me live and die with my memories and my thoughts. What social stays do I need when I may contemplate the purity of the feelings which have guided me ? Ah, yes, but every feeling heart has need of human contacts. I am forming them, these contacts, in a hopeful spirit, with the honest men of all lands, with those—how few is their number ! —whose ruling passion is the love of righteousness on earth."

Much that is difficult to understand in the nineteenth century becomes explicable when it is realised that such men as Jacques Necker and such women as his daughter Germaine, sat, for the most part, in the seats of power during that century.

She had brought with her Jacques' policy for a Constitutional Monarchy on the English plan, newly refreshed and restored by its author. Her great house in the rue du Bac became, once more, immediately the centre of political activity and the real master of the Assembly and the Government. To it came all the most illustrious figures of the hour, Lafayette, Narbonne, Talleyrand, the Lameths, de Montmorency, Lally-Tolendal, Jaucourt, Alexandre de Beauharnais and a hundred others. Germaine moulded them, once more, into a party. She convinced them that the moment had come to put her father's ideas into execution and to set up a House of Commons and a House of Lords. She urged, further, that Mirabeau's gold mine, the new " land-money," ought to be brought under strict financial control, lest the King, or someone even less worthy than he, managed to lay hands on it.

Her anxiety about the " gold mine " gave her no rest. While others were talking about liberty and the rights of man, her keen black eyes remained focused on this new source of

money, the possession of which, as she understood, was equivalent to the mastery of France, perhaps of Europe also. She did
not take many of her friends into her confidence. Most of them
were politicians, drunk with the new political ideas. They went
about with their heads in the clouds, building better worlds on
the insecure foundations of talk. What was essential was to
snatch the " gold mine " out of their reach before they discovered
that the possession of it would enable them to realize their
dreams. Germaine looked about her for allies whom she
could trust. She opened her heart to Talleyrand and Narbonne
and she invited Thérèse, Marquise de Fontenay, the banker's
daughter, to her house. Thérèse knew all about the " gold
mine." Necker's daughter and Cabarras' daughter, little as they
liked one another, served the interests of their respective fathers
and of that class to which their fathers belonged, by acquiring
influence over the representatives of the nation. Thérèse's
beauty made slaves even of the grave Condorcet and the
illustrious Lafayette. Germaine's wit flashed like a sword
among the wittiest company in the world. Intoxicated with love
and language, these noble leaders of a stricken France went to
and fro between the rue du Bac and the Riding School where the
Assembly met, compounding the Constitution which was to
make the King of France a figure head and a fiction and which was
to banish for ever from the eyes of men that Aladdin's cave that
Mirabeau had discovered to them. The Constitution was
finished and presented to the King for signature. In his dark
palace, the blinds of which often remained drawn for days
together, Louis signed it. Instantly the word went out that the
King was a good fellow after all. Necker's newspapers were
filled with praise of the Royal Family and of Monarchy—
Constitutional Monarchy. The Revolution, it was announced,
was over ; the millenium was at the door.

" The King and Queen," Germaine wrote after the event, " had
been urged to go to the Opera. When they arrived at the house
they were greeted with hearty cheers in which the whole

audience joined. The ballet *Psyche* was being given. While the furies danced and waved their torches, filling the theatre with light, I saw the faces of King and Queen lit up by this pale imitation of Hell. A horrible presentiment overwhelmed me. The Queen was forcing herself to look pleasant, but one could see the deep sadness behind her charming smile. The King, as usual, seemed more concerned about what he was looking at than about personal reactions. He glanced round him calmly, even carelessly. He was accustomed, like most sovereigns, to hide his feelings and perhaps that long restraint had diminished their intensity.

" We strolled afterwards in the Champs-Élysées, which was brilliantly lighted. Only the fatal Place de la Révolution separated us from the Palace and its garden. The illumination of the Tuileries and the garden was joined, in admirable fashion, to that of the long avenue of the Champs-Élysées, garlands of lamps being used for the purpose.

" The King and Queen drove slowly through the crowd. The moment their carriage was recognized there were shouts of ' *Vive le roi !* ' But these demonstrators were the same who had insulted the same King on his return from Varennes. Their applause was of no more account than their abuse. . . .

" Our attention was attracted by sounds which seemed to come from all directions at once. The people had begun to sing and the newsboys, singing too, called in loud voices :

" *La grande acceptation du roi. La Constitution monarchique.*"

" It seemed that the Revolution was complete and that Liberty had been established. But all the same people kept glancing at each other as if they hoped to find in their neighbours' expression the security which none of them felt."

Germaine wrote this in her old age when Louis XVI's brother was King of France. Actually on that night, her own anxiety was lively, because all her plans had, suddenly, at the last moment, been upset. Having finished the Constitution, the Assembly was about to dissolve so that new elections might be held under the new Constitution. It had seemed more or less certain that the famous men who had made the Constitution would be returned to Parliament to put it into effect and, consequently, the election had been looked upon as more or less of a formality. Suddenly, at one of the last sittings, Maximilian Robespierre had proposed that no member of the existing Parliament should be eligible for election to the New Parliament.

His motion had fallen like a bomb among Germaine's friends. They refused to believe that it could possibly be carried, but in that they reckoned without the large number of inconspicuous members whom they had treated with contempt and the small number of members who remained faithful to the King and, consequently, disliked the new Constitution. That large number and that small number joined together, to vote for and to carry Robespierre's motion.

Germaine's heart sank. Not her noble friends, all of whom were under strict control, but new, unknown and untried people were to enter into possession of Mirabeau's " gold mine." Worse still, it was obvious that this Maximilian Robespierre had seen through the game and knew to what uses the land-money might be put. In the account of the celebration already quoted there occurs this passage :

" I met a few members of the Assembly during my walk (in the Champs-Élysées). They looked like dethroned sovereigns, very much worried about whom their successors were going to be. Undoubtedly there were good reasons for sharing their wish that they had had the task of maintaining the Constitution, such as it was, entrusted to them, for enough was already known about the spirit in which the elections to the new Assembly were being conducted to dispel any hope of improvement."

CHAPTER XIV

MANON

GERMAINE'S worst fears were realized. The new Parliament (called the Legislative Assembly to distinguish it from the old Constituent Assembly) contained almost no noblemen. It displayed an unruly and radical spirit and showed little inclination to seek advice from bankers. In other words, it held hard to the " gold mine."

Germaine and her friends, excluded from Parliament, proceeded immediately to set up a Parliament of their own in the form of a political club. Their club-house was situated in the rue Saint-Honoré, a big pretentious building which had belonged once to a religious order, the *Feuillants*. They now called themselves " Feuillants." Here were Sieyès, one of the chief architects of the Constitution, Bailly the Mayor, Matthieu Dumas—eight hundred " friends of the Constitution," eight hundred exalted Liberals all of whom had been ready—whether wittingly or unwittingly—to seize "the gold mine" and give it to the Masters of Money. "The People want Liberty," Germaine told them, " but only intelligent men can give it to them."

Meanwhile she kept her eyes fixed on the Parliament and on the Jacobin Club which was situated on the opposite side of the same street. The Jacobin Club had been formed at Versailles two years before by the members from Brittany. It had come to Paris with the King and Queen and at that time, had numbered Mirabeau among its ornaments. Now its chief ornaments were Brissot, Pétion, Condorcet and other representatives of the district of the Gironde. Robespierre was a member ; his influence was growing as the Club grew more and more extreme in its views.

Germaine feared Robespierre. She feared also the woman whose power in the Jacobins was as great as her power in the Feuillants—namely Manon Jeanne, Mme Roland. Manon was thirty-seven, whereas Germaine was only twenty-five; the mistress of the Jacobins had a husband twenty years her senior, who had been more or less a failure all his life—a poor counterpart to the Swedish ambassador. But what Manon lacked in wealth she possessed in passion. Never has frigid woman loved herself with more intense flame of desire; seldom has frigid woman been able to excite so lively an enthusiasm in men's hearts. She told them, and they believed her, that to be free was to be equal since liberty was the sap of human kindness. She was intoxicated with liberty and she intoxicated all those who approached her. Like a medium, she set men *en rapport* with the gods until they babbled the words that came burning from her lips. Her husband obeyed; Robespierre obeyed too, but, somehow, doubted.

Manon's people were middle-class—wine merchants from Bordeaux, lawyers, doctors, substantial tradesfolk. Most of them were revolutionaries from disgust with the breakdown of government, and especially of finance. The debts which Necker had contracted and which, as they supposed, the King and Queen had incurred by their extravagance, horrified them. But like the King and Queen, they had no faith in Mirabeau's money. That " gold mine," in their shrewd judgment, was too good to be true. Like Germaine, therefore, though from different motives, they wished to be rid of it, as soon as possible.

It was an inevitable attitude for merchants accustomed to carry on foreign trade and so anxious to possess gold. The Girondists, as they called themselves, were well satisfied with the bankers who discounted their bills and made them advances; they showed all the bankers' dislike of money that was not as " good " outside of France as inside. Thus, Mirabeau's land-money seemed to them to be a further proof of the rotten state of the government—a shame to which the Queen's profligacy had reduced honest folk.

That was Manon's opinion. Manon hated Marie Antoinette as Germaine had never hated her—as poor women, athirst for luxury, hate rich women. For the same reason Manon hated and despised Germaine—the daughter of the swindling financier. And Manon had a third *bête noire*—the blackest of them all— the barrister Danton, who possessed a club of his own, across the river, called the Cordeliers. Danton was big and loud, handsome as Mirabeau had been handsome, and like Mirabeau, wild and rascally with, nevertheless, a power and weight of loving in his nature which, on occasion, could sanctify him. Manon shuddered in his presence as frigid women shudder in the presence of full-blooded men. Manon called him coarse, bestial, corrupt— and he was all these—but her eyes were blind to the light which sometimes shone on the man's face. Women who are cold always make virtue of their deficiencies. But in Danton's presence Manon's virtues looked lean and unsubstantial, just as Manon's circle of admirers looked weak and effeminate. Germaine had known how to admire Mirabeau, while hating him (she spared some admiration also for Danton), but her rival at the Jacobins could not admire anything which she hated.

There was the difference between the two women. They were egoists both, but whereas Germaine's love of herself was strong and coarse and unruly, Manon's love was precise, delicate, fastidious, humourless. The Feuillants, in consequence, had no dealings with the Jacobins. Indeed, they constituted a direct rival to the older body, a rival, too, which, since Parliamentary honours had been denied them, threatened to become the governing power.

Danton observed that threat ; so did Robespierre ; so did the crazy doctor, Marat, whose paper, *L'ami du peuple*, was demanding already the destruction of privilege and wealth. Robespierre was extraordinarily like Manon, a sour and prim little Puritan who had been " top boy " at the Jesuit school where he was educated and who had resigned the post of Public Prosecutor in his native Arras because one of the duties of the

office was the countersigning of the death warrants of criminals.
This neat little man, whose wig was always powdered and whose
linen was always spotless, felt towards Danton and Marat exactly
what Manon felt. But there was a streak of shrewdness in
Robespierre which had convinced him already that if Germaine
and her friends were to be prevented from seizing Mirabeau's
" gold mine," Danton and Marat and their people must be
enlisted in the task of prevention. Robespierre knew enough
about the Masters of Money to understand that their power was
greater than that of armies. Force must be met with force ;
cunning with cunning. And there was neither real force nor
real cunning in the circle of Manon's friends. Robespierre,
who had been something of a high Tory at Versailles where he
had stated that France could not be imagined without her King,
began to move to the Left. Manon's circle saw him no more.

Meanwhile, Germaine was forcing her friends upon the King as
his ministers. Louis was in no position to resist such pressure because every word of resistance became, in the newspapers which
Necker's daughter controlled, a weapon of offence against the
throne. Nevertheless, there was resistance, especially from Marie
Antoinette. When Narbonne, Germaine's lover and the King's
kinsman, was put forward for the office of Foreign Minister,
the Queen wrote to Fersen, under the date November 7, 1791 :

" No appointment yet. Madame de Staël is working hard for
M. de Narbonne. I never saw a stronger and more involved
intrigue."

A month later Narbonne became Minister of War. The
Queen wrote again :

" Count Louis de Narbonne is at last, since yesterday, Minister
of War. What glory for Madame de Staël and what a pleasure
for her to have the whole army at her command."

It was. Germaine, from day to day, had been growing more
and more uneasy about the political situation in its bearing upon
the financial situation. Her shrewd eyes had observed
Robespierre's move to the Left and she had not for a moment

forgotten that it was he who had plucked the prize out of her hands. She saw that a party which included Robespierre and Danton and Marat would constitute, if in possession of the "gold mine," a force that, within the boundaries of France, would be irresistible. How to break up the combination before it had become established !

She looked at Manon and her Girondists. They had accepted the idea of a monarchy on the English plan, but at heart they were all Republicans. Again, at heart, as has been said, they all feared Mirabeau's money. Merchants and tradesmen like money which they can ring on their counters. Above all they feared, and hated, the mob, the "lower class," the skinny and threatening inhabitants of the rue Saint-Antoine, who ran through the city of a night to listen to Danton's bellowings among the guttering candles at the Cordeliers. Germaine concluded that a diversion which had as its object the destruction of the "gold mine," and which promised, consequently, a period of retrenchment and of discipline would not be unwelcome to these thrifty souls.

Her plan was to form a Franco-Prussian alliance against Austria—the Queen's Austria—and to make war on that country. She and her friends foresaw that, once war had begun, supplies of money which could be used outside of France would become necessary in order to equip the armies. Since the land-money could not be used outside of France—no banker anywhere in Europe would touch it—the land-money would soon depreciate in value, especially as it would be necessary, sooner or later, to offer the Church lands as security for the foreign loans. When that had been done, even French merchants and shopkeepers would refuse to accept the land-money because no security of any kind would exist behind it.

No sooner was Narbonne installed at the War Office, therefore, than he demanded of the Parliament a vote for £2,000,000 for the strengthening of the national defences—a demand which caused sudden great anxiety in Paris and throughout France. Secret agents, Ségur, who had been Necker's right-hand man and

MADAME DE STAËL

obedient slave, and Custine, were sent off to Germany, the former to the King of Prussia and the latter to the Duke of Brunswick. At the same moment the whole Paris Press began to describe the preparations which the Emperor, Marie Antoinette's brother, was making for the invasion of France and the rescue of the Royal Family. These reports occasioned a panic which, since Frenchmen have never lacked for courage, was transmuted, very soon, into a grim demand for war. The Parliament addressed an angry letter to the Queen's brother in which threatening language was employed. When he replied in most conciliatory tones, it was immediately assumed that he was playing a game. Out came the drums and whistles. Mobs, which yesterday had been ready to follow Danton and Marat, cheered Narbonne now and his illustrious mistress. The Feuillants bounded into popularity and Manon and her Girondists—the whole Jacobin club—fell under shadow. They too, all except Robespierre, became war-minded.

Robespierre dared to protest for he had seen the game. Protests came also from the King, who knew how absurd were the charges against Austria, even if he did not know the real reason for these charges. But neither Robespierre nor King Louis possessed the power of propaganda which Germaine possessed. With the help of her newspapers and her nobles she shouted down all opposition. After all, it was natural that the King should try to shield his wife and her brother; natural too that Robespierre, who was a pacifist and a weakling, should dissent from war.

Germaine was about to bear Narbonne a child. But this circumstance did not deter her from accompanying him on a visit to the French armies in the north. She saw with her own eyes how ill-equipped were these armies and how badly disciplined. But she declared, shamelessly, that they were in excellent fighting trim. Narbonne created two new marshals and appointed them, with the illustrious Lafayette, to lead the forces of the Fatherland. Then he and Germaine returned to Paris and testified that all was well. Only the King and Queen and Eric Magnus appear to have been shocked by this escapade ; their opinions mattered nothing at all.

Nevertheless the King of Sweden, Gustavus III, thought fit to recall his Ambassador as a protest against the behaviour of his Ambassador's wife. Eric Magnus left for Stockholm. The French Parliament sent a dispatch to the Emperor ordering him to furnish proof before a given day (March 1, 1792) that he had no hostile intentions. As it happened the Emperor died on the given day ; but that act was not enough to acquit him. A few days later it was learned that Prussia had joined forces with Austria, in face of the threatening attitude of France.

This news caused a chill of anxiety. The King availed himself of the opportunity to dismiss Narbonne, who was immediately hailed in the Parliament as a martyr. Germaine's newspapers bared their teeth and made ugly accusations against Marie Antoinette. Was this alliance between Prussia and Austria her doing ? And did she hope, very soon, to see Paris brought to heel by foreign bayonets—the bayonets of her own Austrian people ? A new, fierce spirit began to infect the mobs which crowded into the galleries of the Jacobin Club (thrown open during some months to the public) and of the Parliament.

The King marked this rising tide of hate against his wife and sent for Manon's friends, the Girondists, who, as he guessed, were opposed to the war. But Manon's friends were frozen with terror. Her husband, Roland, and his colleagues declared that they could not stop the war, and that, too, was the opinion of General Dumouriez who had been appointed Foreign Minister. Germaine watched with delight the impotence of her enemies to extricate themselves from the trap she had set for them. In the end the King was forced to come in person to the Parliament, and declare war on his wife's nephew.

" I was present," she wrote, " at the sitting at which Louis XVI took, under compulsion, the step that was fated to lead him to so many troubles. . . . His face was expressionless, not from any desire to convey a false idea about his feelings, but because

resignation and dignity so informed his bearing that there was
no room for any other expression. As he entered the Chamber
he glanced to right and left with the vague curiosity which people
who are so short-sighted as to be unable to see anything, often
display. He proposed that war be declared in the tone of voice
he might have used about some trifling order. The President
answered him in the arrogant, off-hand manner which the
Assembly had now adopted, as if it was necessary to the self-
esteem of a free people to ill-use the King whom it had chosen
as its Constitutional head. When Louis XVI and his ministers
had gone, the Assembly voted the war with acclamation. A
few of the members refrained from taking part in the discussion, but the people in the galleries were in ecstasies.
Members flung their hats in the air."

Baiting the King now became the recognized method of
showing one's patriotism. Louis, as has been said, was a
Christian. There were things which he would not do, even to
save his life. His enemies knew it and paid him, in consequence,
the noblest compliment which may be paid to mortal man—
namely, the compliment of destroying him by means of his own
goodness. They demanded measures against priests whose
only fault was that they had remained faithful to their vows.
The King refused to adopt these measures, though he knew very
well to what use his refusal would be put. Neither threats nor
cajoleries could move him, and the insolent speech which Manon
wrote for her husband and which Roland read in his presence,
effected no change. Louis saw his duty and saw that it did not
include the betrayal of helpless men who had put their trust in him.

The war began. Manon took charge of it. Emergency and
fear quickened her mind to a panther-like agility. She directed
her husband, now minister of the Interior, in the smallest detail
of his office and she exerted the same direction over all the other
ministers. When bad news came from the front, she contrived
to load the burden of odium on the shoulders of King and
Queen, just as Germaine had done; but at the same time she

managed to make use of such popularity as remained to Louis and Marie Antoinette in the provinces of France. Her enemy, as she knew, was Danton, to whose party Robespierre and Marat had gone over. Fear of Danton made her lean, to some extent, on Germaine and her bankers. Germaine, for her part, was ready to help, provided that Manon's people secured the " gold mine " and set it beyond reach of profane hands.

Had the French armies offered any kind of resistance, Manon might have succeeded. Her party, in that case, would have been compelled to contract foreign loans—as Germaine had foreseen —and the land-money would have been surrendered to the financiers. The necessity of war would have justified this step. But the sudden and complete collapse of the French armies, which took place as soon as the campaign began, changed everything. In face of that collapse, loans were out of the question, and so there was only the land-money between France and abject surrender. Unless surrender was to be made, it was necessary to conscript the whole people and to make of France an isolated unit, cut off from all contacts with the world.

Manon and her people were incapable of that. They were Europeans, traders with all nations, Liberals professing a universal philosophy. Iron circumstance found them helpless.

The fourteenth of July came round—that day of Necker's triumph three years before. Again humiliation had been prepared for King and Queen, in the shape of a celebration in the Champs de Mars. Again Germaine was there to witness their humiliation. This is how, in the reign of Louis XVIII, she described the melancholy spectacle :

" A few feeble voices cried ' *Vive le roi*,' like a last good-bye, a final prayer. I will never forget the look on the Queen's face. Her eyes were veiled by tears. The magnificence of her toilet, the dignity of her bearing, made sad contrast with the crowd by whom she was surrounded. A few National Guards only separated her from the populace. The armed men gathered in the Champs de Mars looked as if they had come to take part in a riot rather than a fête. The King walked from the tent, which had been erected for his use, to the altar ... where he swore again to support the constitution under the ruins of which his throne was soon to be buried. A few children, seeing him, raised a cheer. ...

"Only a man of Louis XVI's character—that of a martyr—could have endured such a position. Both his gait and his expression were characteristic; in other circumstances one might have wished for a little more majesty. But now, he had only to be himself to be sublime. I saw, from far away, his powdered head among those heads of black hair; his coat, embroidered as of yore, among the coats of the common people who jostled him. When he ascended the altar steps, one felt that one was looking at a holy victim offering himself in willing sacrifice. He descended, and passing back through the ranks of disorder, sat down beside the Queen and his children. His people saw him no more till he stood on the scaffold."

Germaine was right in believing that Louis XVI was offering himself. For kingship has ever been sacrificial. The difference between a King and a President is the difference between a spiritual association of men and an association for mutual advantage. Kingdoms, as Louis knew, are not and cannot be commonwealths, any more than the spirit which animates a religious brotherhood can be the same as the spirit which animates a joint-stock company. The reason why the heads of Kings are anointed is that oil was, commonly, poured upon sacrifices to make them burn. Sacrifices, too, were garlanded with crowns. In other words the King was, essentially, the father, he who will give himself, if need be, for his children. His fatherhood was the mirror of human fatherhood on the one hand, and of Divine Fatherhood on the other. The nation was the King's family, and its bonds were love and not hope of mutual advantage. "Nationalism," as that word is now understood, was foreign to this excellent conception which was spiritual and not national.

Louis XVI, therefore, at the altar in Paris, is a challenge to every leadership : are you ready to die for the people ? And the brave figure of the Queen, holding still the great dignity of her office, will stand, for all time, against the rhetorical insincerities of the banker and the banker's women. King and Queen, at any rate, had not made money out of this bemused and befooled populace. They had not stolen the children's bread. They had not tried, with hideous apparatus of terror, to bind men to their policies. When love had perished and loyalty was perverted by scoundrels, they had tried, still, to go in the old ways and hold by the ancient truths, even though these ways led to Calvary and these truths carried promise of sacrifice.

As the tide of defeat surged down from the northern and eastern frontiers towards Paris, Manon's people fell into a palsy of irresolution. Having mobbed and threatened the King during June and July, they began to turn to him for help in August, suggesting that he and the Queen might be able to stay the advancing armies of Austria and Prussia.

That weakness was a signal to resolute men. Danton's partisans seized the Hôtel de Ville and proclaimed the Revolutionary Commune. They set up what was, in effect, a new Monarchy and asserted their right over the persons and property of all Frenchmen. On the morning of August 10, 1792, they launched their mob against the King's palace and the King's Government. By midday, Louis and Marie Antoinette, who with their children had taken refuge in the Parliament, were prisoners. The whole of the King's Guard had been massacred.

The King was suspended in the exercise of his office. He and his family were ordered to be kept in the Temple, and were taken in a closed carriage to that grim prison, through furious mobs. Danton and Robespierre and Marat reigned in his stead.

Germaine watched the downfall of Royalty as she had watched so many of the other great events of the Revolution.

" The Constitutionals (i.e., the Feuillants)," she wrote, " had in vain asked leave to enter the King's palace in order to defend it. The invincible prejudice of the courtiers refused them admittance. Unable, meanwhile, in spite of this refusal, to join the opposition, they wandered round the Tuileries, taking the chance of being massacred since they were not allowed to fight. Among them were MM. de Lally, Narbonne, la Tour de Pin, Gouvernet, Castellane, Montmorency and several others whose names have since been honoured. . . .

" Before midnight on August 9 the forty-eight alarm bells of the sections of Paris began to ring, and all through the night this sound, monotonous, mournful and quick, did not cease for a moment. I was at my window with a few of my friends, and every quarter of an hour the voluntary patrol of the Constitutionals sent us news. We were told that the sections were on the march under the leadership of Santerre, the brewer, and Westermann, a soldier. . . . Nobody could guess what was likely to happen next day, and nobody counted on living more than another day. There were some moments of hope during this dreadful night ; we took heart, I don't know why, perhaps only because we had exhausted our fears.

" Suddenly, at seven o'clock, we heard the terrifying sound of the guns of the sections. The Swiss Guards won the first round and the mob fled through the streets as frightened as, earlier, it had been wrathful. I must say that I think the King ought to have put himself at the head of the troops and driven back his enemies. The Queen was of that opinion, and the brave advice which, in these circumstances, she gave her husband, does her honour and should commend her to posterity."

Another observer, a Captain of Artillery named Napoleon Bonaparte, thus described the unholy scene and, incidentally, threw some light on the characters of some of the women of Paris.

" At the sound of the alarm bell," he recounted, " and on the news that the Tuileries was being attacked, I ran to the Carrousel, to Fauvelet, brother-in-law of Bourrienne, who had a furniture shop there. Bourrienne had been my comrade at the Military School at Brienne. From that house I could, at my ease, observe all the events of that day. Before I had reached the Carrousel I had met, in the rue des Petits-Champs, a group of hideous men with a head on the top of a pike. Seeing me passably dressed and with the appearance of a gentleman, they came towards me to make me cry 'Long live the Nation,' which I did without difficulty as may be imagined.

" The palace was attacked by the vilest of mobs. The King undoubtedly had for his defence as large a force as the Convention afterwards had. . . . The greater part of the National Guard was for the King. One must do it that justice.

" The palace taken and the King in the care of the Assembly, I ventured to enter the Tuileries gardens. Never again on any of my battle-fields did I get such an impression as that given me by the masses of the corpses of the Swiss Guards ; perhaps it was the narrow space that exaggerated the numbers or the effect may have been due to its being my first experience of that kind. I saw well-dressed women indulge in acts of the utmost indecency towards the corpses. I visited all the neighbouring cafés ; everywhere passions were violent ; rage was in all hearts ; it was visible in every face, although they were very far from being the common people."

Danton's wife, Antoinette, and Camille Desmoulin's wife, Lucille, were together during these dreadful hours.

" The alarm bells were ringing on every side," Lucille wrote. " We got up. Camille (her husband) went off assuring me that he would not expose himself. We (Lucille and Antoinette Danton) had breakfast. Ten o'clock, eleven o'clock passed without our hearing a word. We picked up some of yesterday's newspapers, sat on a sofa in the drawing-room and tried to read. Mme Danton made me read an article, and it was while she was doing this that I thought I heard the sound of cannon fire. . . .

" She (Antoinette Danton) listens, hears it, grows pale and falls down in a faint. . . .

" I took off her clothes. I could have fallen down on the spot myself, but I was held up by the necessity of helping her. . . . At one o'clock somebody came to tell us what had happened. Some of the Marseillais had been killed. How cruel the stories were ! Camille came back and told me that Suleau's was the first head he had seen go down. Robert had been in the city and had witnessed the awful spectacle of the massacre of the Swiss Guard ; he came in after luncheon and gave us a dreadful account of what he had seen and all day we heard nothing but details of what had happened. Next day, the 11th, we watched the funeral procession of the Marseillais. God, what a spectacle. How it wrung our hearts ! Camille and I spent the night at Robert's house. I was terrified, I don't know why, it didn't seem that we should be safe at home. Next day, the 12th, when we got back, I heard that Danton had been made a minister."

Danton had not been among the attackers of the palace, nor is it certain where he spent the hours during which monarchy was destroyed in France. He need not be blamed. He was the centre of action and the organizer of victory and had his place, on that understanding, outside of the battle. Nor is it easy to fix upon his shoulders the load of guilt for the day's horrors. That belongs to those merchants of death and of debts who, during years, had destroyed the people's love of their King and filled their minds with poison of hate, and suspicion and fear. Danton had no weapons but massacre; like his wife he was victim of the propaganda which Necker and his daughter had carried on for their personal gain and the ruin of all Frenchmen.

Germaine, meanwhile, was using her influence with those of the Revolutionary leaders who had already been bribed to save her lover, Narbonne, and his friends.

" I was told," she wrote, " that all my friends who had tried to guard the palace from outside had been seized and massacred. I rushed out instantly, to discover the truth. My cab-driver was stopped on the bridge. . . . After two hours uselessly spent in trying to pass, I learned that all those who interested me were still alive, but that most of them had been compelled to go into hiding to avoid the proscriptions with which they were threatened."

A different kind of defence this from that offered by the Swiss Guard, " from inside "—defence very like that which Lafayette had offered against the mob at Versailles. Germaine's "Kindergarten" of pretty lads was snugly ensconced under the sheltering umbrella of finance. She went to see them :

"When I went on foot," she wrote, "that night to see them in the humble dwellings where they had succeeded in finding shelter, I passed armed men lying in drunken slumber on the ground in front of doorways. These only stirred to utter horrible oaths. I saw several workwomen in the same state, and their cursings were more ghastly than the men's. The moment one of the patrols, which had been constituted to keep order, was sighted all honest men fled out of the way ; for what was called 'keeping order' was in fact assassinating and helping assassins."

Germaine's escort, however (to whom she makes no reference), was of so reliable a kind that her safety does not appear to have been in doubt for a moment. Indeed, the more one reads about her peregrinations at night in this stricken and bloody Paris, the clearer it becomes that she stood very well indeed with the successful Jacobins, Danton and Tallien, for example :

"Several of my friends," she wrote, "MM. de Narbonne, Montmorency, Baunets, were threatened personally ; each had gone into hiding in some middle-class household. But the refuge had to be changed daily because the hosts soon became terrified. We decided at first against the use of my house for this purpose because we were afraid that it was being watched ; but on the other hand, as I pointed out, my house was likely to be respected as that of an ambassador, and bearing on its door the name l'hôtel de Suède. This, although M. de Staël was absent from Paris. Very soon hesitation gave way to necessity. Nobody was found bold enough to offer shelter to the proscribed men. Two of these came to me. I told none of my people except the few whom I could trust absolutely. I shut them up in the most remote room in the house and spent the night myself in the rooms overlooking the street, expecting every instant that a domiciliary visit, as it was called, would be paid me.

"One morning one of my servants, whom I distrusted, told me that a placard, describing and denouncing M. de Narbonne,

had been pasted up at the corner of my street. M. de Narbonne
was one of the people hidden in the house. I had the impression
that my servant was trying to frighten me into betraying myself.

" Shortly afterwards the dreaded domiciliary visit took place.
M. de Narbonne had been outlawed. He would therefore be
put to death the same day on which he was taken. In spite of
my precautions I knew very well that if a careful search was
made he was bound to be discovered. It was essential therefore
to prevent such a search. I collected my forces (and I discovered
then that one can always control one's feelings, however violent
they may be, when lack of control is likely to endanger someone else's life). The *commissaires* told off to search all the
houses of Paris for proscribed persons were men of the lowest
class. While they were making their visits, soldiers stood on
guard at each end of the street to prevent escapes. I began by
frightening them as much as I could about the outrage against
the Rights of Man they were committing in entering an
ambassador's house, and, as they did not know their geography
too well, I managed to convince them that Sweden was a power
able to attack them immediately, seeing that her frontier and
that of France were the same. . . .

" Either you get common men at once or you never get them
at all. Ideas and feelings with them are not awakened gradually.
Seeing that my arguments had made an impression I dared,
with death in my heart, to chaff them on the unjust character of
their suspicions. Nothing pleases fellows of this class more
than chaff, because they love to be treated as equals by the
nobles against whom their wrath burns so fiercely. I kept up
my banter until I had shepherded them to the front door, and
I bless God for the wonderful strength he gave me during this
time. Meanwhile it was obvious that this state of affairs could
not continue. The smallest accident must bring death to a
proscribed man who had so recently been a minister and who,
therefore, was very well-known (Narbonne)."

Happily it was found possible to ship Narbonne off to
England and four days later he was safe in London.

CHAPTER XV

A WOMAN AT BAY

FOR Marie Antoinette there now began that long and dreadful martyrdom which is without parallel in the history of modern times. Scourged with the hatred of millions which came up to her prison, day and night, in yells of execration and menace, she entered, clutching fearfully the hands of her two young children, upon her *Via Dolorosa*. Only the King and the King's sister, Madame Elizabeth, remained to her.

Manon's case was not, in fact, much better than the Queen's case. Her party had failed and was already, with the entry of Danton into the Government, thrust aside. But she was not greatly discouraged. Her personal vanity, and the vanity of the class to which she belonged, assured her that men without intelligence could not, for long, remain at the head of affairs. They would make a mess of things. France's trade and commerce would be destroyed and ruined merchants and shopkeepers would soon put an end to mob rule.

This was exactly how Germaine and her friends were calculating. True, Germaine's friends, as noblemen, had, as has been described, been hunted through the streets after the fall of the King. But the wife of the Swedish Ambassador could accomplish much, as her own account shows :

" I was told on the 31st of August," she wrote, " that M. de Jaucourt and M. de Lally-Tollendal had both been taken to the Abbaye (prison). I had information that only those whose assassination had been determined on were being sent to that prison. The quick-wittedness of M. de Lally saved him in a most curious way. He made himself defendant of one of his fellow-prisoners who was brought to the Tribunal before the massacre began. The prisoner was acquitted, as everyone realized, because of Lally's eloquence. M. de Condorcet admired his ability and exerted himself to save him, while at the same time, M de Lally found a capable protector in the English Ambassador, who was still in Paris. M. de Jaucourt lacked their help. I got a list of the members of the Commune of Paris, now the masters of the town. I knew none of them except by their horrible reputations and trusted to chance to give me a cue. Suddenly I remembered that Manuel, one of them, had dabbled in literature, having published some of Mirabeau's letters with a preface—a bad preface, truly, but showing some signs of a desire on its author's part to pass for a wit. I felt that if the man was greedy of applause, he was probably accessible to flattery. I wrote to him and asked for an appointment. He gave me one for the next day, at his house at seven o'clock in the morning, rather a democratic hour, perhaps, but I was punctual.

" He was not yet out of bed when I reached his house, and I had to wait for him in his study. There I saw his portrait standing on his desk and felt really hopeful that his vanity would come to my help. He entered. . . . I drew a picture of the distressing changes of popular feeling of which examples were being furnished every day.

" ' Six months from now, perhaps,' I said to him, ' you yourself may have lost your power.' (Before that time he had perished on the scaffold.) ' Save M. de Lally and M. de Jaucourt ; lay up a sweet and consoling memory against the day when, perhaps, you will be proscribed in your turn.'

" Manuel was an emotional man, easily carried away by his passions, but capable of honest behaviour ; it was for defending the King that he was condemned to death. He wrote to me on September 1st that M. de Condorcet had obtained M. de Lally's liberty and that, at my request, he was about to set M. de Jaucourt free.

" Thankful to have saved the life of so splendid a man, I made up my mind to leave (Paris) the next day. I had promised to pick up the Abbé Montesquieu, another proscript, outside the barrier and take him with me, in the disguise of a servant, to Switzerland. . . . The news of the fall of Longwy and of Verdun reached Paris on the morning of September 2nd. Again one heard everywhere those terrible alarm bells. . . . My passports were in perfect order, and I conceived the idea that the best way of travelling would be in my *berline*, with six horses and postilions in full livery. I thought that this equipage would impress people with the idea that I had a right to travel and that, in consequence, they would not try to impede me. . . .

" Scarcely had my carriage moved four paces when, hearing the postilions' whips, a posse of old women, who looked as if they had sprung out of hell, flung themselves on my horses, shrieking for my arrest and declaring that I was making off with the nation's gold and was going to join the enemy. . . . These women attracted a crowd in an instant, and gutter-boys, with ferocious faces, jumped up beside my postilions and compelled them to take me to the headquarters of the Section in which I lived (the Faubourg Saint-Germain).

" I entered this place and saw in progress what looked like a permanent riot. The man who called himself President informed me that I had been denounced as likely to try to take proscribed persons out of the country, and that they were going to examine my servants. . . . He ordered that I should be taken to the Hôtel de Ville. Nothing could have been more terrifying. I should have to cross Paris and to get out (of my carriage) at the Hôtel de Ville ; I knew that several people had been massacred on the staircase of that building on August 10th. No woman, it is true, had so far been killed, but, in fact, on the following day the princesse de Lamballe was murdered by a populace whose rage was already of so dreadful a character that everyone seemed to thirst for blood.

" It took me three hours to go from the Faubourg Saint-

Germain to the Hôtel de Ville. A man on foot led my carriage through an enormous crowd which howled for my death. It wasn't me they were troubling about; very few of them knew me; it was my fine carriage and smart liveries which, in the mob's eyes, had become challenges to massacre. Not yet fully aware of the brutalizing effects of revolutions on men's hearts, I asked help on several occasions of *gendarmes* who passed near my carriage windows; they answered me with gestures of contempt and menace. I was pregnant, but that fact didn't disarm their wrath. Quite the contrary, the more ashamed of themselves they felt, the more exasperated they became. Meanwhile the *gendarme* who had been posted in my carriage, being removed from contact with his fellows, took pity on me and promised to defend me with his life.

" I descended from my carriage in the middle of an armed mob and walked under an arch of pikes. As I mounted the stair, which bristled with spears, a man thrust at me. My *gendarme* protected me with his sword. But if I had stumbled at that moment my life would have been lost, for it is of the nature of the common people to treat with respect anybody who still remains standing, but to kill anybody who has been struck down.

" At last I reached the Commune, over which Robespierre presided, and breathed again at my escape from the populace. What a protector to have found! Robespierre! Collot d'Herbois and Billaud-Varennes were acting as secretaries. The latter had not shaved for fifteen days to avoid the least suspicion of being an aristocrat. The room was full of common people— women, children, men, yelling 'Long live the Nation' at the pitch of their voices.

" I pointed out the right which I had, as Swedish Ambassadress, to leave the country, and displayed the passports given me because of this right. At that moment Manuel arrived. He was very much astonished to see me in so melancholy a position, and having answered for me until the Commune should have decided upon my fate, he took me away from this terrible place and shut me in his own room with my maid.

" We had to wait there six hours, hungry, worried and afraid. The window looked on the Place de Grève, and we saw the assassins coming back from the prisons with bare and bloody arms. They uttered horrible yells.

" My carriage with its luggage remained in the middle of the *Place*. The crowd was making ready to pillage it when I saw a big man, in the uniform of the National Guard, jump into the driver's seat and forbid anybody to touch anything. He spent two hours defending my luggage ; and I confess I found it difficult to understand how so trifling a matter could be attended to in the middle of events of so horrifying a nature. Towards evening this man came to my room with Manuel. He was the brewer, Santerre, so hideously famous since. He had seen and distributed in the Faubourg Saint-Antoine, where he lived, the wheat sent there by my father during the famine, and he remembered these occasions. He had had no wish to go to the help of the prisoners (who were being massacred) as was his duty as a commandant, and had found in my carriage the excuse he wanted for remaining. He wished to boast about it (his guardianship of my luggage), but I could not refrain from telling him what I thought he should have done. As soon as Manuel saw me, he exclaimed with much feeling :

" ' Ah, how thankful I am that I was able to set free your two friends yesterday.'

" During the night Manuel drove me back to my home in his own carriage ; he had been afraid to do it in daylight, and so, perhaps, lose his popularity. The street lamps had not been lit, but we passed many men carrying torches. The light of these torches was more terrifying, even, than the darkness. Again and again Manuel was stopped and asked who he was. When he answered : ' The procureur of the Commune,' this worthy revolutionary was saluted with respect.

" When we reached my house, Manuel told me that a new

MADAME ROLAND

passport was being given me, but that I would not be allowed to take anybody with me except my maid. A *gendarme* had been told off to accompany me to the frontier.

" The next day Tallien came to my house under orders from the Commune to escort me out of the city. Every moment was bringing us news of fresh massacres. There were several people, some of them very much compromised, in my room. I begged Tallien not to mention that he had seen them ; he promised, and kept his word. I got into my carriage with him ; we, my friends and I, took leave of each other without being able to speak, for our words were frozen on our lips."

All her friends, however, were spirited out of France by persons who, in other days, had been her father's and her own agents, but who were now turned revolutionary. Tallien was one of the chief authors of the massacres ; his complaisance, where Mme de Staël's friends were concerned, is therefore all the more astonishing and makes it obvious that throughout the whole course of her visit to the Hôtel de Ville she was in perfect safety, except, perhaps, from a stray shot by some drunken mobsman. These mobs were Necker's ; the same who had cheered the banker and savaged his enemies on so many earlier occasions, the same who had plucked the leaves in the Tuileries Gardens to make " Necker cockades." Where there is a mob, there is also a mob master.

Meanwhile, in the prisons, red massacre was afoot—massacre, as many witnesses attest, arranged by Germaine's friends, Manuel and Tallien—among others. These scoundrels had had graves dug in advance for the victims ; they had engaged the butchers ; they supervised, at a distance, the butcheries.

" What preoccupied us most," wrote M. de Saint Méard, who was a prisoner in the Abbaye, " was to determine what position we should assume in order to receive death in the least painful fashion when we arrived in the arena of the massacre. From time to time we sent some of our comrades to the turret window to inform us as to the position adopted by the unhappy people who were being killed, so that from their report we could decide which one we should do best to choose ourselves. They reported to us that the people who raised their hands suffered much longer, because the force of the sword strokes was deadened before it reached their heads. . . .

" The heartrending cries of a man who was being hacked to pieces with swords drew us to the turret window, whence we saw the dead body of a man lying in the road, opposite the door of our prison ; a moment later another was massacred, and so it went on.

" It is quite impossible to describe the horror of the profound and gloomy silence which reigned during these executions ; it was only broken by the cries of the victims and by the sound of the swords striking them on the head. As soon as they fell to the ground a murmur was heard from the crowd, mingled with cries of ' *Vive la Nation*,' which were infinitely more terrifying to us than the horror of the previous silence. . . .

" We saw two men come in holding swords in their blood-stained hands ; they were guided by a turnkey, carrying a torch, who pointed out to them the bed of the unfortunate Reding. At this terrible moment I held his hand and tried to reassure him. One of the men made a movement to pull him up ; but the unhappy man stopped him and said in a faint voice :

" ' Ah, sir, I have suffered enough. I do not fear death ; for pity's sake kill me here.'

" At these words the man stood still, but as his comrade looked at him and said : ' Come on,' he made up his mind. He picked up the Swiss (Reding), took him on his shoulders, and carried him down into the street, where he was put to death."

In all, some 1614 persons were massacred, in circumstances of horror which have few parallels in human story. But the tigers did not possess claws strong enough to strike at Germaine and her group of lordlings. As has been said and must be repeated, the mobs which Danton commanded had been recruited in the first instance to serve Necker. There were plenty of officers and non-commissioned officers still in these ranks who were ready to serve Necker's daughter. Leaders come and leaders go, but money is eternal. Shrewd men took care to stand as well as possible with those who to-morrow or the next day might be their masters once more.

Among the shrewd men, as has been seen, were Tallien, one of Robespierre's henchmen, a printer's devil turned statesman. Fouché, too, ex-Oratorian, the Comte de Barras and Stanislas Fréron. These scoundrels were up for sale; and with the fear of the " gold mine " in every financial centre, there was plenty of money available to buy them. They sold life to those who were able to pay for it, provided always that such sales could be effected without danger to themselves.

Consequently, on the second day of the " September Massacres," as has been said, Germaine took the road in her great *berline* with its team of big horses, for the Swiss frontier. She who had played lead in the first acts of the tragedy heard only the sound of hooves on the good highway; the shrieks and sobs of the victims, who were her father's victims and hers, were muted for her ears. They killed that day in one of the prisons, the beautiful princesse de Lamballe, Marie Antoinette's friend. They hacked off her head and stuck it on the end of a pole. As evening began to fall, bloody hands raised the pole up to the Queen's window in the Temple. On that day, too, a woman cut out a man's heart from his chest and ate it.

The September Massacres were part of Danton's plan to force Paris to defend herself. The butchers who committed the massacres had been hired; but the spectators were ordinary citizens, crazy with fear of the foreign armies that were approaching the capital. Danton and Marat had filled the newspapers for days with accounts of these foreign armies and the vengeance they would wreak on the Parisians. They had hinted at Royalist plots, hatching in the prisons where the " vile aristocrats " were lying. They had declared that the Queen, even in her downfall, was planning the ruin of France when her nephew and his soldiers should have triumphed.

Fear, in short, was Danton's recruiting sergeant. By fear he gathered reinforcements, armed them, and sent them to the front; by fear he compelled the reluctant to meet his demands ; by fear he made cowards brave so that, as partners in his massacres, they cut themselves off from any hope of retreat. And he sent out his fear to all the towns and villages of France so that a people, bemused by Manon's doctrines of liberty and equality, was whipped back, suddenly, to action.

He had the means to propagate fear, because, on the first day of his coming to power, he had possessed himself of the land-money. At last, Mirabeau's " gold mine " was being put to use. Its immense resources, rich as the good soil of France itself, had scarcely, until this hour, been guessed at. Armies arose, as if by magic. By the same magic Government was clothed in power.

Manon's heart began to fail. Was it possible that after all Danton would succeed ? The news of the great French victory at Valmy came to drive the blood out of her cheeks. The invaders had been checked and were retreating towards the frontiers.

Instantly Danton turned on Manon's people, those good Liberals who, amid the hurricane, had continued to dream of a new heaven and a new earth. He snatched away from them even the appearance of power. He began to utter threats that the mobs in the galleries applauded. Manon, like the King and Queen before her, began to look beyond Paris towards the provinces of France where substantial merchants still bought and sold and where the silk trade and the wine trade still flourished. Secret means of communication were established with Lyons and Marseilles and Bordeaux and Nantes and a hundred other centres.

This woman, in other words, who for a few weeks had ruled Paris, became Paris' enemy. Her party, which included the most illustrious names of the Revolution, became the spearhead of counter-revolution in the Gironde, in the Midi, on the Rhône. Nearly all the merchants and tradesmen in these areas rallied to it, not only because it promised stable government, but also because it was the enemy of the land-money.

The battle which Germaine had, perforce, relinquished was thus taken up by her one-time rival. Manon's energy and resourcefulness had never been so conspicuous, nor had her power over her husband and his friends ever been more complete. That power, in its exercise, was not limited to men. The party of the Gironde possessed many female agents, notably Thérèse de Fontenay, Cabarras' daughter.

This girl had not fled from Paris when the Royal House was overthrown. She had lingered on, in her big mansion, through the days of massacre and horror, maintaining some sort of social life. Men from all parties visited her—the same who had helped Germaine and her friends to escape ; and she enjoyed immunity from rough handling. That, certainly, was due to the fact that her father was one of the great international bankers and that her brother and uncle were important people in the Bordeaux wine-trade. If the dictators were overthrown these were the people who would rule France.

Danton, Robespierre and Marat watched Manon and Thérèse with ever-increasing suspicion. Their own position, in spite of the victory of Valmy, was too insecure to allow them any sense of confidence, and they realized that, if the great cities of France revolted against their rule, the task of defence might become impossible. In such circumstances it was necessary to break Manon's power without, if possible, drawing upon themselves, in the process, the hatred of the provincial towns. It was decided to bring the King to trial.

The snare, for the Girondists, in this move, lay in the respect for the Throne which still existed in the provinces of France—especially those provinces which were remote from the danger of foreign invasion. Even if most Frenchmen believed that the

Queen had been plotting against their country, there were comparatively few Frenchmen outside of Paris who desired to see the monarchy destroyed. There were still fewer who wanted action against the King's person. If, therefore, Manon's people voted for the King's death they would, by that vote, alienate their moderate supporters, the merchants and shopkeepers; if they voted against the King's death the Parisian mob would accuse them of being Royalists at heart. In the first case their influence would be gone, and with it their leadership; in the second their lives would be in danger.

King Louis was brought from his prison and placed on his trial as had been King Charles I of England before him. During several days Marie Antoinette suffered the distress of seeing him led away from the Temple—for it was quite likely that the mob would assassinate him. She displayed the heroic and lovely courage which was become, now, her habit, comforting Madame Elizabeth and the children. The King was condemned as a traitor to France and the voting began on the punishment which he must suffer.

In vain Manon's people tried to escape from that terrible vote by proposals that the matter should be referred to the nation itself. Danton would have none of these evasions. He forced them to go, one by one, to the tribune, and to pronounce, one by one, for or against the King's death. All, without exception, voted for the King's death, though there were many brave men of other parties who voted against it.

Marie Antoinette broke down at the news, but only for a few moments. The King had been removed from his family. He was permitted to spend some part of his last night with them. They all tried to be brave. But when he went away to his solitary room on the upper floor, nature asserted herself. Next morning Marie Antoinette heard the coming of soldiers and the going of a carriage. They told her, later in the day, that she was a widow.

Louis XVI died as he had lived, calmly and with an excellent courage. They had set the guillotine in the great square which is now the Place de la Concorde ; an immense crowd surrounded it. The King was driven down by way of the rue Royal in a closed carriage with two horses. Silence greeted the carriage and it was not broken when its occupant descended. As Louis mounted the steps of the scaffold, bands began to play. He raised his hand and, instantly, the music ceased. He appeared to be about to address the people. An officer rode up, shouting :

" I brought you here to die, Capet, not to make speeches."

The bands played again. Sanson, the executioner, approached the King to remove his collar. It seemed for a moment as if Louis would resist that indignity, but his confessor murmured :

" The Saviour, Sire, suffered a greater humiliation."

The King then submitted. As the axe was about to fall, the priest cried in a loud voice :

" Son of St. Louis, ascend into Heaven."

Sanson showed the King's head to the people, wading through the Royal blood which poured from the scaffold on to the handkerchiefs outstretched to receive it.

CHAPTER XVI

"THE ANGEL OF THE ASSASSINATION"

ON the day of the King's death Germaine de Staël was at Juniper Hall, Leatherhead, England, with her lovers Louis de Narbonne, Talleyrand and Mathieu de Montmorency. She had followed these lovers to England in defiance of the entreaties of her parents, chiefly because she had begun to fear that Narbonne, to whose babe she had just given birth, no longer cared for her.

Both Necker and Suzanne had been compelled to listen to their daughter's views about love.

" Love," she had told them, " is above laws and man-made opinion. It is the truth, the flame, the essential stuff, the basal idea of the moral world. Heaven itself has no right to condemn it."

Pious Jacques was shrewd enough to relate this truth to the circumstances of the case. He knew his daughter :

" My daughter," he wrote to his friend Meister, " is about to leave us to go and spend some months, not indeed in London, but in the English countryside where several of her friends are now gathered. Not from you, sir, whom I love and who love us, would I seek to hide how much this journey saddens us. I have done everything in my power to prevent it ; but all to no purpose. She will have to travel through France, and that is an added anxiety even though she won't go through Paris. Her confinement passed off excellently, but a journey undertaken so soon after it, at this season of the year, is necessarily a matter of distress. One must be resigned to what one cannot help."

Suzanne wrote to her old lover, Gibbon, the historian.

" After having exhausted uselessly all the resources of mind and reason in attempting to dissuade my daughter from her insensate project, we had an idea that a short stay at Geneva might, by bringing her under the influence of public opinion, make her more docile. She profited by that freedom to set out on her journey sooner even than we had feared. How badly she has begun the year (1793) and made us begin it. I say no more."

Meanwhile Gibbon had received a letter from Germaine herself :

" There are feelings," this letter ran, " which, uniting every aspect of love and friendship become yourself . . . and more than yourself. When unheard of conditions, such as have arisen in the Revolution, have welded together the minds and souls of two people during five years, when these conditions have produced mutual dependence, so that it is impossible for the two people to live apart, when, finally, everything known as propriety and worldly consideration and advantage has tumbled into a ridiculous heap of ruins, I can see no reason why he and I should go on living if we are to be separated."

Narbonne, however, was in no mood for love-making. Indeed the King's trial and the King's death had struck horror into every heart. Germaine, though she was ready to sentimentalize over fallen Royalty, was exasperated. Her sole concern was Narbonne, whose coldness infuriated and humiliated her. Later she wrote the whole story into a novel, thus :

" I followed Fernand (Narbonne) into the desert (England). A woman surrounded him with all the tender joys of love. In the desert he was still a sovereign : he saw happiness and a whole existence hang on one look from him : power and glory were restored to him by my ardent and complete yielding. My love was his shield from the injustice of man, as it tried to attack him in his thoughts. In my heart he read himself . . . he loved me . . . he lived.

" Fernand suggested an absence of a few days from me. I

opposed this project. I complained of it bitterly. No, I did not demand rights from Fernand on the strength of my benefits to him . . . It seemed to me that I carried such a power and weight of love within me that it must dominate him, that a man loved with such a strength of passion could never dream that he was free."

Germaine, at Juniper Hall, was removed from politics and finance and was, in consequence, bored as well as distraught. She seems to have looked upon the visit as a holiday (she was paying all expenses) and to have felt resentment that her guests exerted themselves so little to amuse her.

In Paris, Manon was trying to reorganize her party. The King's death had been a heavy blow. The continued success of the French armies was increasing Danton's popularity. Some kind of counter-attack against dictatorship was necessary if ruin was to be averted. Agents, consequently, were sent out to refresh the enthusiasm of the provinces for liberal, as opposed to dictatorial, principles. Thérèse de Fontenay was one of these. She applied for and obtained permission to travel to Bordeaux to visit her brother and she took her husband, from whom she had obtained a divorce, and her child with her. Very soon her house in Bordeaux became a centre of intrigue against Danton and Robespierre to which the wine merchants and their bankers resorted eagerly. She got rid finally of her husband. A kind of rage of devotion, inspired by her exquisite loveliness, infected the town, which, for that matter, was already in a frenzy of hatred against Paris.

Hatred, as has been said, was not confined to Bordeaux. It was seething, also, in Marseilles, in Toulon, in Lyons, in Lille and on the frontiers. All these centres were in touch with one another. All demanded the suppression of the dictators and the closing down, once for all, of that " gold mine " by which the dictators lived. Take the land-money away from them, the merchants of the Gironde and elsewhere assured one another, and their power is bound to collapse.

Those who were not merchants held the same ideas upon different grounds. Manon's party, like Manon's mind, was built upon a classical foundation. Its heroes were the philosophers of Greece and Rome and its ideals, the ideals of the Platonists and Stoics. Authority, this philosophy ran, was at best a necessary evil since it interfered with liberty. Any kind of dictatorship was hateful. These doctrines were very widely held in France, especially by young people, who saw in them the expression of their own generosity. Few young people penetrated to the basal fallacy—namely, that generosity is a feeling and not a system of thought, and that, consequently, every attempt to provide a philosophical basis for feelings is, in its essence, an attempt to dictate. Manon and her friends never tired of proclaiming what noble-minded people would do, if restraint was removed from them. They explained the obvious fact, that the world was full of people who were not noble-minded, in terms of oppression and despotism. It is an easy step from that idea to the idea that the sons and daughters of liberty belong to a class by themselves and have laid upon them in consequence the duty of opposing and, if possible, destroying all who stand in their way. Men, such as Mirabeau, who have loved greatly never fall into this error because they know that the real motive of humanity is ecstasy—that condition in which self is effaced and intellectual subtleties are thrust away.

Manon had never loved. She lived among abstractions, shadows, names. Her world was peopled not with red blood but with Liberty and Beauty and Truth. And since all these possess reality only for the generous and the loving, she lived alone, with ghosts. Her party, indeed, proclaimed her isolation for it was as bitterly opposed as all the other parties of the Revolution to the free movement of human nature expressed in loyalty and veneration and worship.

It was in this net of false thinking that so many of the ablest minds of France were ensnared. Nor were simpler minds exempt from danger as the case of Charlotte Corday proves. This was a girl of old family who had been brought up in a convent and then had gone to live with her aunt in Caen in Normandy. Charlotte was gentle and good, with a great eagerness to improve her mind and with a habit of hard thinking. She read the works of Manon's people and passed from these works to the study of the Greek and Roman philosophers. She became a Stoic, abandoning the Christian order of ideas, her indignation was aroused when, after the King's death, it became clear that power had passed to Danton, Robespierre and Marat.

Marat especially interested her because he was a native of Caen. She followed, morbidly, all his speeches and actions and came to the conclusion that he was a tyrant standing in the way of the millennium which the Girondists had been about to initiate.

Most of the people of Caen, like most of the people of Bordeaux and the other provincial towns, held, as has been said, the same opinion. All were making ready to throw off the authority of Paris and put an end to the dictators, nor did the fact that foreign armies were threatening the fatherland seem to weigh with them. Like other theorists, they were blind to unpleasant reality. But reality, in the shape of the Masters of the Jacobin Club, was watching them.

That Club, since the King's death, had become frankly extremist and Manon's people were withdrawing from it. Robespierre was its oracle. Marat, in his newspaper, bellowed its decrees. And since it had branches all over France, it became, very soon, the centre of a great spy system. Robespierre's agents in the provincial towns kept him fully informed about the activities of such people as Thérèse. Unfortunately for Robespierre, however, many of his agents were in the pay, also, of his enemies. The information he received was not always accurate.

Consequently it was not until the Austrian and Prussian armies began a new offensive against France in the spring of

1793 that he and Danton awoke to the full extent of their danger. They could no longer count upon Marat, because he had been smitten by a disease which kept him confined to his house. Nor did they feel sure of such members of their party as Tallien and Barras and Fouché. Exactly the same position as had attended the last days of King Louis' reign faced them— an enemy rushing down upon Paris ; Ministers of doubtful loyalty ; the prospect of rebellions and insurrections all over France.

But Danton had not lost his courage. Now, as in the previous year, he launched his mobs against the weaklings. Manon's party was attacked in the Parliament House on May 31. Next day the whole body of the Girondists was prisoner, in the sense that all were placed under guard in their own dwellings. Once more the alarm bells rang monotonously, night and day, pro- claiming treachery and danger. Once more there was murder afoot in the streets, with bloody heads raised on poles ; once more companies of recruits marched through the streets on their way to the front.

The news ran swiftly across France. Bordeaux revolted, Lyons revolted, Marseilles revolted, Toulon, the greatest of French naval bases, opened its harbours to the English and Spanish fleets. In a night, as it seemed, the foreign invader found allies in all the provinces of France. In Bordeaux Thérèse became more than ever the inspiration of the young man who should defend the city against Robespierre ; in Caen, Charlotte Corday took a decision to put her faith into practice for the sake of all her fellow-citizens. She obtained a passport, on the plea that she wished to visit relations in the capital. When she reached Paris she wrote to Marat asking for an interview. The same day she bought a large table knife with a sharp point. Her request was refused because Marat was ill. She repeated it, saying that she wished to bring him news of his friends at home. Again she was refused. She went to his house and was turned from the door. Her voice rose in pleading for admission.

Marat heard it. He called to his servant to admit her and bring her to his bedroom. She found him in a bath, wrapped in blankets—that treatment alone giving him any relief. She sat down beside him and talked to him for a few moments about Caen and its reactions to the attack on the Girondists. Suddenly she plucked her knife from her dress and struck him through the left breast, piercing his lung and opening the largest of his blood-vessels. He sank back, crying for help. She tried to escape ; but his attendants captured her.

It was July 13, 1793. Next day she was brought before the Revolutionary Tribunal. Foquier-Tinville, the public prosecutor, in his black-plumed hat, questioned her closely but obtained no information beyond an avowal of guilt. She refused to express regret for her crime. She was condemned and taken to the Conciergerie, where an artist, with her consent, painted her portrait. On July 15 she rode in one of the red carts which now served the guillotine. The executioner showed her head to the mob and, brutally, struck her dead face with his fist. Hysterical onlookers declared that her pale cheeks flushed at the insult.

Marat's mobs went mad with rage. But Manon's people shuddered. One of them called Charlotte " the Angel of the Assassination." " She has ruined us," another declared, " but she has taught us how to die."

CHAPTER XVII

MANON, meanwhile, had been arrested. Danton's eloquence had shattered her party. Her husband, Roland, and many of her friends were fugitives. The rest were in prison.

In these circumstances Manon allowed herself to indulge in an affection which, while at liberty, she had held in restraint. She wrote passionate letters to Buzot, whom she had known during a long period—and with whom, as she had told her husband, she had been in love ever since she had known him. This love-affair was characteristic of Manon. For it was not an affair of the heart but of the head. Buzot's views were identical with her views and Buzot, in the Parliament, had never failed to support her ideas. Therefore she adored him. He was a married man and she was a married woman. She had no intention of sullying her own or his purity. But she did not spare poor old Roland a confession which shattered him.

" I honour, I cherish my husband," she wrote, " as a sensitive daughter adores a virtuous father to whom she would sacrifice even her lover. But I have found the man who could be that lover and, while remaining faithful to my duties, my ingenuousness has not known how to hide the feelings which I subdue to them. My husband, extremely sensitive, affectionate and proud, could not endure the least change in his empire ; his imagination depressed me and his jealousies irritated me. Happiness fled away from us. He adored me. I sacrificed myself to him and we were unhappy." Nevertheless, she achieved her ambition " to keep my soul pure and to see the glory of my husband intact."

The contrast between this stoicism and Germaine de Staël's blazing indulgences is so striking that the connecting link between the two is apt to be overlooked. Germaine declared that she loved her father but she sacrificed nothing to him. Manon declared that she loved her fatherly husband but she sacrificed his happiness as well as Buzot's happiness to her own virtue. Germaine devoured her lovers; Manon froze love with her self-esteem. Far apart as libertinage and puritanism may seem to stand from one another, they have their roots in the same soil.

Manon did not, at first, take her imprisonment very seriously. She had friends even among the dictators, and though she loathed Danton she knew that, like her own Girondists, he was now in touch with the international money masters. Danton was becoming as anxious as her own people to put an end to the " gold mine." But she would not ask favours of him.

" I looked upon that repulsive and atrocious face," she wrote of Danton, " and although I told myself that a man should be judged only on his words, that I knew, for certain, nothing against him, and that even the most honourable of men is likely to have two reputations in time of party strife—that in short one ought to disregard appearances, nevertheless, I could not reconcile the idea of any good man with that face. I have never seen anyone who so perfectly expresses (in his features) excess of brutal passions. My lively imagination . . . has often depicted Danton to me, dagger in hand, exciting by voice or gesture a band of assassins more timid or less ferocious than himself.

Had Danton been better-looking he might have led—and saved—Manon's party, for they had much in common. As it was the despot covered his own increasing transactions with the Money Power by denouncing the Girondists' transactions.

But there was one observer of these antics who was not deceived—namely, Robespierre. Robespierre, as has been seen

MAXIMILIAN ROBESPIERRE

had rescued Mirabeau's " gold mine " from Germaine de Staël
and her nobles and bankers ; he supported Danton while that
uneasy patriot was striking at the Girondists and so willy-nilly
rescuing the " gold mine " from Manon and her merchants.
But when the Girondists had been destroyed, Robespierre
stretched out his hand, lest Danton himself should make away
with the spoil. Suddenly and mysteriously the great leader who
had organized and equipped fourteen armies for the salvation
of France ceased to be a member of the supreme governing
body, the Committee of Public Safety. Robespierre reigned in
Danton's place.

Danton offered a woman as the explanation of his conduct.
His wife had died ; he had fallen in love again, madly, reck-
lessly, with a girl of seventeen years, named Louise Gély.
Louise was beautiful, gentle and gay. Danton married her and
declared that his interest in public affairs was grown tepid. He
absented himself from the Parliament and displayed to all the
world a lively uxoriousness. And meanwhile he tried to save
Manon and her people, using as before the method of attack to
cover his true purpose. The Parliament shared his views and
would certainly have accepted his leadership had not the state
of France been so desperate. For the fires which Manon had
lighted were blazing furiously. Everywhere at home was revolt
and civil war ; on every frontier a determined enemy. France
was at war with England and Prussia and Austria and Spain—
to say nothing of a host of smaller states. She was blockaded
by sea and by land, while half her population had turned against
her. The Government in Paris, the Committee of Public Safety,
with Robespierre and Carnot at its head, was fighting desper-
ately, backs to the wall.

What a moment to suggest that the " gold mine," the sap and
marrow of resistance, by which all the armies were being
nourished, ought to be closed down in favour of a loan. But
Danton, newly wed and pretending a great detachment from
politics, made the suggestion.

" I am no great financier," he told the Parliament, " but I can see the importance of putting our money on a sound foundation."

He proposed, with Cambon, that the land-money, the assignats, should no longer be legal tender in amounts exceeding a hundred francs. Notes of greater value than a hundred francs would be allowed to rank as payment of taxes but not as ordinary money for buying purposes.

In other words, the hard-pressed Government was to relinquish its source of wealth and to become dependent on loans from bankers for the means of carrying on its resistance. Danton defended his proposal with great cleverness by pretending that if the Revolution possessed " sound money " (i.e., bankers' money) its enemies would be dumbfounded.

" These excessive issues of paper money," he cried, " are endangering the Revolution, that Revolution which was made by men who never had as much as a hundred francs in their pockets but who, all the same, managed to succour the wretchedness of the people while they themselves were shedding their blood for the Fatherland."

He then suggested that the " gold mine " was of use only to " financiers," and urged the Parliament to :

" Be like Nature ; she cares nothing for individuals, only for the species. What will they say at the Court of St. James if this reform of Cambon's is put into execution ? They will be dumbfounded to see a nation strong enough, in the middle of the convulsions which are shaking it, to rectify, by a single decree, the financial system and so to bring comfort to the people, to restore the national credit and to achieve fresh resources for use against the Allied powers."

The Parliament passed Cambon's motion. But Robespierre brushed it aside. Robespierre went on digging in the " gold mine," creating money against the public land and spending that money on the armies of France. Toulon capitulated to the artillery-fire of Captain Napoleon Bonaparte. Marseilles submitted, then Lyons, then Bordeaux. The English blockade was raised. The foreign armies on the frontiers were driven back across Rhine and Pyrenees. Danton came no more to the Parliament House. He and his girl-wife went to his mother's place at Arcis-sur-Aube, the little town at which Necker fleeing from France had been placed under arrest.

Louise loved her husband and tried to comfort him. But the giant was shaken. He who, by means of the land-money, had armed and saved France at the time of the King's downfall, saw another repeat his achievement on a greater and more splendid scale. And he knew in his heart that this had been done because the advice he had given had not been taken.

There was no hope now for Manon and her people. Those of the party who had not managed to escape were brought to trial on October 24, 1793. On the 30th they were sentenced to death. At noon next day they were taken to the guillotine. A few hours later Manon was taken from her prison, Saint-Pélage, to the Conciergerie from which house of death her friends had, that day, set out on their last journey. A week later her trial began. She was accused of having played a part in fomenting the rebellions of the provincial towns. Sentence of death was pronounced on November 8, in the morning, and the hour of execution fixed for the same afternoon. Manon displayed a great courage.

She had already asked her friend, Sophie Grandchamps, " to be present at my last moments in order to give authentic evidence of them."

When Sophie demurred, she had cried, suddenly :

" Ah, it's frightful. My own request terrifies me. . . . Only promise to watch me pass. Your presence will lessen my terror. I shall at least be sure that one worthy soul will render homage to the firmness which will not desert me, even in that dreadful moment. You will be satisfied with me, I promise you."

And so it was. Manon had kept a white dress for the great

occasion. She put it on to hear her sentence, which she received with dignity. Then she took luncheon with a fellow-victim, a forger of the land-money, who was in extreme terror. She sustained the poor man with banter and her big black eyes seemed to hold their mirth resolutely. Sophie was waiting at the Pont Neuf, having strengthened herself with "the great lessons of philosophy." The chain of red carts with their shorn victims, most of them standing, a few collapsed on the benches, came slowly into sight amid cries of "Here they come," from the spectators. Manon was standing up in one of the carts :

"She was fresh, calm and smiling," Sophie testified, "I could see that she was trying to infuse some courage into her unhappy companion whose pallor and weakness made a striking contrast to her own firm bearing and brilliant colouring."

Sophie fled homewards. Manon rode proudly on to the *place* where the long uprights of the guillotine stabbed the dark sky. She mounted the scaffold with her dignity unfaltering and answered the howls of the mob with scornful eyes. Her eyes rose to the big, dirty statue of Liberty, made of stucco, which pious hands had erected.

"O Liberty," she murmured, "how many crimes are committed in thy name !"

CHAPTER XVIII

GERMAINE'S stay in England occasioned so much scandal that, at long last, Jacques asserted himself by cutting off supplies. Juniper Hall was then unavoidably bereft of its châtelaine, and the kindergarten was dispersed. Several of its members followed her to Switzerland.

" There's only one good thing left in the frightful upset of the Universe," she wrote to a friend, " only one thing worth living for, and that is to give happiness to one's friends and get happiness from them. You know the position in which my friends find themselves ; my house is their only shelter. And I am almost wholly ruined by the confiscation of my father's property in France. Two noblemen, de Montmorency and de Jaucourt, have been living under Swedish names in my house for the last two months. M. de Narbonne, under a Spanish name, has just arrived . . . But the Bishop of Autun (Talleyrand), whom I love so tenderly, has been refused admission because of his erstwhile democratic opinions. . . . This body of emigrants which willed the Revolution, but whose revolutionary activities stopped short at the point where self-sacrifice ended and oppression of others began, this body, so small in respect at any rate of its noble members, ought to be specially acceptable to the wise and moderate of (Switzerland). These emigrants feel that they ought to avoid the places where emigrants of a less desirable kind are assembled, for, situated as they are between two extremes, they knew the price of that moderation which the two opposing factions are pleased to regard as a crime . . .

" Things are all right here ; but I have not succeeded in getting permission for the Bishop (Talleyrand) to join me and I won't stay anywhere without him."

Germaine was living, on her own showing, simultaneously with the Bishop, de Narbonne and de Montmorency—not to mention de Staël. Nor could she bear the idea of the loss of any one of her lovers. Her husband, whose gambling debts made a slave of him, ventured to suggest that she might rent a house in Geneva. She replied :

" I must confess that the society of Genevan people is insupportable to me. Their freedom of speech simply results in insolence, and their impeccable morals in infinite boredom. In any case a small town is the worst scene of action in the world for exceptional people. Every word they say is bound to be torn to shreds by the gossips. I am sure that, in Geneva, my father and I assume the significance of the States General in Paris. To create a stir without achieving fame is only an unmitigated nuisance."

A heavy blow fell upon her. Talleyrand was ordered out of England as an undesirable alien, and had to take ship to America.

"Ah, England," cried his bereaved mistress, " they've robbed me of my beloved, my excellent friend . . . It was the Emperor's minister (i.e. the Austrian Ambassador) who asked them to apply the provisions of the Aliens Bill against him. There is the greatest calamity for me since the Revolution ; there was not a single interest of one of his friends with which he was not tenderly occupied at the time of his going. What a misunderstood character ! And his mind, so richly endowed, so charming, is even more remarkable. Nothing shall prevent me from seeing him again ; and it may be that other reasons will force me to go in search of him. I begin to loathe Europe . . . But who, at twenty-seven, can agree to break completely with the past ? How to love as one has loved ! How to experience feelings as vivid as one's memories ! "

Meanwhile the outbreak of civil war in France had brought

tragedy to a greater than Manon. On the night of Sunday, October 13, a paper was handed to Marie Antoinette in her prison, charging her with being implicated in the risings against the Republic. She was ordered to appear and defend herself on the following day.

Nothing had been spared to the gay Queen. Nothing was to be spared. Widowed, torn from her helpless children, she faced her accusers in the horrible court house. Volleys of oaths and curses mocked her distress as she stood, white-haired and haggard, in her carefully mended rags while the vile Hébert made suggestions about her relations with her little son that froze even Foquier-Tinville's blood.

" You do not answer me," the horrible creature demanded.

" I have not answered," replied the Queen, " because Nature refuses to answer to such a charge brought against a mother. I appeal to all the mothers who are here."

The trial dragged on during two days. The Queen held her dignity unwearied to the end. At four o'clock on Wednesday morning a verdict of " Guilty " was returned.

" Have you anything to say ? " the Court demanded.

Marie Antoinette shook her head. Outside the drums were beating. Their sound was multiplied all over Paris. The marching of troops made time for the heavy beating. Thirty thousand horse and foot gathered into the streets and the *place*, between dawn and eleven o'clock, when the tumbril drove out from the prison. The Queen stood up in the cart, with her hands bound. She had a priest with her—one of the Revolutionary kind. She did not seem to notice him. She wore an old white dress, mended often. The serenity of her face declared her thought.

" Down with Tyranny " and " Long live the Republic " yelled the people, upon whom, as upon sheep, the wolves of finance were about to feed.

The cart lumbered into the *place* and she saw the palace where she and the King and their children had lived. Tears filled her eyes. She mounted the scaffold, unflinching. Sanson showed her head to the people.

The people were beginning, already, to weary of death. The old women who surrounded the guillotine were not always now on duty. They came, only, for great occasions. But the knife was never idle. Prisons were emptied only to be filled again. In November, three weeks after the Queen's death, as has been described, Manon suffered, the last of her party. At that time Alexandre de Beauharnais, he who had presided over the Parliament when the King and Queen were fleeing out of France, was arrested as a General who had failed and as a person suspected of sympathy with the Girondists. His wife, Rose, was arrested at the same time, though she had not again lived with him. Madame du Barry, too, who had returned rashly from her asylum in England in order to help some of her friends, was seized and flung into prison.

Rose de Beauharnais, since her return from Martinique, had spent most of her time with Tallien, Robespierre's friend. Robespierre suspected Tallien and the fact that Rose called herself a Jacobin did not exempt her from trouble. Her husband was soon brought to trial and executed.

Alexandre had not changed during the period of his calamity. He remained the same stiff, learned, brave prig. On the eve of his execution he wrote to his wife, in his best copy-book style, a letter which was designed to be shown to his children and by them cherished as a precious heirloom. Alexandre thought of everything, especially his reputation. The spirit of the new Liberalism and the new finance has never found a worthier temple. The letter ran :

"*4th Thermidor of the Second Year of the Republic, one and indivisible (July* 22, 1794).

" All the evidence given at the so-called examinations, which have been to-day inflicted on a number of prisoners, shows that I am the victim of foul calumnies spread by certain aristocrats who pretend to be patriots and are now confined here. The knowledge that this infernal conspiracy will not cease until it has brought me before the Revolutionary Tribunal deprives me of any hope of ever seeing you again, dear friend, or of ever again embracing my children. I will not dwell on my regrets ; my tender love for my children, the brotherly affection I have for you, must convince you of my feelings in this respect.

" I grieve also to leave a land I love, for which I would willingly have laid down my life a thousand times. Not only can I no longer serve France, but the manner of my death makes me appear an unworthy citizen. This torturing thought does not allow me to refrain from begging you to clear my memory. Strive to rehabilitate it. Prove in the eyes of all men that a life-time spent in serving our country's cause and in assuring the triumph of liberty and justice should outweigh the slanderous accusations of a few individuals most of whom belong to a class upon which we look with suspicion.

" This task of yours must be postponed, for in the midst of revolutionary temper, a great nation seeking to pulverize its chains must ever be watchful and must be more afraid of sparing a guilty man than of striking the innocent.

" I die not only with the serenity that allows us to think fondly of our dear ones, but also with the courage that animates a man who recognizes no master, whose conscience is clear, whose spirit is upright, whose most ardent wish is the prosperity of the Republic.

" Farewell, dear friend. Console yourself in our children. Console them by enlightening their minds and, above all, by teaching them that, by their courage and patriotism, they may efface the memory of my execution and recall my services and my claims to our nation's gratitude. Farewell, you know those I love : be their comforter and by your care prolong my life in their hearts. Farewell, I press you and my dear children for the last time to my breast.

" ALEXANDRE B—— "

Alexandre, as has been said, was unaware of Rose's arrest, just as he was unaware that she had become a Jacobin. His children, however, knew better. Hortense, his daughter, recounts how, after her mother had been taken to prison, her brother, Eugene, " rushed off alone to see Tallien and tell him of our misfortune. I waited impatiently . . . but, alas, he, who would have been willing to help us, was already powerless to do so. Terror had frozen every heart."

There was no doubt about it. Paris lay like a sheep on the butcher's trestle, with the red knife to her throat. None dared to breathe. None heard any sound except the trundle of the red carts and the thud of the knife.

Among hundreds less famous Jeanne du Barry was called to account. The lovely girl, who had ruled France and directed the efforts of Louis XV to restore his power by obtaining money from his nobles, came, on December 6, 1793, to the Revolutionary Tribunal. Foquier-Tinville accused her of all her sins with the sin of treachery to the Revolution added. The Jury condemned her to death.

She was fifty now, still beautiful, if rather matronly. Nor had she lost the innate courage and pugnacity which long before had carried her from the gutter to the King's house. She fought for her life. When sentence was pronounced she fell to the floor, making a terrible screaming which shook the onlookers. Next day, when the executioners came to cut off her hair and dress her in the rough white robe of the condemned, she screamed so that even these hardened men were shaken. She continued to scream all the way to the guillotine and aroused so much sympathy among the onlookers that it became necessary to set the carts to a trot. She mounted the scaffold bravely, but once there began to scream again so that the crowd in the *place* was stricken with horror. A few days later the guillotine was removed to a new site near the Bastile, an out-of-the-way spot where its operations were less likely to attract attention. It was the first sign that Paris was weary.

Nor was Paris alone in this reaction of weariness. As soon as the rebellions throughout France were quelled, Robespierre had sent agents to the provincial cities to punish the inhabitants. These agents took guillotines with them. In addition they employed powder and shot and, occasionally, drowning. Fouché and Collot d'Herbois blew some thousands of men and women to pieces in Lyons, and, in addition, massacred a great company of school children who were made to stand together and then mowed down with cannon. In Toulon, Barras killed more than a third of the inhabitants. Fréron, at Marseilles, effected a heavy slaughter, chiefly by means of the guillotine. The most dreadful massacres, however, took place at Nantes (where Carrier filled barges with victims, scuttled the barges and amused himself by shooting the swimmers), and at Arras, Lille and along the Eastern Frontier. Only Bordeaux escaped lightly.

This is the more remarkable when it is realized that Bordeaux was given over to the mercy of Tallien, Rose de Beauharnais' friend. He was a coarse fellow, with an itching palm, whereas Fouché, Barras and Fréron were all men of conspicuous ability and some little refinement. Fouché, in addition, was an excellent father to his own children, who appear to have loved him deeply. Why were the milder men less merciful, while the less mild man displayed gentleness ?

The answer is to be found in the fact that, at Bordeaux, Tallien met, not for the first time, Thérèse de Fontenay, That girl, as has been seen, had made herself, in a fashion, queen of the Girondists in the City. With the fall of Manon's people she was arrested and imprisoned. The guillotine awaited her.

But she was the daughter of Cabarras. No sooner was Robespierre's Pro-Consul established in Bordeaux than he began to see a way of combining business with pleasure which was exceedingly agreeable to him. He visited the prisons, came to Thérèse's cell, at the end of a long round, and asked, artlessly, for the papers relating to her case. These were brought to him.

Tallien expressed his surprise at the paucity of evidence contained in them. He ordered an inquiry. Thérèse was set free.

Next day the suggestion was conveyed to her that if she chose to go into residence at the Pro-Consular hotel, much honour and glory would belong to her. The girl was very young, greedy of life and ambitious of power. She had no scruples because, from her cradle, she had imbibed the doctrine that the sole object of life is gain. The idealism of the Girondists, barren as it was, found no place in her heart. Instead, she conceived the evangel of Liberty as a licence to universal piracy, the piracy of hearts and the piracy of purses. Not that she was greedy, or base, or vulgar. Thérèse believed herself to be made of a superior clay. She had courage and great strength of character. The blood of adventurers flowed in her veins, assuring her that she was born to possess and rule.

And so she accepted Tallien's offer and became Tallien's mistress. She sat beside him at the festival of Liberty and was, herself, worshipped in the Cathedral as the goddess of Reason. But she refused to attend the guillotine and she constituted herself immediately the good angel of the rebellious Bordellais.

Great numbers of respectable and wealthy citizens bought their lives at his hands and even the poor were not turned away. Tallien's money-bags grew fat, and not all this fat was remitted to Robespierre in Paris. Tallien was well pleased because his faith in Robespierre was anything but robust. The man would come to grief. And what then? The lover of Cabarras' daughter and the saviour of the good citizens of Bordeaux might find salvation where others perished. Very soon the clemency of Thérèse's lover warmed the heart of a France sick with the horror of the shootings and drownings and decapitations of all the other lords of the Jacobins. Bordeaux was the bright spot in the night of terror. Nor was its brightness dimmed by the fact that the loveliest daughter of France was Queen of the Carnival of Forgiveness. Thérèse's beauty, coming to its first flowering, made men gasp and wrung the hearts of women. Her exquisite features, framed in hair which fell to her feet, proclaimed unearthly goodness. Nor did her big eyes, limpid as a child's, betray that quick impression.

But Robespierre was watching her. Robespierre distrusted all women, for he had known no woman. The Spartan soul rejected the things of women as it rejected corrupting and corroding pleasure, and besides, how thin were the money-bags from Bordeaux as compared with those from Lyons and Marseilles and Toulon! He sent messages to Tallien, urging a greater severity. His spies were ordered to keep their eyes open.

Robespierre had need of money. For though the " gold mine " was amply sufficient for all internal needs, there were purchases to be made outside of France. Neither England nor the world at large would accept payment in Mirabeau's land-money. Without gold, therefore, the Government in Paris could not obtain Colonial produce and certain essential munitions of war. Robespierre had already seized every ounce of gold in France upon which he could lay his hands. Every additional ounce, as he assured his Pro-Consuls, was vital to the safety of the Republic. His Pro-Consuls were his gold diggers, charged with the duty of stripping gold and silver from churches and mansions and shops and even tombs, to say nothing about such minor sources of supply as bric-à-brac and jewellery.

Bordeaux had been a rich prize ; the thin bags which reached Paris proclaimed a great lack of diligence in collection, that is to say in the use of terror. Let the guillotine be kept busy. Tallien became afraid and hardened his heart. But Thérèse relaxed nothing of her clemency. Bordeaux was filled with her goodness. She managed, in addition, to get much of Tallien's gold out of France into the safe keeping of the London banks, thus, by the same act, securing her lover's and her own future and weakening the resources of the Parisian dictator. Robespierre could endure no more. Tallien was recalled to Paris.

Thérèse was now isolated and helpless and those who had

praised her began to call her names. She packed up, leaving her child with friends, and took the road for Versailles. She arrived there and hid herself in a cheap lodging—which, had she but known it, was kept by a relative of Duplay, Robespierre's landlord in the rue Saint-Honoré. She tried to communicate with Tallien, but her letters never reached him.

Tallien was sick with fear. He watched in agony of apprehension, Robespierre's swift attack on the supporters of Hébert, he who had flung the foul accusation at the Queen. This man was in Money's pay, entrusted with the duty of discrediting the Revolution by driving it mad. Livid and gibbering, he went to the guillotine. The trial of Danton, on a charge of being a corrupt person, also in English pay, followed immediately, and was pressed with a vigour which left Paris breathless. When the jury showed signs of unbelief that the great Tribune of the People could have been bribed with gold, they were taken aside and shown a letter which had been found in Danton's house at the moment of his arrest. It ran :

" We wish you to pursue your efforts and to advance the sum of £750 to M. C. D., £3000 to W. F., and £250 to de M. We accede to the request of C. D. Please advance him £4500 and be so good, yourself, as to find out in what directions money can most usefully be disbursed."

The letter was dated from " Whitehall, Friday 13" (? September, 1793), and came from the Foreign Office. It was addressed to the French banker Perregaux. The payments, it was stated, were being made on account of " essential services " rendered in " fanning the flames and driving on the Jacobins (i.e. Hébert) to a paroxysm of fury."

This letter decided Danton's fate. He was convicted as an enemy of France, acting on behalf of the English money-lenders. Since he had done his best to close the " gold mine " against the French armies, the sentence cannot be looked upon as wholly without justification, for the " gold mine," as has been seen, was the indispensable means of salvation.

Louise watched her husband go to his death. Danton's huge form towered above his companions in the cart. As he passed Robespierre's house he shook his fist at the shuttered window, shouting :

" Robespierre, you will follow me."

Then he began to sing and came, singing his death song, to the *place*. The song went out wildly over the great, silent, terrified crowd. Danton went up last of his friends to the scaffold that was carpeted deep with their blood. It was evening, and the sun was going down behind the hill where the Arc de Triomphe now stands. Danton's head and shoulders were silhouetted against the sun. He glanced across the *place*, perhaps to bid his wife good-bye. It is said that he crossed himself, saying :

" Now then, Danton, no weakness."

To Sanson he said :

" Show my head to the people. It's worth it."

CHAPTER XIX

THE WOMAN-HATER

TALLIEN'S fear quickened from day to day as the Reign of Terror gathered force and Paris became more and more a desert watered with blood. Robespierre was winning the war. On every frontier his well-led, well-disciplined and well-found armies were driving back their enemies. The land-money had been protected from destruction by the guillotine, by stern laws which checked any rise in the price of food and by a rigid exclusion from every market of gold and silver money. There was no choice open to Frenchmen, therefore, but to accept land-money in exchange for their goods. Moreover, to refuse that money was to die. And meanwhile the Government had wrung enough gold out of the rebellious cities to pay for all the foreign goods of which it stood in need.

Opposition was dead. Corruption had been rooted out and destroyed. The patriots alone survived in this bloody modern Sparta, where even the women had been whipped into submission. Paris, the city of women, was denatured because Robespierre mistrusted the whole sex. All mistresses and all women of notoriously loose morals were sent to the guillotine. Love, outside of the marriage bed, became a crime, the punishment of which was death. Chill fell upon every heart and there was silence by day and by night such as Europe had not known in any city since Puritanism held London in its first frost. Robespierre decreed a reign of virtue.

The little man was as tidy and trim as ever, his linen spotless, his hair powdered beyond reproach, the gold-headed cane in his hand a King's sceptre of elegance. He minced along the rue Saint-Honoré from Duplay's house, through the public gardens, across the bridges, stopping often to play with children, who liked him, troubled much by the vagaries of his dog. And women hid themselves, haggard with fear. He had no need of women. Almost, he had abolished them from Paris. His system was based on fear, stark and swift, and by fear he had achieved the regeneration of his countrymen. Fear had cast out corruption, treachery, cowardice, greed even. It was casting out love too. The little Stoic smirked at the children.

But the work of purgation was not yet complete. There was Tallien, still alive, and Thérèse and the butchers of Lyons and Marseilles and Toulon. Rose de Beauharnais, too, and other false Jacobins of her kidney. Robespierre's thin lips were pressed tightly together. That power, which had broken Danton and was driving human nature itself into new ways of perfection, would make quick work of the Pro-Consuls.

Robespierre slept soundly in these genial days of early summer, for " the sleep of a labouring man is sweet whether he eat little or much." Not so the butchers. Like Tallien they had all been recalled to Paris ; unlike him they were being hunted and hounded already by the citizens of the towns which they had ravished. Now that the danger of rebellion was over, Robespierre would have to listen to these complaints. He would have to find scapegoats. The butchers felt the knife upon their throats.

None more so than Joseph Fouché. That good father and family man was in distress because his little daughter lay dying. The fear of Robespierre, for whom he had murdered a thousand boys and girls, gripped his heart. He crept about Paris, at night, stealthily going from butcher's house to butcher's house and then from deputy's house to deputy's house. He carried a list of names with him. The list was long and distinguished.

" These," he told each of the men whom he visited, " are the names of the next batch of victims."

Each of the men whom he visited read his own name.

" What are we to do ? " they asked Fouché in shuddering tones.

The man who had once been a lay brother of the Oratorians shrugged his shoulders.

" If he doesn't die," he told them enigmatically, " then you will."

Fouché's list shook the Parliament. It dried every throat in that Assembly. But it failed to inspire courage. As Robespierre's green and incorruptible eyes swept the benches, sweat broke out on every brow, and each man in his heart hoped against hope that, when the others were taken, he might be spared. There was Robespierre's strength. Fouché had ceased to attend the Parliament but he heard the news. He went, secretly, to Tallien.

" Thérèse de Fontenay," he told him, " has been arrested. What will she say when the guillotine draws near ? "

Tallien shook his head. He was in collapse, helpless, dumbfounded. But Fouché did not lose hope. On the contrary, he wrote to his brother telling him that Robespierre's end was near. Fouché knew all the power of money ; his list of names had taught him where money might be distributed to the best advantage. And he had vast quantities of money to distribute— all the resources of those who desired to make an end of Mirabeau's " gold mine " and so achieve the conquest of France. He began to promise and to pay. Deputy after deputy pocketed the gold and swore to save his own skin. Then Fouché bought a Spanish dagger and went back to Tallien. He told the terrified wretch that, in a day or two, Robespierre would ascend the tribune of the Parliament and propose his own and other people's arrest. That would be the moment to strike. Fouché then produced his dagger. He recalled the fact that, alone among the Pro-Consuls, Tallien had a reputation for mercy. Bordeaux had been the happy exception among the cities of

MADAME TALLIEN

France; and that was due to the girl who, already, was being spoken about in Paris as his, Tallien's, good angel. Thérèse lay under sentence of death. If her lover brandished this Spanish dagger in the moment of crisis, all men would believe that Thérèse had sent it to him so that he might accompany her into Eternity. Thus Robespierre, in his moment of crisis, would be confronted by the love of woman.

Tallien was far from understanding the deeps of Fouché's wisdom. But he was desperate and, in his desperation, prepared to try any remedy. He promised to flourish the dagger at the right moment. Fouché hid himself again, but, at night, resumed his activities.

The great day arrived. It was the Revolutionary month of Thermidor (July), and Paris lay under a cloudless sky. The members of the Convention, as the Parliament was now called, came early because it was known that Robespierre meditated a new slaughter. All were white, shaken, tortured by anxiety, the more so that they had yielded, in the majority of instances, to Fouché's persuasion. Robespierre, on the occasion of his recent " acknowledgment of the Supreme Being," had spoken darkly about " corruption." Were their names really upon the list ? The little man arrived, fresh and confident as ever. His friend, St. Just, who was good-looking, ascended the Tribune and began to read a speech full of vague threats. The members wetted their dry lips. Then Tallien sprang to his feet and shouted for the names of those who were thus menaced. All the members began to shout: " Names, Names ! "

St. Just tried to resume his reading, but the Chairman rang his bell continuously and silenced him. And the shouting went on. Tallien leaped up and whipped out his Spanish dagger. He swore to kill himself there and then if this horrible tyranny of fear was continued. This was a challenge to Robespierre. Robespierre accepted the challenge and rushed to the Tribune. He faced Tallien and stood, glaring at the dagger. The Convention saw the man, who had purged Paris of love, face to face

—as they supposed—with a desperate lover. The gleam of the dagger was a light of passion in a frozen world. Hearts began to thump and feelings were unloosed. The red tide of life flowed again in men's veins.

Never was antithesis sharper or more deadly. For this dagger of love was set against the mechanism of the knife. Tallien's corn-coloured head, in that hour, was a halo. His fellows shook their fear away and forgot the red carts and the red valets, the ritual of preparation and the blank instant of fulfilment. They shouted down the little Robespierre, whose face grew livid with his rage.

" The blood of Danton chokes you," a deputy cried.

It was the signal of release. A moment later Robespierre was under arrest. But his corps of gaolers refused to receive him at the prison. He went free again, to the Town Hall, where the Revolution had had its earliest lair. He gathered his friends and prepared to resist. The bells began to toll. The mob came up from its kennels. Terror seized upon all those who had dared to attack him.

In this extremity Barras, the butcher of Toulon, asked leave of his fellow-members to lead the attack on Robespierre. He went away into the night ; in his absence Robespierre and his supporters were outlawed. The Parliament continued to sit. They heard the rain begin to fall and then a clap of thunder. Torrents descended. After a long time Barras came back. He announced that the rebels were taken and that Robespierre, who had received a shot in the jaw, was lying on the table in a neighbouring committee-room. Many of the deputies hurried out to gaze upon fallen greatness. Next morning Robespierre was brought to the Revolutionary Tribunal and formally identified by Foquier-Tinville.

" Are you Maximilian Robespierre ? " the prosecutor demanded.

There was no trial because all the prisoners were outlawed and therefore condemned already. The red carts awaited them.

In the streets women were gathered with fluttering handkerchiefs, and smiling lips to see the man go by who had despised
and condemned all women. They cheered and laughed and
danced so that the carts could scarcely proceed.

Robespierre, weak from loss of blood, was carried up the
steps of the scaffold. He had spoken no word. Sanson bound
him to the plank and then tore away the bandage from his
broken jaw. The poor man uttered a scream of agony. The
thud of the falling knife was lost in women's laughter.

CHAPTER XX

NEXT day Tallien and his Thérèse were hero and heroine of all Paris. He was the Knight who had slain the dragon ; she the fairy princess who had inspired the splendid deed.

Tallien was greatly embarrassed, because he had lost interest in Thérèse. The hunger of the Parisians for emotional satisfaction, of which Fouché had taken so careful account, was incomprehensible to this stupid fellow. He shrugged his shoulders and spent the day following Robespierre's execution in going through Robespierre's files and burning all the evidence against himself which they contained. He was not alone in that work. All the butchers were there, Barras and Fréron and Fouché. They made clean work of it so that no other dictator should possess record of their shame.

That day lost from love disturbed and distressed Paris. Why had the lover delayed to rescue his beloved ? There were murmurings, which grew so active that the man was forced to heed them. It was made known that Thérèse's birthday fell upon the morrow. Her lover had contained himself that he might the more splendidly celebrate the occasion. This explanation answered. When the carriage of the bridegroom, drawn by two horses, appeared in the streets, on its way to the prison, a great crowd greeted it. There were crowds all the way. Tallien was compelled to acknowledge so generous a welcome. He strode, amid cheering, through the grim iron gates. He was taken at once to Thérèse's cell.

She started up at sight of him and began to accuse him bitterly. Why had he not communicated with her? Why had he done nothing to help her? Why, after Robespierre's fall, had he not ordered her immediate release? He fumbled excuses which she brushed aside. Then, uneasily, he told her the story of the Spanish dagger.

Thérèse's eyes began to glow. She realized, suddenly, that what this man had brought was not an offer of marriage but a throne. Her quick wits transformed the situation in an instant and Tallien saw, before his astonished eyes, the fairy princess for whom Paris was waiting. Thérèse's loveliness grew more ravishing every moment. She took his arm and leaned upon it. When she came to the prison gate her pale cheeks and sad expression wrung every heart. Tallien handed her into the carriage and got in beside her. A great cheer speeded them on their journey to his mother's house.

The streets, already, were full of joyous crowds and there were bonfires preparing on all the heights. Away with Puritanism. With Terror. With blood. Away with the guillotine and the red carts. The butchers, who had not foreseen this popular outburst, hid their long knives and set doves' feathers in their caps. Barras proclaimed the end of tyranny. A few days later Fréron and the band of young men he had recruited, went down, at night, to the Jacobin Club and turned its mourning members out into the street. Thérèse had accompanied the young men. They gave her the key of the grim building and she locked the door.

Barras was master now, with Fréron and Tallien as his lieutenants, for Fouché had thought it prudent to disappear for a time. Barras persuaded the convention to remove Robespierre's restrictions on the free circulation of gold and silver. Gold began to flow into France from England. Within less than a month, so eager was everyone to acquire the precious metals,

Mirabeau's " gold mine " had been destroyed.   The land-paper lost the whole of its value because nobody would accept it. All those who held their savings in the form of the land-paper were ruined, just as modern Germans were ruined when the mark lost its value after the Great War.   France was helpless at last in the hands of her enemies.

BOOK III

THE BLOOD-SUCKERS

CHAPTER XXI

QUEEN BEE

THE Parisians forced Tallien to marry his Thérèse—a sign that the campaigns which had been waged against marriage and family-life had convinced nobody. The young couple went to live in a charming little house near the Champs-Élysées. To this house, very often, came Rose de Beauharnais, whom Barras had taken as his mistress.

Rose was a good ten years older than Thérèse but she remained, nevertheless, a very lovely and most seductive woman. As a guillotine widow she had acquired a certain *réclame* by virtue of which, and with Barras' help, she had secured possession of her husband's estates. But they were worth very little and she had two young children, Eugene and Hortense, who were growing up and, consequently, growing expensive. Rose was fond of her children in a good-natured, careless way. But she was fonder still of herself, of luxury, of comfort. Though she had not seen her husband for many years, she invented a story that they had met in prison. She was Jacobin no longer, but noblewoman of the old France who had suffered in prison because of her rank and title. She let it be known that she and Thérèse had shared the same cell, though, in fact, they had been incarcerated in different districts of the city, and had not met until after the death of Robespierre.

Thérèse did not resent these inaccuracies upon which her friend was building her life, because Thérèse was always good-natured and always inclined to generosity. After all, Rose could never be rival to " Our Lady of Thermidor " as the

Parisians called her, Thérèse, in acknowledgment of her victory over Robespierre.

Tallien, married, sank into insignificance. The Pro-Consul of Bordeaux became, soon, the humble servant of his wife, whose connexions with international finance were now—with Mirabeau's " gold mine " extinguished—so important to France and to the French Government. Thérèse possessed the power to obtain loans, and loans were what Barras and his supporters needed more than anything else on earth, seeing that, though the land-money had gone, the armies remained.

The girl understood all her power—as indeed was to be expected of Cabarras' daughter. Barras, as she knew, was surrounded by enemies, Robespierre's bereaved followers for example and the remnants of the old Royalist party. If he lacked money, the Jacobins or some others would savage him. He was, therefore, in the hands of the woman who, to her popularity, added the power of the purse. Thérèse was Queen as Marie Antoinette had not been Queen.

She proceeded to pick Paris out of the gutter by recreating a social world. Very soon, so eagerly did she strive, it cost more to dress and feed and horse her than it had cost to maintain the Royal Family. She made Barras pledge France for loans and more loans and still more loans. The money-lenders came flapping into the stricken city. The armies on the frontiers began to suffer privation.

Thérèse did not think about the armies. Under Robespierre, they had achieved so mightily that their enemies were afraid of them. Prussia made peace with France and this example was followed by Spain and other countries. There was nothing to fear. Thérèse and Rose competed with one another as leaders of fashion and expended their nimble wits devising new modes, new dishes and new amusements. One night a little officer with a lean, half-starved face came to Thérèse's salon and told fortunes ; as a payment for a length of cloth obtained for him earlier in the day to make an overcoat. He was, so he said, a

Corsican whose family had lost all its possessions when that island went over to the English.

Thérèse saw his gratitude but not the criticism in his grey eyes. This little officer, whose name was Bonaparte, had witnessed the march of hunger across France. He was sick with contempt for " the women." A Stoic cast in the ancient mould.

Barras had met this little General Bonaparte at the Siege of Toulon and testified that he was a good gunner. But since nobody now wanted gunners, nobody bothered about him. Thérèse did not invite him again. She gathered round her instead, bankers and financiers, theatrical managers, newspaper men, writers, artists, poets, actors—representatives, in short, of the apparatus of money-lending as applied on the national scale. It was a less select company, certainly, than that which Germaine de Staël had entertained in the rue du Bac, but it served the same purpose in circumstances which had changed.

What was the purpose? In these latter days the woman of the suburbs lives upon the " Society Gossip " of the daily and weekly Press as the worker bee, busy and sterile female, lives by and through the influence of the queen. For woman, as for bee, ecstasy of some sort is an ingredient of living as essential as food or air or water, so that if it cannot be obtained at first hand, then it must be had vicariously. The " Social Gossip " column, in other words, is the most vital part of the newspapers, since it supplies the communication between the society queen and the household drudge. Abolish it, the hive will be dispersed.

Thérèse understood all this instinctively. She knew that, in the bitter days of deflation and privation which lay ahead, Paris would need a vicarious queenship, a beautiful and splendid being whose doings would excite the interest and enthusiasm of all, so that all would sit at her table and, in her bounty, forget their own emptiness. She would clothe and feed and amuse all France at second-hand, through the ink of a hundred pens.

The Press of Paris began to discuss Thérèse as if she was,

indeed, Queen of France. No detail of her toilet but merited and received attention. No visitor to her house but became an object of public solicitude. In her lovers all were satisfied with love. Baby-linen after her marriage to Tallien assumed an importance in the news sheets comparable to that of the guillotine under Robespierre ; and, indeed, the comparison is warranted. For there is an ecstacy of fear as well as of reproduction and the one, for a time, can make the cement of society as well as the other.

Meanwhile, the " queen " having been established and proclaimed, the money-lenders made preparations to take the honey what time the busy workers should have gathered it. Loans to farmers, loans to factory owners, loans to the Government, loans to the army contractors, these, like the bee-farmers' frames, were set up in every corner of France. And needy men and women, stripped of their possessions and even of their flesh, made haste to fill the gaping frames. Thérèse's salon grew more and more brilliant as more and more emigrants returned to Paris, to share in the honey harvest. Among them Ouvrard, wizard of finance, and Germaine de Staël, newly come from Geneva where the ageing Necker, who called himself Baron de Coppet, spent his days gazing at Suzanne's body in its glass coffin filled with spirits of wine and quarrelling with two or three old butlers whom he had brought with him from France. Germaine did not like the glass coffin. She did not like Coppet. She had shed her former lovers—not without violent efforts to keep them. Narbonne and Mathieu de Montmorency and the others remained in the refuge she had found for them in Switzerland but, rather ungratefully, perhaps, had ceased to adore her. Another more recent lover, the Count de Ribbing, a Swede, with very yellow hair, who had played a part in the murder of his King and thus prevented the dismissal of the Baron de Staël from his post as French Ambassador, had not proved satisfactory. Germaine had gone out into the highways and hedges and found a tall, weedy youth with a most insolent wit, whose views upon politics, and everything else, corresponded to her views. This was Benjamin Constant. Necker detested the fellow and even Mathieu de Montmorency, who had become exceedingly religious, spoke hard words about him.

Mathieu happened to be living at Mezéry, Germaine's house in Switzerland, when Benjamin began to pay court to Germaine. The nobleman, in his new-found piety, felt nothing but horror for this vulgar and irreligious young man. He allowed Germaine to know what he felt and for a time she held Benjamin at arm's length. But Benjamin was persevering and artful.

" At midnight on a day on which his (Benjamin's) bitter humour had degenerated into hatred of human kind," wrote Norvins, " agonized and terrifying cries were heard proceeding from his bedroom. Everybody had gone to bed. The servants rushed to his room and found him lying on his bed, pale, with distorted features, raving and in convulsions. They gave the alarm, shouting : ' Help ! M. Constant is killing himself.'

" People in their nightwear came rushing from all parts of the house. I went to call Mme Rilliet, who hurried with me to the sick man. Constant directed what appeared to be his last glance towards her and murmured in tones that were scarcely audible :

" ' Ah, Madame, tell her that I am dying for her. Ah, beg her in the name of a dying man to come and, if time is given me, bid me a last farewell. Say that I shall die happy when I have seen her.'

" Very much moved, Mme Rilliet hurried from the room. Mme de Staël was in bed :

" ' Get up, my dear,' she cried, as she rushed to her, ' Constant has committed suicide ; he begs to see you before he dies.'

" Mme Rilliet had no difficulty in inspiring so impressionable a soul as Mme de Staël with her emotion.

" ' He's dying ? ' Mme de Staël cried. ' I'll come.'

" Meanwhile I had gone to Mathieu's room. I found him in a white dressing-gown, seated, reading the *Confessions* of Saint Augustine. At my first words he emerged at a bound from the beautiful serenity of Christian charity, which the news I brought had profaned, and exclaimed in the accents of the old nobility :

" ' Fling the fellow out of the window. He does nothing but give bother. His suicide will bring scandal on the house.'

" In spite of the seriousness of the position I couldn't help smiling at this frank outburst. Meanwhile, when he heard Mme de Staël's name, Mathieu rose from his chair, coolly lit his candle and accompanied me to Constant's room.

" The entire household, masters and servants, surrounded the bed, on which the patient flung himself about, uttering heart-rending shrieks. At the sight of this horrifying spectacle Mme de Staël exclaimed :

" ' Poor soul, what have you done ? A doctor. A doctor.'

" These breathless words which were interrupted by sobs produced a magical effect.

" ' Ah, is it you ? ' whispered the dying man. ' Is it you ? You call me back, for a moment, to life.'

" ' Ah, live, live, dear M. Constant. I call you to live.'

" These words were spoken in accents of the liveliest despair, for the change in Constant's face gave us no hope of his recovery. As for him :

" ' Ah, since you order it,' he exclaimed, ' I shall try to live.'

" And he succeeded so well that, clutching at the hand of Mme de Staël with a kind of nervous spasm which terrified her, he imprinted a big kiss upon it. . . .

" When the doctor came none of us felt that the miracle of his (Constant's) resurrection would fail to be accomplished. We all retired in a state of mind rather less sympathetic, for we didn't wish to embarrass Constant in his explanations. Mathieu remarked :

" ' What a farce. Good God,' relit his candle and went back to his room."

Benjamin's progress into Germaine's heart was now rapid, though she had confessed, quite recently, that she felt a personal antipathy to him " which nothing can overcome." The fellow

JOSEPH FOUCHÉ

had read her secret. He knew that into that heart there was only one way open, ever, to all comers—namely, flattery of a vanity which had never yet been sated. He helped her to write and taught her how to write effectively. She produced a pamphlet, the modest title of which was *Thoughts on Peace addressed to Mr. Pitt and the French.* The preface declared :

"During the bloody reign of Robespierre, when each new day brought a fresh, appalling list of victims, I could do nothing but long to die myself. . . . I should have reproached myself for mental effort which was independent of this all-absorbing pain."

The pamphlet showed that what was now necessary for the salvation of the world was a union of blood and intellect— herself and Benjamin.

"My authorship of the pamphlet," she wrote to a friend, "has been recognized by my father. He has read it and forgives me. . . . I want to go to France at the end of April. . . . M. de Staël is delighted with Paris and believes that everything is perfectly safe there. Well-known people, rich people have gone back to France and recovered their possessions. So far as I can see all there is to fear now is the nature of things ; the Government is well-intentioned."

Jacques was opposed to this project but, as usual, was over-ridden. Germaine could not remain away from the scene of her glory. But she did not find Paris so delightful as she had expected.

"There are districts in Paris," wrote her father's friend, Meister, who visited the city about this time, "which seem to be entirely deserted. The most deserted of all is the Faubourg Saint-Germain where, in streets of palaces, only a house here and there is occupied—as a rule by officials of the Government. If you happen to enter one of these houses across the façade of which is written in huge red and black letters : 'For Sale : National Property,' you will be horrified at the state of disrepair in which you will find it. Most of these houses have been stripped of furniture, glass, fixtures; and, on the pretext of getting lead from the roofs and saltpetre from the cellars, the woodwork has often been ruined and the very walls have been broken down.

"Evening began to draw in. Passing near the dome of the Invalides—that wonderful House of God which they have treated as if it was the house of a nobleman or an emigrant— I saw a biggish group of huge figures, of a shining whiteness, crowded together like sheep in a fold. I couldn't make out, at first, what they were, but when I got nearer I recognized the enormous marble statues of saints which had formerly occupied the niches of the superb church. They were up for sale, these saints, like so many other objects of all kinds which one sees everywhere. But these poor saints? Who will buy them? Who will dare to buy them?

"It is at ten o'clock at night that the sadness and bareness of Paris are most apt to strike a visitor who has known her in happier times. In the old days, at that hour, one was hurrying off to sup or to amuse oneself. The wheels of a thousand carriages filled all the streets with a sound which expressed the joy and the gaiety of a light-hearted, care-free, contented people—or at least of a people which seemed to be contented. To-day, after the emptying of the theatres, silence reigns everywhere, and if a carriage does happen to pass you, you notice it. With the exception of the patrols there are scarcely any foot passengers either.

"There are very few cabs for hire. For people who kept their own carriages in better times, don't reconcile themselves easily to paying £4 for a journey, even though, when exchanged for goods, these £4 are now scarcely worth a shilling.

"Almost all the spaces in front of the houses and all the important streets have become markets for furniture, china, pictures, etc. You see, everywhere, the same sort of stuff that we used to see, in the old days, for sale on the Pont Saint Michele, the quai de la Fervaille and under the piliers des Halles.

The Capital of the World looks like an enormous old curiosity shop.

"Fear of dying of hunger has driven people to invent all sorts of ways of feeding themselves. One often sees a cage of rabbits at a house door or outside of a shop, and one sees, too, skinny goats whose milk may, easily, be very precious if things go wrong.

"What strikes me most, in a general way, in Paris, is the queer look of uncertainty, of 'uprootedness' on almost every face, a look at once restless, defiant and tormented, often haggard too, and convulsive. I believe that anyone, who had never before seen, or even heard of Paris, on seeing it to-day, would echo the remark of M. de Jussieu to some man whose name I don't know :

"'Sir,' said he, 'I have not the honour of knowing you ; but I find you very much changed.'"

Benjamin, in his new, very distinguished company, found Paris exciting.

"I have not seen," he wrote to his aunt, "a single pinched face or a single beggar. The Jacobins are detested ; the Royalists are laughed at and despised ; peace, order and the Republic are what people want and what they mean to have."

But he added a few days later :

"Freedom of speech and of the Press is extreme here ; it is unheard of, this union of the most arbitrary power that ever existed on earth, with a licence complete in every direction."

Benjamin had bought himself some fine clothes. He always scented himself and wore his hair in curls. This was Germaine's doing for she was determined to make a " gentleman " of him.

"The influence of women," she wrote, "and the ascendancy of good company—what were called the 'gilded *salons*'—seemed very formidable to the people who were not admitted to these *salons*. They accused us, when we happened to invite some of their friends, of trying to seduce them. You saw on the 10th Days, for Sundays no longer existed, all the elements of the old and new *régimes* gathered together at parties ; but they were not reconciled. The charming manners of well-brought-up people shone through the humble clothes adopted during the Terror, which these people still wore. The converts from the Jacobins found themselves for the first time in the society of the *grand monde* and were more disturbed about the *bon ton* which they wished to imitate than about anything else. The women of the *ancien régime* paid court to them, to secure the recall of brothers, sons, husbands ; and the gracious compliments which they knew how to pay them exerted a profound effect on rough ears, inclining even the bitterest partisans towards conduct of which we have since seen so many examples."

Germaine did not care what people said about her Benjamin. He might not be beautiful ; he was the cleverest man in Europe with pen and tongue and his strange relations with the illustrious Mme de Charrière, to say nothing about his German wife, were material of excitement. The alliance of virtue and intellect which they formed took the town by storm. Both were determined to have their share of honey.

Both adhered to Necker's plan for a monarchy on the English pattern. Thérèse was not averse from that idea because it was obvious that Barras' Government was not strong enough to contract more foreign loans; and loans and still more loans were urgently necessary. Nor was Barras himself ill-disposed. He and Tallien were ready to restore the monarchy at once, provided that their share in King Louis' death and their subsequent butcheries were forgiven. Louis XVI's little son, called Louis XVII, had died in prison—or more probably been abducted from prison ; the heir to the throne was the late King's brother who, already, called himself Louis XVIII. They approached him. He sent them about their business and, with English help, attempted an invasion of France by way of Quiberon Bay. That attempt failed. It was followed by a massacre of prisoners in which Tallien played a part.

Instantly Paris was in an uproar, Royalists and Robespierrists once more at each other's throats.   Barras felt his power slipping away from him.   He turned against Tallien who had shown himself too much of a Terrorist, and against Germaine and Benjamin who had tried to bring back the King.   Then he hunted up the little gunner, General Bonaparte from Corsica, and put him in charge of the troops that were to defend the Government and Parliament against attacks by the mob. General Bonaparte smashed the mob to pieces with cannon and in twenty-four hours had reduced Paris to abject submission.

CHAPTER XXII

JOSEPHINE

GERMAINE and Benjamin were ordered by Barras to leave Paris at once—and this, though De Staël was still the Swedish Ambassador and Germaine, therefore, Ambassador's wife. But these two had no further dealings with one another.

"My daughter," wrote the ageing Jacques bitterly, on January 2, 1796, "has arrived after a long journey which has, happily, been free from accident. M. Constant was her travelling companion. They are both wonderfully full of republican ideas and hopes and seem to forgive a trifle too easily the methods employed by Governments to attain these objects. I am very far from seeing eye to eye with them . . ."

As soon as they arrived at Coppet the house became a political club, full of Germaine's admirers.

"They gathered for breakfast," wrote Frédéric de Château-vieux, "in Mme. de Staël's room. They drank only coffee then. This breakfast lasted two hours, for as soon as they assembled, Mme. de Staël raised a question, more often chosen from the realms of literature or of philosophy than from that of politics—and this out of consideration for her father whose career on the political stage had ended so unhappily. But whatever the subject of discussion, it was attacked with a liveliness of imagination and a profundity from which Benjamin Constant derived his best training and from which gushed forth all that the human mind could conceive and create . . .

"Each then retired until luncheon, which passed off in a

perpetual quarrel between M. Necker and some aged butlers, deaf and complaining, relics of the *régime* that M. Necker had overthrown, who, in their embroidered liveries, had followed M. Necker to Coppet. The afternoon was devoted to work until seven o'clock, when M. Necker's whist began. This whist was stormy. M. Necker and his daughter quarrelled, got angry and left the table, vowing never to play with each other again, and began to play again the next evening. The rest of the evening was devoted to conversation."

Rosalie Constant, Benjamin's cousin, who came sometimes, was less easily impressed :

" It is impossible," she wrote, " to live peaceably with these queer people. With enough to make ten fools happy, she (Mme. de Staël) is perfectly miserable, but she loves Benjamin passionately. God knows where this will end. . . .

" She (Germaine) was seated between the ' fox ' and the ' kitten ' and the other one (i.e. three of Germaine's men friends), with an elbow on the chest of one, the other grasped by the head, and the third holding the back of her neck and calling her ' a nice little pussy ' . . . I quarrelled horribly with them about our country, which they look on as the home of boredom and emptiness . . . I did not convince Benjamin. I came away so as to avoid having supper there."

Benjamin felt the strain too much for him—Germaine was writing a book on " The Influence of the Passions on the Happiness of Individuals and Nations," in which the confession occurred :

" Perhaps at this moment of writing I wish to be loved once more ; perhaps at this very moment I resign my destiny to my love."

He fled to Paris, saying he was going to persuade Barras to allow her to return. He found everything in a state of flux. Tallien remained in some sort of possession of Thérèse, and Rose de Beauharnais still passed as Barras' mistress. Barras now confirmed in power, wanted to be quit of Tallien so that he might possess Thérèse. He invited Thérèse to share his triumph and hinted to Rose that little Bonaparte, who had been rewarded for his services against the mob with the Command of Paris, would make a not too impossible husband. There were tears and hysterics, but in the end Rose yielded her place to Thérèse.

Barras now declared that he had never had anything to do with Louis XVIII, and that he remained a Republican. But such declarations did not help to fill the Treasury and the lack of money was becoming acute. If only they had not been in such a hurry to destroy the land-money. Thérèse busied herself to wring loans out of her father and his friends. Ouvrard, who was in touch with the Hopes of Amsterdam and, thus, with the Barings in London, exerted his utmost endeavours. France was pawned like old furniture. Even so, the armies had to be denied almost everything—weapons, boots, clothes, horses, even food. The intelligence services were cut down and the regiments began to dissolve. Robespierre's invincibles became bands of brigands who lived by pillaging Frenchmen. On every frontier the enemies of France took heart.

Meanwhile, Thérèse affected a more splendid luxury. She had tables built for her under vines and orange trees 'so that the guests might pluck their fruit as they sat at meat. Silver and gold were wrought cunningly to supply her with cups and plates. The world was ransacked to carpet her floors and decorate her walls. And Paris laboured day and night to provide enough new frocks of enough splendid stuffs.

"The fair sex in France," wrote a Royalist, "naturally coquettes, vain, dashing and bold, are now more inclined towards the naked than the clothed system. Nakedness, absolute nakedness and nothing but nakedness was therefore seen at the playhouses, at the opera, at the concerts, at the routs and in public walks as well as in private assemblies. Where one lady left off a fichu, another laid aside a petticoat. Where one uncovered her arms, another exposed her legs. Mme Beauharnais, the gay widow of the guillotined Vicomte, put on flesh coloured satin pantaloons under a clear muslin frock, leaving off all petticoats, but at the same time lowering the sleeves of her gown to her elbows. Her long elastic gloves of Grenoble (silk) combined to hide even her clumsy fingers. Mme Tallien, who prided herself on the beauty of her arms, in her turn wore gowns without sleeves, and to detract the notice of admirers from the flesh-coloured pantaloons of her rival affixed borders of large and open Brussels lace to her under-garments."

Rose de Beauharnais had been permitted by Barras to keep the little villa in the Chaussée d'Antin, which he had given her, and to retain, also, her carriage and two black horses. It was thus, as a great lady of the old nobility, that General Bonaparte met her. He knew little of social uses, nothing of the lady's past, nothing of her relations with her late husband, not much, perhaps, about her relations with Barras. He saw only the loving mother of a boy and girl whose misfortunes had not spoiled their youthful charm. He fell head over ears in love.

Rose was very hard up, for Barras had been proving more and more difficult about money and the estates of the late Alexandre were yielding little. Indeed it had been necessary to draw upon her mother, a lonely widow now, living still in the sugar refinery at Martinique to which the Tascher-la-Pagerie family had resorted when their own mansion was burned down. Old Mme Tascher-la-Pagerie was, herself, in sore straits because of the ruin of her plantations which had been caused by the war between France and England, but her daughter showed her small mercy.

" I shall be happy," wrote Rose to her, " if this letter reaches you, with the assurance that your daughter and grandchildren are well. You are doubtless already aware of my misfortunes ; that I have now been four months a widow and left with only my children to console me, and my dear mamma as my sole support."

Things were not quite so bad as this, however, as Chancellor Pasquier, a sober witness, has testified :

" We had as a neighbour," Pasquier wrote, " Mme de Beauharnais, whose high fortunes we were far from foreseeing. Her house (in the country outside of Paris) adjoins ours. . . . At early morn we used to watch the delivery of baskets full of provisions ; and these were followed soon by mounted gendarmes patrolling the road from Nanterre to Croissy—for the young director (Barras) usually came on horseback.

" The house of Mme de Beauharnais displayed, as is somewhat the fashion with Creoles, a kind of showy luxury. Side by side with the superfluous there was often a lack of the most necessary articles. Poultry, game and rare fruits would be piled up in the kitchen (we were then passing through a time when provisions were very scarce) while, on the other hand, there were not enough saucepans, glasses or plates and she borrowed these from our poor little household . . . Our intercourse was limited to these neighbourly acts, although Mme Pasquier had met Mme Beauharnais before the Revolution.

" France resembled a fortified city after a long siege, when there is a lack of everything at one and the same time. The products of the soil and groceries brought their weight in gold. Even soap was sold at exorbitant prices and then part of it was clay. The most serious and hardest privation to endure was that of bread. One must have suffered from that privation in order to conceive the patience demanded of the poor who, nevertheless, endured it with admirable fortitude."

Rose, who was called " Geyette " by her family, meanwhile kept up her correspondence with her mother, thus :

" I hope this letter from your poor Geyette and her children will reach you ; for she has great need of your sympathy ; her heart yearns for that of which she had so long been deprived. You must be aware by this time of the misfortunes which have befallen me, and must know that I have no other recourse than you for the means of my existence . . .

" I am not only widowed, but I am deprived of my husband's property . . . I know too well your regard for my honour to have the least doubt that you will supply me with the means of subsistence. I shall have to depend on your bounty entirely and must beg that you make me a remittance once at least every three or four months."

A little later she wrote :

" You will receive then, my dear mamma, three bills of exchange drawn upon you from Hamburg, October 25, at three months' sight, in my favour, in three sums as follows, £400, £350 and £250 sterling . . . I need not remind you how necessary it is to honour these drafts, since they are for the reimbursement of friends who have so generously supplied me and my children.

" Why do you hesitate to rejoin us, my dear mamma ? Think how much trouble and vexation your coming would save your dear Geyette, who lives only in the expectation of soon seeing you and of realizing the hopes she has so long and so ardently cherished. It is also the advice of our friends to convert everything possible into money and to come to us as soon as you can—to rejoin your own children, who love you and will ever cherish you."

Mme Tascher-la-Pagerie did not adopt this advice, and money grew more and more difficult to obtain.

" Mme de Beauharnais," wrote Mme de Rémusat viciously, " was not well off and her love of dress and luxury made her dependent upon those who would help her to satisfy her passion."

Consequently the advances of the little Corsican gunner had to be listened to.

" My mother," wrote Hortense, " told us that she was dining with the Director Barras and that she would take us with her. ' What,' I cried impetuously, ' you actually associate with such people ? Have you forgotten our family misfortunes ? ' ' My child,' she answered with the angelic gentleness which never left her, ' you must remember that, since your father's death, I have done nothing but try to save the remains of his fortune which we feared would be lost. Must I not be grateful to those who have helped and protected me ? '

" I recognized that I was wrong. I begged my mother's pardon and went with her to the Directory, established in the Palace of the Luxembourg. Barras had invited a number of guests, of whom Tallien and his wife were the only ones I knew. At dinner I found myself placed between my mother and a general who, in order to talk to her, kept leaning forward so often and with so much vivacity that he wearied me and obliged me to lean back. Thus, in spite of myself, I looked attentively at his face, which was handsome and very expressive but remarkably pale. He spoke ardently and seemed to devote all his attention to my mother. It was General Bonaparte."

Thérèse and Barras encouraged this happy ending to a considerable difficulty. They praised General Bonaparte, saying that they had heard that he was a great landlord on his native island. To the General they said that Rose had expectations from the family estates and plantations in Martinique. But Bonaparte needed no tempting. So violent was his affection that he actually bestowed a new name on Rose so that she might the more exclusively belong to him. For some reason she had been baptized : " Rose Joseph." He called her Josephine.

A few days after her engagement was announced Rose Josephine received this letter :

" *Seven o'clock in the morning.*

" My waking thoughts are all of you. Your portrait and the remembrance of last night's delirium have robbed my senses of repose. Sweet and incomparable Josephine, what an extraordinary influence you have over my heart ! Are you vexed ? Do I see you sad ? Are you ill at ease ? My soul is broken with grief and there is no rest for your lover.

" But is there more rest for him, when delivering ourselves up to the deep feelings which master me, I breathe out upon your lips, upon your heart, a flame which burns me up. Ah, it was during last night that I realized that your portrait is not yourself.

" You start at noon. I shall see you in three hours. Meanwhile, *mio dolce amor*, accept a thousand kisses but give me none for they fire my blood.

"N. B."

" *Un millier de baise* " (*sic*). What bad French he wrote ! All the same it was a love letter of a kind new in Rose Josephine's experience.

They were married a few days before he was due to leave for a new command—that of the " Army of Italy "—a band of half-naked robbers who were gathered, hopelessly, at Nice to oppose the entry into France of an Austrian and Piedmontese army that was threatening to cross the Maritime Alps. This " Army " did not possess a single horse. Bonaparte's lively affection annoyed his " Joesphine " and she was glad to see him go. As soon as his back was turned, she spent the money he had given her on a bunch of new frocks.

But she was wrong in supposing that she had heard the last of her husband. Scarcely a month elapsed before the news reached Paris that he had destroyed all his enemies, and more or less, conquered Italy. Paris, weary of hunger and shame and Thérèse, bounded from despair to confidence. Crowds began to fill the rue Chantereine where Josephine lived, to mob her when she drove out and to demand sight of her at all hours. She heard herself called—" Our Lady of Victory "—which was as good a title, after all, as " Our Lady of Thermidor." But Josephine did not want titles, especially such as might awaken the jealousy of Thérèse and Barras. She wanted money and lovers.

Useless to protest. The flood of victory rose higher and higher and swept France off her feet. A flood of gold followed— Austrian gold. Barras pocketed a tip of £1,000,000 ; Thérèse bought more frocks and more jewels. It became much easier to raise new loans.

Meanwhile letters from the little soldier had been arriving by every post :

"CHANCEAU POST HOUSE,
"*March* 14, 1796.

"I wrote you at Chatillon and sent you a power of attorney to enable you to receive various sums of money in course of remittance to me. Every moment separates me farther from you, my beloved, and every moment I have less energy to exist so far from you. You are the perpetual object of my thoughts. I exhaust my imagination in thinking of what you are doing. If I imagine that you are unhappy, my heart is torn and my grief overflows. If you are gay and lively among your friends—male and female—I reproach you with having so soon forgotten the sorrowful separation three days ago ; in that case you must be fickle and incapable of deep emotion. So you see I'm not easy to please. But, my dear, I feel quite differently when I imagine that your health may not be good or that you have reason to be upset ; then I deplore the haste with which I was torn away from my darling. I come to persuade myself (at such moments) that your natural goodness of heart no longer enfolds me. It is only when I am certain that you are not upset that I get peace.

"If I was asked how I slept, I feel that before replying I should have to get a message from you to tell me that you had had a good night. The diseases and the passions exert influence on my thoughts only when I torture myself with the fear that they may reach you, my dear. May my good genius, which has always preserved me in the midst of great dangers, surround you and enfold you ; so, I will go unguarded to my fate.

"Ah, don't be gay. Be sad a little. But may your soul be as free from worries as your body from illness. You know what our good Ossian says on the subject. Write me, dear, a long letter and accept the thousand and one kisses of your most devoted and faithful friend."

He had actually addressed this letter to the "Citoyenne

Beauharnais." Josephine understood how anxious he was and guessed that, perhaps, he was not so ill-informed about her ways of life as she had supposed. He had made her write a dutiful note to his mother. She soon got a reply from Marseilles, where Mme Bonaparte was living in a cheap lodging.

" I have received your letter, Madame," it ran, " which could only confirm the opinion I had already formed of you. My son (on his way to Nice) has informed me of his happy marriage ; from that moment you possessed my esteem and approval. Nothing is lacking to my happiness except the pleasure of seeing you. Be assured that I feel a mother's tenderness towards you and that I love you as much as I love my own children.

" My son gives me hope, and your letter confirms it, that you will pass through Marseilles on your way to join him. I look forward, Madame, to the joy that your stay here will give me. My daughters join me in hoping that you will hasten the happy moment of your journey. In the meanwhile, rest assured that my children, like me, have dedicated to you the same friendship and tenderness that they feel for their brother.

" Believe, Madame, in the attachment and affection of

" LETITIA BUONAPARTE (*Mère*)."

This copybook letter was not, certainly, the work of " Mama Letizia," as her children called her. Napoleon had probably written it himself. Perhaps, too, he had dictated the letter which soon followed from his elder brother, Joseph.

" Madame," this letter ran, " I have learned with the warmest interest of your marriage to my brother. The friendship which unites me to him does not allow me to be insensible to the happiness that he will find with you. Of this I am as sure as he, from the opinion I have formed of you."

It was like being back again in the sugar refinery at Martinique, among all her respectable relations. Only much worse. She did not answer many of Bonaparte's letters. They multiplied in number and in passion, thus :

"I am not satisfied with your last letter; it is as cold as friendship. I have not found that flame which kindles your expression and which I have sometimes imagined that I lighted there."

Again:

"*Mio dolce amor*, my brother will give you this letter. . . . I have received yours of (April) 5th and 10th. You have been several days without writing to me! What are you doing? Oh, my kind, kind love, I am not jealous. Only uneasy sometimes. Come soon. I warn you that if you delay you will find me ill; I cannot endure fatigue and your absence at the same time.

"Your letters are my day's happiness, and these happy days are few. Junot is taking twenty-two flags to Paris. You must come back with him. Do you understand that? Be ready, please. If (Junot) doesn't come back, woe without remedy; if he comes back without you, grief without any consolation, anxiety without end.

"My dear, he will see you; he will breathe upon your face. Perhaps you will grant him the unique and priceless favour of kissing your cheek. And I? I shall be alone and very far away; but you are going to come, aren't you? You will soon be beside me, on my breast, in my arms, mouth to mouth. Take wings. Fly. But travel gently. The road is long, bad, fatiguing. If you should be overturned or be taken ill, if fatigue—go gently, my beloved.

"I have a letter from Hortense. She is entirely loveable. I I shall write to her. I love her dearly and I'll send her the perfumes she wants.

"N.B.

"I don't know if you want money, because you never mention such matters. If you do want it ask my brother for it—he has 200 louis of mine. If you want a job for any of your friends, send him to me. I'll find one for him."

It became necessary to lie now in order to avoid going to

NAPOLEON AS A YOUNG GENERAL

Italy. So Josephine wrote to say she was pregnant. This news threw her husband into transports of anxiety interspersed, at moments, by equally violent transports of suspicion :

" My life," he wrote, " is an unending nightmare ; a foreboding of evil oppresses me. I can't see you any longer. I have lost more than life, more than happiness, more than peace of mind. I am almost without hope.

" I am rushing to send a courier to you. He is to stay only four hours in Paris and then bring back your reply. Write me ten pages. That is the only thing that can comfort me in the smallest degree. You are ill. You love me. I have made you miserable. You are in delicate health and I can't see you. That thought breaks me.

" I have wronged you so terribly that I can never atone for it. I accused you of lingering in Paris and you were ill. Forgive me, my dear. The love you have roused in me has robbed me of reason. I shall never be sane again—I am victim of incurable disease. My forebodings are so black that I would content myself if I could merely see you and press you for a couple of hours to my heart. Then I would be ready to die with you.

" Who is looking after you ? I imagine you must have sent for Hortense. I love that sweet child a thousand times more when I think that she can comfort you a little. For me there is neither comfort nor rest nor hope till the courier I have sent comes back and till, in a long letter, you tell me fully all about your illness and whether or not it is serious. If it is really serious, I warn you I start instantly for Paris. My coming or not coming is contingent on your state of health.

" I have always been lucky. Never yet has fate resisted my will. To-day I am wounded in the deeps of my spirit. Josephine, how can you go on so long without writing to me ? Your last, laconic note is dated May 22. It is a sad letter so far as I am concerned, but I always carry in it my pocket. Your portrait and your letters are always beside me, under my eyes.

" I am nothing without you. I can scarcely realize how I

lived without knowing you. Ah, Josephine, had you known my heart would you have delayed from May 18 till June 4 before beginning your journey? Would you have listened to false friends who are, perhaps, trying to keep you away from me? I tell everyone here that I hate anybody who approaches you. I expected you to set out on May 24 and to arrive here on June 3.

" Josephine, if you love me, if you know how everything depends on your health, take care of yourself. I dare not tell you not to undertake so long a journey, and that too in the hot weather. At least, if you are fit to undertake the journey, come by short stages ; write to me at every sleeping place and send on your letters in advance.

" All my thoughts are concentrated in your room, on your bed, on your heart. Your illness! That is what torments me night and day. Without appetite, without sleep, without care for friends, glory, fatherland—you, you alone. The rest of the world exists for me no more than if it had been destroyed. I value honour since you value it, I value victory since it pleases you ; but for these considerations I should leave all to rush and fling myself at your feet.

" Sometimes I rebuke myself that I get needlessly alarmed ; I say : now she is better, she is starting, she has started, already, perhaps, she is at Lyons. Vain imaginings! You are in bed, suffering, more beautiful, more interesting, more lovable. You are pale and your eyes have become more languishing. But when will you be better? If one of us must be ill, it should be I who am more robust, more courageous. I could endure illness more easily than you. How cruel is Fate which strikes at me through you.

" What consoles me sometimes is to think that while it is in the power of Fate to make you ill, it is in nobody's power to compel me to survive you.

" In your letter, dear, tell me that you know that I love you more than can be imagined ; that you know that all my moments are consecrated to you ; that no thought of another has so much as entered my head—all others seem to me graceless, witless, unlovely. You, you alone, as I see you and as you are, can please me and command all the faculties of my spirit. Tell me that you know this, that you know you possess the whole of my mind ; that my heart has no recess from which your gaze has been excluded, no thoughts which are not yours to command ; that my strength, my powers, my spirit are all yours ; that my soul is in your body ; and that the day on which you change or cease to live will be my death day ; that nature, that earth is beautiful only because you dwell therein. If you don't believe all this ; if you are not convinced in the deeps of your soul, penetrated through and through, then you break me, when you do not love me. There is a magnetic fluid between people who love one another. You know that I shall never endure a rival—much less go on enduring. To tear out his heart and to see him would be, for me, the same thing ; and then if I were to raise my hands against your sacred person—— No, I should never dare to do that ! But I would quit a world in which the most virtuous of women had deceived me.

" But I am sure and proud of your love. Misfortunes are the trials which reveal to each, mutually, the force of passion. A child as adorable as its mamma will soon see the light and will pass many years in your arms. Hapless me ! I would be satisfied with one day. A thousand kisses on your eyes, your lips, your tongue, your heart. Most adorable of your sex, what is your power over me ? I am very ill of your illness ; I am in a burning fever. Don't keep the courier more than six hours. Let him rush back to bring me the letter I so long for.

" Do you remember my dream in which I saw myself your boots, your dress and in which I forced you to come bodily into my heart. Why has not Nature arranged things in this way ? She has much yet to accomplish.　　" N. B."

France and Europe were ringing with the fame of the young

general whose triumphs wore a supernatural aspect. But that was no help to Josephine in her astonishing and most unwelcome struggle with a Corsican clansman whose every word breathed fire and fury and passion. She put the struggle away from her with a gesture of helplessness :

" *Il est drôle, Bonaparte,*" she remarked.

She had lived her life and found money better than love-making. What a calamity to have caught this Tartar just when she most wanted to enjoy herself in Paris. But he gave her no respite.

" You were to have left Paris on the 5th (of June)," his next letter ran. " You were to have left on the 11th. You had not left on the 12th. My soul was full of joy ; it is full now of pain. The couriers come, but they do not bring me letters from you. When you do write a word or two your style expresses no depth of feeling. You loved me as a child loves a new toy. You feel, already, that to hold such a love in your heart would be to make yourself ridiculous. It appears to me that you have chosen (someone else) and that you know to whom to address yourself in order to replace me. I wish you happiness—if frivolity can achieve happiness—frivolity and perfidy. You have never loved.

" I had hastened my operations. I calculated that you would be at Milan on the 13th. You are still in Paris. So I take counsel with my own soul. I resolve to strangle a feeling which is unworthy of me. If glory is not enough for my happiness, at least it constitutes an element of death and immortality. As for you, I pray that the memory of me may not be hateful to you. It is my misfortune to have known little about you—yours to have supposed that I was like the men who surround you.

" My heart has never felt any frivolous emotion ; it denied itself love. You inspired it with a boundless passion—a frenzy which degraded it. The thought of you filled my soul to the exclusion of the entire world. To me your whims were a sacred law ; the sight of you a supreme joy. You are lovely, beautiful.

Your sweet and heavenly soul is expressed in your face. I adore everything about you. Had you been more naïve, had you been younger, I should have loved you less. Everything ravished me—even the memory of your faults, even the memory of the afflicting scene which took place a fortnight before our marriage. Virtue, so far as I was concerned, was what you did ; honour was what pleased you. Glory attracted me only because it was agreeable to you and flattered you. Your portrait rested, always, on my heart. Never a day, but I gazed on it ; never an hour but I covered it with kisses. You left my portrait neglected for six months ; you did not once take it out of its case. Nothing (of all you did) escaped me. If I continued to live, I should love only you ; it is the only part I can play.

" Josephine, you would have made a man less fantastic than I happy. I tell you you have made me miserable. Cruel, why have you enticed me to set my hope on a feeling which you do not possess ? But it is unworthy to reproach. I have never believed in happiness. Every day death gallops round me. Is life worth making so much fuss about ?

" Adieu, Josephine. Stay in Paris. Don't write me any more. But do, at least, honour my hearth. A thousand daggers tear my soul. Don't drive them in any farther. Adieu, happiness, love, everything that earth had to give me. . . .

" BONAPARTE."

She wrote him three lines in reply and repeated that performance after a week.

" You ought," his next letter ran, " to have started on May 22. Being good-natured, I waited till June 1—as if a pretty woman would consent to give up her habits, her friends, Madame Tallien, a dinner with Barras, a new play, and Fortuné[1]—yes, Fortuné whom you love much more than your husband. For your husband you have only a little of the liking, a small share

[1] Her lapdog.

of the benevolence, with which your heart abounds. Every day I count up your misdeeds. I lash myself to fury in order to cure myself of love of you. But have I ceased to love you ?

" My peerless little mother, I'll tell you my secret. Defy me, stay in Paris, have lovers—let everybody know it—never write me a monosyllable. Then I shall love you ten times more. It isn't madness ; it isn't delirium of fever ; I shall never be cured. Oh, would Heaven I could be cured. But don't tell me you are ill. Don't try to justify yourself. . . ."

Josephine was frightened at last. She began to pack. There was a final supper at the Luxembourg at which everyone flattered her and gave her kind messages for her very illustrious and very glorious husband. She choked ; if only somebody else had married Bonaparte. She went home and wept over the bust of Socrates which stood in her bedroom.

Next day she took the road with Joseph Bonaparte, her husband's elder brother, and came sobbing to Milan where all the bells were ringing in honour of her spouse. The Italians mobbed her just as the French had mobbed her. Even that was endurable, when compared with the General's embraces. The poor woman tried to shelter from the hurricane by having an affair with a lieutenant named Hippolyte Charles, a clever little mountebank.

" I am fêted wherever I go," she wrote in despair to her aunt, Madame Renaudin, now, at long last Marquise de Beauharnais. " All the princes of Italy give me entertainments, even the Grand Duke of Tuscany, brother of the Emperor. Ah well, I prefer being a private individual in France. I don't care for the honours they give me in this country. I get dreadfully bored. My health has undoubtedly a great deal to do with making me unhappy ; I am often out of sorts. If happiness could give health I ought to be in the best of health. I have the most amicable husband imaginable. No time is given me in which to want anything. My wishes are his. He is all the day long in adoration before me as if I was a goddess. There could not

possibly be a better husband. M. Serbollini will tell you how
he loves me. He often writes to my children too; he loves
them dearly. He is sending Hortense, by M. Serbollini, a lovely
repeater watch, jewelled and enamelled; to Eugene a splendid
gold watch."

She wrote to Bonaparte in Italy as little as she had written in
Paris. But the battle-fields were nearer to Milan than to the
French capital. She got plenty of " refreshers " from her
husband. Thus :

" No letters from you, which really makes me uneasy ; yet
they all tell me you are fit and that you have actually had a trip
to Lake Como. Every day I wait, impatiently, for the post
which, as I hope, will bring me news of you."

She had kept putting him off. But his victories were so
numerous that his opportunities of leisure began to increase.

" I write very often and you seldom," he reproached. " You
are naughty and undutiful, as well as thoughtless. It is disloyal
to deceive a poor husband, an affectionate lover. Ought he to
lose his rights because he is far away, up to the neck in worries
and anxieties ? "

The Battle of Arcole followed. Bonaparte became the idol of
his soldiers and of France by rushing forward, alone, with a
standard when the tide seemed to have turned against him. All
Italy gave herself to bell-ringing in his honour. With the
sound of the bells in her ears Josephine read a despatch, to
herself, from the field. It ran :

" I don't love you an atom. On the contrary I loathe you.
You're a good-for-nothing, graceless, tactless, tatterdemalion.
You never write me ; what is your husband to you ? You
know what joy your letters give him and you write a bare
half-dozen lines, thrown off anyhow.

" How are you spending your time, Madame ? What is this
absorbing business which makes it impossible to write a line
to your very kind husband ? What feeling is it which is
alienating and stifling the love you promised me ? Who is this

paragon, this new lover, who engrosses all your time, is master of your days and prevents you from troubling yourself about your husband ?

" Josephine, take care. One fine night the doors will be broken in and I shall be before you."

That decided it. She packed up, and with Hippolyte Charles for escort, bolted from Milan to Genoa. Bonaparte, full of victories and glory, found himself publicly ashamed :

" I get to Milan," he wrote to her, " I fling myself into your room ; I have left all in order to see you, to clasp you in my arms. . . . You are not there. You gad about the town, from entertainment to entertainment ; you run away from me when I approach. What do you care for your ' dear Napoleon ' ? You loved him as a passing fancy dictated ; your fickleness has blotted him from your thoughts.

" I know the remedy for weariness and the ills of life because I am accustomed to dangers. Have your fling of pleasure ; happiness was invented for your use. The world asks nothing better than to amuse you. Only your husband is very, very unhappy."

Next day he wrote :

" I have received the courier whom Berthier sent on to Genoa. You had no time to write me ; I feel that instinctively. Certainly, in your case, with so many pleasures and amusements claiming your attention, it would be absurd to make the smallest sacrifice on my behalf. Berthier has been good enough to show me the letter which you wrote to him. Do not, please, make the smallest change in your plans nor do anything to upset the parties arranged in your honour. I am of no consequence. The happiness or misery of a man whom you do not love is, necessarily, a matter of no moment.

" For my part, to love you only, to make you happy, to do nothing which might vex you—these are the objects and goals of my life.

" Be happy. Don't reproach me or indeed concern yourself at all with the happiness of a man who lives only in your life and rejoices only in your pleasure and happiness. When I demanded from you a love like my own I was wrong. Why expect lace to weigh as heavy as gold ? When I dedicate to you all my desires, all my thoughts, every moment of my days, I yield to the power which your nature, your charms and your whole personality have so effectively exerted over my unfortunate heart. I do wrong, since Nature has not given me attractions with which to captivate you ; but I do deserve Josephine's regard and esteem for I love her frantically and uniquely.

" Farewell, beloved wife ; farewell, my Josephine. May Fate gather within my breast all the griefs and troubles, but may it give Josephine prosperous and happy days. Who deserves them more ? When it shall be quite certain that she can love me no more, I will hide my deep grief and will be content to be useful and serviceable to her.

" I reopen my letter to give you a kiss. Ah, Josephine . . . Josephine."

Josephine learned that Thérèse and Barras were so furiously jealous that not even the Austrian gold could mollify them, plentiful as was the supply of it. She wrote to assure them that she looked on her husband's success as a mere flash in the pan and that she had no joy of it. But the flash could not be extinguished though three separate Austrian armies were sent to quench it. Italy was wholly conquered. The General, awaiting a treaty of peace, sent for his widowed mother and sisters and told his wife, in tones that frightened her, that she must show them due respect and, while they remained, behave herself.

She obeyed ; but it was an ordeal. Madame Bonaparte, senior, was a woman of iron who had brought up her large family of sons and daughters on the pittance left to her when the Corsicans, who had gone over to England, had driven out of the island the Corsicans who were for France. She was tall, handsome, stern. Virtuous as a Spartan and thrifty as a bone. Pious, too, in her own narrow, obscurantist fashion. She did not approve of Josephine.

Disapproval had many counts. The woman " painted." She was over-dressed, lazy, pleasure-loving. And she was a widow with two children and without substantial resources. Again, she was older than " Napoleone," and there were bad reports about her conduct in Paris. Mme Bonaparte, senior, was well informed owing to the curious accident which had brought Fréron, Barras' friend, to her lodging in Marseilles during the period before the General had become famous.

Fréron had fallen in love with Pauline Bonaparte, the second girl, who for her part had completely lost her head. Pauline was only sixteen, and already conspicuously beautiful, Fréron was forty with the reputation of a libertine as well as a butcher. " Napoleone " forbade the marriage. Pauline and her mother saw the hand of Josephine in this refusal. They passed on Fréron's stories about " Rose " and Thérèse to the General and Pauline lost no chance of insulting her sister-in-law.

It was a difficult time for Bonaparte, but he had his reward when the Austrian Government agreed to his peace terms. He hurried back to Paris, leaving Josephine to follow slowly behind him. The Capital received him as a Saviour.

In the circumstances Barras and Thérèse had to swallow their feelings. Talleyrand had come limping back from America— where he had gone after leaving England—and was now Foreign Minister. He gave a great ball in the General's honour and invited Germaine de Staël who, with her Benjamin, had returned to Paris. (It was Germaine who had obtained from Barras the portfolio of Foreign Affairs which Talleyrand carried.) Thérèse was present, among the bankers. So was Josephine. Josephine had evidently been weeping because her eyes were red. Everyone crowded round the General and neglected Barras. Germaine actually elbowed her way through the crowd to his side.

" Ah, General Bonaparte," she asked him, " whom do you admire most among women ? "

The answer came like a pistol shot :

" My wife."

" I said admire, not love ? "

" She who has borne the most children."

There was a laugh. Germaine nodded and went away. After all, she had not lacked in this respect. But Josephine was furious. She made Bonaparte take her away at once.

Next day the General was made aware of the desperate condition of the nation's finances. He had sent much gold from Italy, but much more was needed, since France remained still at war with England and consequently exposed to the risk that a new Coalition might be formed against her. What is needed, Barras declared, is peace with England.

The General had already, and independently, reached the same conclusion. He told the Government that if a French army seized Malta and Egypt, England would make peace because she would have great difficulty, in such circumstances, in maintaining communication with India. It was from India that the goods came which the London merchants sold to Europe and it was from India that, in an emergency, gold could be drawn to replenish the British banks. Her bankers, said Bonaparte, rule England. If they cannot get colonial goods from India they will have to part with gold in order to pay for the wheat they import from Poland and Russia. But the same force which is shutting out the goods—namely, the French army in Egypt, will also be shutting out gold.

General Bonaparte was told to undertake the Egyptian campaign. He sailed from Toulon with a fleet of 501 vessels, took Malta and reached Alexandria without sighting a British ship. Josephine went to Plombières to drink the waters in the hope that they might enable her to bear a son when her husband returned. She fell from a balcony while at the spa, owing to the breaking of a railing, and did not, therefore, get back to

Paris for some weeks. She heard on arrival that Bonaparte had conquered Egypt.

She was tired and uneasy and would fain have joined herself once more to Thérèse's gay company at the Luxembourg. But Barras was frightened of her and did not welcome her. So she bought—on mortgage—a small place named Malmaison on the outskirts of Paris and went to live there. Very soon Hippolyte Charles, the young officer whom Bonaparte had sent home from Italy, was installed at Malmaison.

This means of escaping from loneliness caused some scandal and filled the Bonapartes, some of whom were in Paris, with rage. But the news that the General's great fleet had been destroyed in Aboukir Bay by Nelson drove other matters from their minds. It was obvious that " Napoleone " was done for, seeing that he could not now escape from Egypt.

Thérèse heaved a sigh of relief. She had been afraid of the little General on the few occasions when she had met him. Now that he was ruined professionally, she could address herself to her own life and to the anxious conditions which bore upon it. Barras' powers as a borrower were exhausted ; with the defeat of the navy to add to the other misfortunes, hope of obtaining any more loans could be abandoned. She decided to abandon Barras and to accept the offer of Ouvrard, the banker, to become his mistress. Ouvrard had a wife who lived in the country. He was tall, handsome, cultured, a lover of music and art and his wealth was beyond computation. Thérèse felt sure that she would be safer in his big mansion than in the Luxembourg.

Her decision was not at all an unkind one. Barras was tired of her. But he needed her help with the money-lenders and she was ready still to give him her help. Was not Ouvrard associated closely with the greatest bankers in the world, the Hopes of Amsterdam and the Barings of London ?

Ouvrard did not want to lend to Barras, but he did want to establish relations with Cabarras, Thérèse's father, Banker and

Financial Adviser to the King of Spain. And he was as violently in love with Thérèse as it was possible for him to be in love with anybody. She had obtained a divorce from Tallien. Her child by Barras was dead and she had, therefore, only two children, Fontenay's boy and Tallien's girl. Ouvrard welcomed these children to his house and constituted himself their father, offering to bring them up with any children whom Thérèse might bear to him. In view of all these circumstances Barras' government was accorded some further help on condition that strict economy was exercised.

Josephine, meanwhile, received a strong hint to send Hippolyte Charles out of her house. She was so much distressed by this order that she drove to Paris and saw Gohir, one of Barras' colleagues in the Government. He spoke plainly. The Austrians had again declared war and were advancing upon the frontiers. General Bonaparte's army was locked up in Egypt. Food in Paris was in short supply, prices were rising and the Government was almost without financial resources. In such circumstances a public scandal was scarcely to be endured. When she protested that she was deeply in love with Charles, Gohir advised her to divorce Bonaparte and marry him.

She returned to Malmaison in great agitation. A few days later she visited a lawyer and told him to draw up a petition, asking for a divorce from her husband. The document was duly executed. But at that moment the news reached Paris that General Bonaparte had returned from Egypt and had landed at Fréjus on the Mediterranean coast.

Bonaparte, meanwhile, had received reports from his family about Josephine's behaviour.

" I saw Bonaparte," recounts his friend, Bourrienne, "walking alone with Junot as was his custom. I was not very far away from them and I know not what made me watch him during their conversation. The General's face which, for some unknown reason, was always pale, suddenly became still paler. The muscles of his face seemed to contract, his eyes became fixed and he struck his forehead several times. After talking for about a quarter of an hour he left Junot and returned to me. I had never seen him look so angry or so distracted. I advanced to meet him; as soon as we were together he said in a harsh, brusque tone :

" ' You are not my friend. Oh, women, women. Josephine. . . . If you really had been my friend you would have told me all I have just learned from Junot. He is a true friend. . . . Josephine ! And we are parted by six hundred leagues ! You ought to have told me. Josephine ! To think that she should deceive me so. . . . She ! Woe betide them ! I will exterminate that breed of effeminate puppies and coxcombs. As for her, I'll divorce her. Yes, a divorce. And everybody shall hear of it. I must write. I know everything now. It is your fault. You ought to have told me.' "

Bourrienne tried to pacify the unhappy man and mentioned the fame which he had won in Egypt. Bonaparte swept his words away.

" My fame ! " he cried. " What wouldn't I give to know that what Junot has just told me is not true ! So dearly do I love that woman. If Josephine is guilty, a divorce shall separate us forever. I won't be the laughing-stock of all the good-for-nothing lazy devils in Paris. I'll write to Joseph. He'll get us divorced."

This letter to Joseph was not written until the first gust of feeling had blown by. It ran :

" I have a great deal of domestic trouble because the veil is now entirely rent. Arrange for a country house for me, either near Paris or in Burgundy. . . . I mean to pass the winter in the country and to make a hermit of myself. I am sick of my fellow-creatures. I need solitude and isolation; earthly splendours weary me. My heart is worn out with suffering. At twenty-nine, glory is a trumpery thing. I have drained the cup of human bliss ; what I must now become is a completely

selfish creature. I mean to keep my house to myself; I will
share it with none. I no longer have anyone to live for.

" Farewell, my only friend. . . ."

But if Josephine was coy, Germaine was solicitous. Germaine
had been in great agitation about Bonaparte ever since their
meeting in Paris at Talleyrand's ball.

" General Bonaparte," she wrote, " had become as famous by
reason of his character and mind as on account of his victories,
and the imagination of the French was stirred by him in the most
lively fashion. People kept recalling his proclamations to the
Cisalpine and Ligurian Republics. In one of these the following
phrase had been specially remarked : ' You were divided and
bound by tyranny ; you were in no condition to regain your
freedom.' In the other : ' The true conquests, the only ones
which leave no regrets, are those we win over ignorance.' There
was a tone of moderation and nobility in his style which
contrasted strikingly with the revolutionary bitterness of the
French civil chiefs. The soldier spoke like a magistrate, while
the magistrates were expressing themselves with soldierly
violence.

" General Bonaparte had not put the laws against the
emigrants into execution in his army. It was said that he was
deeply in love with his wife, whose nature was full of sweetness ;
it was said again that he was charmed by the beauties of the poet
Ossian ; people took delight in convincing themselves that he
possessed every generous quality capable of throwing his
amazing powers of mind into high relief. Finally everybody
was so tired of oppressors who borrowed the name of Liberty,
of oppressors who wept for the loss of arbitary power, that
admiration had no bounds since General Bonaparte seemed
to unite in his own person every quality capable of winning it.

" In my own case, at any rate, I saw him in Paris for the first
time with such feelings in my heart. I could find no words to
answer him when he came up to me to tell me that he had called
on my father at Coppet and was sorry he had passed through

Switzerland without meeting him. But when the agitation caused by the admiration I felt had subsided a little, a lively sense of fear followed. Bonaparte, at that moment, had no power ; indeed it was generally believed that the dark suspicions of the Directory constituted a real danger for him. So that the fear which he inspired can only have been due to the singular influence exerted by his personality on almost all those who approached him. I have met men worthy in every way of respect, I have met fierce men ; there was nothing in the effect exerted on me by Bonaparte which in any way recalled the impressions made by either of these types. I soon saw, on the different occasions on which I met him during his stay in Paris, that his character could not be described in ordinary words ; he was neither good, nor violent, nor sweet-tempered, nor cruel as ordinary men are. He was more, or less, than a man.

" Far from becoming easier in his company as time went on, I grew more afraid. I had a vague feeling that no emotion could exert any influence on him. . . . Each time I heard him speak I was struck by his superiority. . . . The difficulty of breathing which I felt in his presence never became less. . . . His face, thin then and pale, was pleasant enough."

In fact Germaine flung herself at Bonaparte's head. She followed him about and sat, always, staring at him until he became embarrassed.

" I examined Bonaparte's face with attention," was her own way of expressing this attempt at conquest, " but each time he noticed me looking at him, he had the art to blank out all expression from his eyes so that these eyes might have been carved in marble. His face at these moments was quite still except for the faint smile with which he met and defeated my every attempt to read his thoughts."

When he went to Egypt she wrote to him, offering herself as a worthy substitute for Josephine. Bonaparte was horrified and outraged, though she had assured him that he was :

" Greater than Alexander ; greater than Cæsar. . . ."

She went about both in Paris and in Switzerland praising him to the skies.

" He is," she wrote, " the most fearless warrior, the deepest thinker, the most amazing genius that history has ever known. . . . What Republican has not felt regret that he is not yet forty."[1]

Madame de Chastenay, hearing these praises, remarked :

" How she would have loved to go and join him among the ruins of Thebes and share his destiny."

One day she heard that he had sent for her book on the *Passions*. She passed on the splendid news to her father who replied :

" So, your glory has spread to the banks of the Nile. Alexander of Macedon called philosophers and wise men from the four corners of the world to argue with him ; the Corsican Alexander, to save time, enters only into communication with the mind of Madame de Staël. *He knows how to do things.*"

---

[1] And so eligible for a seat in the Senate.

CHAPTER XXIII

WIFE AND MOTHER

JOSEPHINE, in face of Bonaparte's return, became panic-stricken. She decided, again on Gohir's advice, to withdraw her petition for divorce and to go out to meet her husband. Bonaparte had taken her son, Eugène, with him to Egypt as his aide-de-camp. She rushed off to the boarding-school kept by Mme Campan, one of Marie Antoinette's Women of the Bedchamber, and bade her daughter, Hortense, who was at the school, accompany her. They drove out, together, on the road to Lyons.

Meanwhile " Napoleone's " mother and sisters were gathering in his house in Paris to await his coming. They wore grim expressions because they were resolved to enlighten him fully about Malmaison and thus to counteract any effect which Josephine's journey might have produced. Josephine's luck was out. She took the wrong road and Bonaparte got to Paris without having seen her.

He was in excellent spirits because the country people had welcomed him with a frenzy of joy and hailed him as " the Saviour." But what he heard in the rue des Victoires killed all his joy. He vowed that never again would he have dealings with this woman who had so callously betrayed him.

" Divorce," he cried. " Divorce and the sooner the better."

Into this atmosphere Josephine and Hortense plunged two days later and, at the first contact with it, Josephine gave herself up for lost. Bonaparte refused to see her. Though she knocked humbly upon his study door again and again she got no answer. A message was sent to her to pack up and go back to Malmaison.

And meanwhile France was giving herself to the man she, Josephine, had rejected. Fear and a frenzy of bitterness divided her mind. She wept and begged and implored—always behind the door. The door, locked on the inside, refused her. When she retired to her rooms upstairs, she heard the coming and going of numberless visitors, all the leaders of all the parties in the State.

The day fixed for her departure arrived. The study door was still shut. She called her son and daughter and begged them to plead for her. They went down together to their step-father's room and craved admittance. He opened the door. Hortense threw her arms round his neck. He saw Eugène, of whom he was fond, standing miserably behind his sister. Behind Eugène, at the foot of the stairs, and weeping hysterically, was Josephine. His courage broke. He called Josephine into the room and sent the children away.

And she confessed everything while he strode about breaking small ornaments. He told her that only the fact that she was a Frenchwoman had saved her. Could he preface his mastery of France by casting a Frenchwoman out of his house? She saw, suddenly, the fear of him and the strength and, for a moment at least, was faithful. Next morning when his brother Lucien called to congratulate him on having got rid of Josephine he found a united and apparently happy couple.

A few days later Josephine was helping her husband to put an end to Barras' rule. The tide of plotting and counter-plotting flowed between their house and the Parliament and then from the Parliament to Marie Antoinette's palace at St. Cloud. Once or twice it seemed that Bonaparte had over-reached himself and that his cause was lost. But he returned nevertheless from this, his first political battle, as he had returned from his wars, the undisputed victor. Josephine was the wife, now, of the First Consul of the French Republic. They moved their home to the Luxembourg Palace.

Ouvrard at a window of his great house, saw that move and

observed the little General ride past. He had his man of business with him.

" Buy ! " he ordered laconically.

He presented himself to the First Consul and offered a loan. Bonaparte received him ungraciously declaring that he did not wish to borrow. But the banker knew better. The Treasury was empty and the Austrians were advancing upon Genoa. Bonaparte would have to borrow.

Nevertheless, as he returned home, Ouvrard felt uneasy. He had heard that Josephine had been forbidden, absolutely, to receive Thérèse or even to speak to her. He foresaw that men who, notoriously, lived with mistresses, would not be welcome at the Consular Court. He hinted to Thérèse that it might be necessary to provide her with a house of her own.

Germaine's adoration bounded up once more. She had gone to Switzerland. She dashed back to Paris and reopened her *salon*. So violent was her approval of Bonaparte that her father actually reproved her.

" Your nerves have got the better of you," he wrote. " It's true, everything hangs on a single life. But he's young and fate will take care of him for us."

And again :

" The general delirium which surrounds you . . . your enthusiasm for Bonaparte . . . I congratulate you on being so greatly rejoiced of his glory."

Again :

" You're all spellbound. I congratulate you—not on feeling so uplifted, but on feeling so happy."

Happiness, however, was short-lived. Many were called to help the First Consul in his work of saving France from ruin, Mme de Staël was not one of them. The light ebbed from her black eyes. She was living now in the rue de Grenelle, in a house of her own and her *salon* was as brilliant as ever. To her house came nightly Talleyrand, confirmed by Bonaparte in his post of Foreign Minister, Fouché, now Minister of Police,

PAUL BARRAS

Lucien Bonaparte, Minister of the Interior, Joseph Bonaparte Elise Bonaparte, Benjamin, Mathieu de Montmorency, Sieyès, whose help had been so valuable to the new ruler is securing his success. Only Bonaparte himself did not come.

What did it mean? Germaine had felt sure that the First Consul would lose no time in setting up her father's system, with its loans and its banks, its parliaments and its constitution. She had said, following Sieyès, that what France needed was " a sword and a head," while Jacques had called Bonaparte " the necessary man "—necessary, that is to say, to money-lenders and their system. It could not be possible that he was going to disappoint them.

A few days passed. The First Consul issued his own consti- tution as he might have issued a prohibition to keep off the grass of his garden. His constitution restored absolute power to the head of the State—himself—abolished popular election altogether, and set up a Council of State, to be nominated by the First Consul, and two Chambers to be nominated by the Council of State. The " sword " had become the " head " also, the whole body, indeed. There was not even a niche for money- lenders in this temple.

But how was he going to do it? Where was the money to come from? The day when paper-money based on land (or any other commodity) could be used had passed for ever. Where ruined currencies are concerned there is no resurrection. Bonaparte would have to obtain gold and all the gold was in the possession of her friends.

This mood of anxiety gave place to new hope. After all, Ouvrard was prepared to lend, the Hopes too, and others. So perhaps Bonaparte's constitution was only a temporary measure of precaution. If only he would send for her ; if only he would avail himself of her wit and wisdom.

He did not send for her. She bestirred herself to secure a place for Benjamin in one of the new councils so that her views might not lack for a mouthpiece. Her friend Chabaud-Latour was pressed into service.

"M. Chabaud-Latour," recounts Aimé-Martin, "took Benjamin Constant to the First Consul and introduced him. Bonaparte remarked that he had read Constant's works and had been much interested in them. He congratulated him. Benjamin returned compliment for compliment and then expressed his wish to be made a member of the Tribunate.

"'And why not?' said Bonaparte. 'Yes, that can be arranged. I'll see to it.'

"At these words Benjamin warmly assured the General of his devotion to him, exclaiming :

"'Believe me, I'm with you. I'm not one of those ideologues who suppose everything can be put right by thinking about it. Give me deeds. If you appoint me you can count on me.'

"They parted. M. Chabaud-Latour happened to say, as they were going down the stairs, that he was about to call on Sieyès. Benjamin insisted on going, too. . . . They crossed the street, ran up the steps and entered. Benjamin Constant succeeded in getting a short interview. He asked Sieyès also to have him appointed to the Tribunate, declaring :

"'You know that I detest force. Never will I be friend to the sword. What I care about are principles, ideas, justice. So, if I'm lucky enough to get your support, you can count on me, for I'm Bonaparte's strongest opponent.' "

Bonaparte nominated Benjamin. Instantly Benjamin began to oppose Bonaparte.

"At eleven o'clock at night," declared the First Consul bitterly, " he begged me, on his knees, for a post. At midnight, when he had got it, he began to insult me."

Germaine made up her mind that Bonaparte would have nothing to do with her. She was " woman scorned " as well as money-lender's daughter. All the rich resources of her hate were drawn upon to hamper and thwart this latest enemy. Her *salon* was transformed, overnight, to plotters' den, and she gathered into it Bonaparte's enemies, Thérèse, disgraced and ostracized that Josephine might be the more effectively white-washed, Juliette Récamier, a lovely girl with a sharp tongue, who had married an elderly millionaire-banker, General Bernadotte, the husband of Desirée Clary, whom Bonaparte had jilted to marry Josephine. Desirée, as it happened, was Joseph Bonaparte's sister-in-law; she continued to adore Napoleon in spite of his fickleness. Bernadotte's vanity was wounded.

These disgruntled people spent their time making the First Consul and his " virtuous wife " and " lady mother " ridiculous. It was the same method as that which Germaine had used, years before, against Louis XVI and Marie Antoinette. She who had destroyed the ancient Household of France had small fear of " the Dynasty of Ajaccio."

" When people talk," one of her friends remarked, " about an idol fifteen days old, one can remind oneself of another idol, aged fifteen centuries, which was shattered to atoms."

Bonaparte heard this challenge. His newspaper, the *Moniteur*, called public attention to the " restless and disturbing ambitions of a well-known person," who was talking already about " organized opposition."

That night there was a big reception at the rue de Grenelle and the huge rooms glowed with light. Germaine's fire-works of wit and sarcasm outbid the candles. Benjamin came in, from the Chamber. Germaine declared, years afterwards, that he said :

" You see your drawing-room is full of people whom you like. But if I deliver, to-morrow, the speech we have agreed upon, your drawing-room will become a desert. Have you thought of that ? "

To which, she declared further, she replied :

" One must be true to one's principles."

There is no reason to accept this account and every reason to reject it. Germaine believed that Bonaparte would be forced, by Benjamin's eloquence, to make terms with her. She supposed that the old " challenge to tyrants " by which money-lenders had destroyed the monarchy and every attempt made, subsequently, to replace it, would achieve its usual success.

" This is not our own cause," cried Benjamin next day. " It is the People's cause. There is only servility here and silence, a silence to which all Europe is listening."

Bonaparte, too, was listening.

" Lice on my clothes," he remarked, " but I'll get rid of them. Do they suppose that I'm going to allow myself to be attacked as Louis XVI was attacked ? "

A Royalist writer, who was watching the battle with joy, wrote of Germaine :

" She writes about philosophy which she doesn't understand, about morality which she doesn't practise, about the virtue of women which she doesn't possess. ' Benjamin,' says she, ' shall be Consul. I'll give the Finances to Papa, Justice to my uncle, an ambassadorship, somewhere, to my husband. As for me, I'll keep an eye on the lot.' "

A Jacobin writer was even less complimentary :

" It isn't your fault that you're fat," he declared. " But it is your fault that you're a plotter. Mend your manners, because in the present state of society you have no empire. You know the way back to Switzerland. Be off, before something nasty happens to you. . . . And take Benjamin with you. . . ."

She gave a dinner in Benjamin's honour. Ten guests, including Talleyrand and Fouché, asked to be excused. She took fright and began to whimper.

" Who has been more enthusiastic for Bonaparte than me ? " she wrote to Roederer, his friend.

She was answered by Fouché, Minister of Police, in his official capacity. He called during the morning to suggest that a stay in the country . . . Anguish turned to despair after she reached Saint-Ouen. She wrote to Talleyrand—the beloved Bishop—" in the name of our old friendship," soliciting an invitation to his ball at which Bonaparte was expected to be present. Talleyrand advised her to keep away " in the name of our old friendship." She rushed back to Paris and ordered new dresses of still more violent hues. She went forth to visit. Doors were closed, discreetly, in her face. At Mme de Montesson's nobody would speak to her except the gentle and very good Delphine de Sabran. She called her next novel after that girl.

" Fouché," she wrote, " often spoke of virtue as of an old wives' tale. But a very wise head made him choose decent behaviour as the most rational so that his wits brought him where other people arrive under the promptings of conscience. . . . I had rendered M. de Talleyrand the most vital services and, what is more important, had been his unflinching friend for years. He was going to give a ball and Madame B. (Josephine), who was always kind to the underdog when possible, had promised that she would arrange for me to have a talk with the First Consul and had expressed a hope that this talk would completely remove the anxiety I felt that I might be sent into exile.

" I counted the days to the ball, never dreaming that M. de Talleyrand might not invite me. But he didn't invite me. No, not even after one of my friends had explained to him how much my peace of mind depended on being invited. That man, who during ten years had spent most of his life in my house, who had me to thank for his return from America, for the management of his business affairs in his absence. That man, to whose good fortune, I swear it, I had powerfully contributed and from whom I received ten letters in which he swore that he owed me his life—that man gave the signal to my persecutors. . . .

" There is a man very well fitted for this world's commerce. He says little and so is able to weigh his words. As he never learns anything except by listening, he hates arguments, wherein his lack of solid knowledge is exposed. He has no eloquence, because eloquence demands movement in the spirit and he has disciplined himself to such an extent as to be unable, even if he wishes to do so, to let himself go. He cannot express himself because to speak easily, one must be able to write easily, and with all his gifts he lacks the capacity to write even a page of all the works which have been published under his name.

" But when he likes, his smallest gestures possess an inimitable good taste. He knows how to possess himself of the intelligence of the whole world. And yet, excellent judge and most discerning critic as he is, he is also strangely barren, a man who needs both power and riches for his mind's as well as for his body's comfort. Possessed of these he will let fall, as occasion offers, sarcasms or compliments, having taken care, beforehand, to be surrounded by people ready to pick them up and prepare the way for more. . . . Mask-like face, silent when it suits him, insolent in the most calculated fashion when that is necessary, displaying polished and charming manners when he wants to . . . he cannot inspire trust in anyone."

Alas, poor, dear Bishop. The truth, of course, was that Talleyrand had been forbidden to invite Germaine to his ball. Her hatred of Bonaparte grew from day to day. She watched him ride by when he moved house from the Luxembourg to the Tuileries and, cat-like, noticed the well-drilled behaviour of the lackeys who attended him.

" As for him," she remarked bitterly, " he looked at nobody and thanked nobody."

She was not, however, wholly absent from his mind for one day he sent his brother Joseph to her with the following letter :

" M. de Staël (her husband) is in destitution while his wife is giving dinners and balls. If you are still in communication with this woman, you might suggest to her the propriety of making her husband an allowance of from £500 to £1000 a year. Or have we reached times when people can trample underfoot not good manners only, but duties also as sacred as those binding children to their fathers, without at the same time forfeiting the regard of honest folk ? One doesn't, of course, judge Mme de

Staël's behaviour by male standards, but would any man who was heir to M. Necker's fortune, and who had, for long, enjoyed the privilege attaching to a distinguished name (de Staël) leave his wife in penury while he lived in abundance and expect at the same time to be received in decent society ? "

Eric Magnus was, indeed, in penury though, to do Necker justice, he had given his son-in-law £2000 and a small pension —to keep out of Germaine's way. That money had soon been lost on the tables and the banker's heart had hardened. Germaine, in despair, wrote to her father, who replied :

" Your hero, Bonaparte, is admired by all. Be wise, be prudent."

The letter had evidently been written with one eye on Bonaparte's postal censor. Meanwhile, Joseph Bonaparte urged his brother to be merciful.

" She'll adore you," he declared, " if you show her the smallest kindness."

" No good," replied the First Consul. " I don't want her adoration. She's too fat."

His hatred of the woman, of her father, of all she represented, of all her money-lending friends was implacable. Nevertheless he tried to read a book she had just published called : *The Relations of Literature to Social Institutions.*

" I sat down with it (the book)," he told his brother Lucien, " for at least a quarter of an hour, in the hope of making something of it. Devil take me, if I can make head or tail. Not that there are not plenty of words—big ones, too. But all the concentration of which my mind is capable has not been enough to make sense of a single one of these ideas which I am told are so deep."

The necessity of defending France once more had arisen because as has been said an Austrian army was approaching Genoa through Northern Italy. Bonaparte prepared for battle by suppressing sixty-three Paris newspapers including the whole of Germaine's Press—a wise precaution seeing that he was at war, still, with England, Austria, Spain, Portugal, Naples, Russia, Sweden, Holland and Turkey. Germaine saw the complete ruin of the machinery by which, so often, she and her father had destroyed their opponents. Bonaparte left to join the army ; she followed him. He reached Switzerland long before her and actually stopped at Coppet to visit Necker, whom he afterwards described as " a big, fat, wheezy headmaster, rather ill-informed even on financial matters." Jacques offered himself once more as the servant of France but, since the occasion of Bonaparte's visit was the behaviour of Germaine in Paris, he did not get far on that road. Instead he had to plead humbly for his daughter and beg the new master of France to forgive her. This, in the end, Bonaparte promised, if there was no more trouble. Jacques' opinion of his visitor was not high, " nothing very wonderful."

Germaine, when she heard about the visit, was in new ecstasies.

" Did you resist the temptation," she wrote to Meister, " to get a glimpse of the hero. He's off to conquer Italy for the second time and sign a new peace of Campo-Formio. Isn't it historic ? "

When she heard about the Battle of Marengo, she wrote to Juliette Récamier :

" This man has a will strong enough to lift the world."

And to Gérando :

" The marvels of this Italian campaign would turn any head. Enthusiasm has wrung from me—even from me—praises which spring from my amazed wonder. The supporters of the Government will be pleased with me in the coming winter— those of them at any rate who want praise without servility."

But she had her moments of gloom and weariness—the offspring of her wounded vanity.

" I've come to the conclusion," she wrote to Gérando, " that sorrow is the portion of humanity. Oh, do you think the heart can ever free itself from such griefs as mine ? The three men whom I have loved the most, whom I have loved since I was nineteen or twenty, are Narbonne, Talleyrand and Mathieu. The first is a graceful figure ; the second no longer even boasts a figure ; and the third has abandoned his old tastes, though his adorable qualities remain to him, unimpaired. I've got new friends who are very dear to me ; but it's the past which really bids our dreams and stirs our hearts."

Narbonne was, in fact, lost to a new mistress—Mme de Montmorency-Laval, Mathieu's mother. Talleyrand had gone over to Bonaparte. Mathieu had become a religious zealot. She was thirty-four, with all her looks gone, tired, bedraggled. Only Benjamin remained to her and she was no longer sure of him. But her native pugnacity remained. She packed her boxes and took the road, once more, for Paris. Poor Jacques was disconsolate :

" My daughter," he wrote, " is ready to go away again to the Great City ; it isn't without searching of heart that I shall see those high mountains thrust between her and myself."

Meanwhile, the Financiers had been looking about for a new ally, to help them curb the power of Bonaparte. Fouché was their man. He began to establish close relations with Josephine who, though quelled, was secretly full of rebelliousness. It was pointed out to the wife of the First Consul that the only real solution of the difficulties of France was a restoration of " Louis XVIII " to the throne of his ancestors. Bonaparte, in other words, must play the part of General Monk, and bring back the King. Josephine and her daughter Hortense ventured one day to urge this course upon him. In addition, Josephine told him that she had received a promise from the Comte d'Artois, Louis XVI's younger brother, to make him High Constable of France, and to erect a statue in his honour.

Bonaparte gazed at her. He knew, if she did not know, that " Louis XVIII " was receiving a pension from the English Government, through the instrumentality of the Rothschilds.

" Tell the Comte d'Artois," he said, " that he will have

to kill me first and use my body as the pedestal of his statue."

" These obstinate women," he remarked later, " are quite crazy. The Faubourg St. Germain has turned their heads. They both want to act as guardian angel to the Royalists. But they won't hurt me. I bear them no ill-will."

Josephine bided her time and kept in touch with Fouché. When Bonaparte went away to his campaign in Italy she gathered her old friends, including Thérèse Tallien, round her once more and, in addition, became friendly with Talleyrand. She did not trouble to write to her husband, who, as usual, protested :

" I have not received a single letter from you ; that is bad. I have written you by every courier. . . . My very kindest regards to you, my good little Josephine, and to all who belong to you."

CHAPTER XXIV

DISCIPLINE OF DAMES

BONAPARTE raised his loan and defeated the Austrians at the Battle of Marengo. He made peace with Austria, then with Prussia, at last with England. He recalled the exiles. He rebuilt the altars which the Jacobins had cast down. The French made him Consul for life and gave themselves wholly into his hands.

But the difficulty about obtaining money remained, even after every department of Government had been reformed and reorganized. It was impossible now, since Barras' destruction of the land-money, to issue paper. Gold and silver were terribly scarce. Bonaparte ordered that foreign goods were not to be allowed to enter France and demanded payment in gold for such French goods, for example wines, as foreign countries chose to buy.

Instantly he found himself involved in a quarrel with the London bankers who foresaw a draining away to France of their precious metal. They bade him remove his prohibition. When he refused they threatened to resume the war.

There need be no surprise at this attitude. What Bonaparte was doing was to challenge the Money Monopoly just as Mirabeau and Robespierre had challenged it and just as, a century before, it had been challenged by Louis XIV.

For if the London merchants could not get their goods into France they would be forced to pay for such French goods as they bought with gold or silver. Bonaparte, in consequence, would obtain a supply of the precious metals which he could use, in the fashion of the bankers, as the basis of credit. Louis XIV had tried to seize gold by force of arms. Louis XV and Louis XVI had tried to obtain it by taxing their nobles and the Church. Mirabeau, with his "gold mine," the land money, had shown how one could get along quite well without it. Bonaparte—the gold mine being now destroyed—hoped to get it by trade.

But since the possession of gold had become a monopoly of a small number of people, including the Barings, the Hopes, Ouvrard, Necker, Cabarras and others, and since, by their monopoly of gold, these bankers ruled the world and all its rulers, it was certain that any statesman who tried to get a store of the metal for himself would be most violently attacked.

In Bonaparte's case attacks came from the Royalists and the Jacobins indiscriminately, both parties being in receipt of money from the secret agents of finance. The Royalists tried to blow up his carriage; the Jacobins tried to upset his government. Finally, Royalists and Jacobins joined hands in a plot to murder him on his way from Paris to Malmaison. All these attempts failed. But he was less successful in saving himself from war. Early in the year 1804 he realized that he would have to face and fight a Coalition consisting of England, Austria and Russia with, possibly, Prussia as well.

In such circumstances his determination never to borrow money had to be suspended. He sent for Ouvrard once more and asked for a loan, telling the banker, at the same time, that in no circumstances would he allow his wife to receive Thérèse who had just borne Ouvrard a child. New orders to this effect had already been issued to Josephine.

Thérèse was greatly distressed. She tried to enter the Tuileries, to which Palace Bonaparte had transferred his court, but was turned from the door. She wrote to Josephine. She sent mutual friends to plead for her, all to no purpose. Bonaparte was "purging" Paris and would have nothing to do with her. Josephine experienced great embarrassment because she liked her old friend and longed to talk things over with her. She discussed her trouble with Fouché. It was arranged that Thérèse should be brought into the palace by a back door when Bonaparte was out of the way.

Fouché, who remained in close touch with the bankers in Amsterdam and London, was finding in Josephine, as has been said, a most useful tool. The woman cared nothing for her husband except in so far as he possessed the means to gratify her tastes for expensive clothes and beautiful jewels. She was ruinously extravagant—so much so that even her husband's prodigal generosity could not satisfy her. Always, she wanted money and more money and still more money. Fouché told her that money could be earned : there were people who hankered after information about Bonaparte and who were ready to pay for it. Some kind of bargain was struck and Bonaparte had, if not a spy, at least an informer in his family circle. Josephine used her new-found power to get rid of her brother-in-law Lucien, who was one of her bitterest enemies. He had been mixed up in a financial scandal. He was ordered to Spain.

Madame Bonaparte, senior, who loved Lucien more than any other of her sons, discovered that Josephine had had a hand in his disgrace. She drove to the palace and demanded to see " Napoleone." In quivering tones, and with raised hands, she told him, in Josephine's presence, exactly what she thought about Josephine. Her daughters added their testimony. Josephine found it prudent to keep Fouché at arms' length for a time. But she continued to see Thérèse when opportunity offered.

There was something very human about Josephine which condoned even her treachery. Quite unconscionable, she was nevertheless good-natured and kind. And though her idleness and laziness concealed a strong and determined will, her natural grace went far to excuse her. Bonaparte continued to adore after the last rags of illusion had been stripped from his mind.

Indeed he seemed, at times, to enjoy the insolent deceptions which she practised upon him. But he took the precaution, nevertheless, of having her watched and thus soon found out what she was doing. A terrific storm followed his discovery of Thérèse's visits.

Nor was he any better disposed towards Germaine de Staël, who had not kept the promises which her father had made on her behalf. Their war began once more as soon as she was re-established in Paris. He disapproved of her relations with Benjamin Constant, of her books, of the influence of her *salon* on Parisian Society. He ordered her to retire to Coppet. She refused to go and begged Joseph Bonaparte to plead for her.

" I get stupid," she confessed to Lucien one day, " in your brother's company because I want so much to please him. I want to talk to him and my mind becomes a blank. I try to wing my words. I want to compel him to give me his attention ; when the blank in my mind is filled I'm as stupid as ever—as stupid as a goose."

But she was not always so flattering. When she heard that Bonaparte had called her an " ideologue," she called him " Ideophobe," and spoke sweetly about his " virtuous wife." Joseph's pleadings were not successful. " Forcibly remind this woman," Bonaparte declared, " that I am not a Louis XVI. Counsel her not to stand in the way along which I wish to go. If not, I'll crush and break her. The best course for her at present is quietness. . . . I won't hurt her if I don't have to."

He informed Fouché, at the same time, that Mme de Staël disturbed people's minds. He had not lived through the whole course of the French Revolution for nothing. It was his belief that the Revolution was due, first and foremost, to the weakening of the Church, secondly, to the growing influence of money-lenders and their womenfolk. He had re-established the Church ; he meant to abolish the philosophers and the money-lenders and turn France again into a country of peasants. If these ideas were not as yet very clearly formed in his mind he felt instinctively that the banker's women, Germaine and Thérèse and the rest, were his natural and inveterate enemies. They served the purposes of their men-folk both by their intrigues and by their profligacy. They corrupted Society; they weakened the State; they betrayed the fatherland. In addition they were lewd and scandalous, imbued with the idea that anything and everything may be bought with money.

" If you look closely at these women," he got a journalist friend to write in the *Mercure*, " you will see how unruly are their lusts and with what imperiousness they conduct their liaisons. Listen to them carefully; you will hear them complaining against everybody; you will hear them sighing in deepest melancholy; their hearts they will tell you are bleeding from the wounds of ingratitude. They keep shrieking for peace of mind, that peace which they say they will never enjoy till they lie in the grave towards which the grief that consumes them is slowly bearing them. Look at them! They are big, heavy, fat and strong. Their faces glowing with a superfluity of health show not a trace of that anguish which heartache always leaves behind it. And why? Because the only trouble they have ever known is wounded vanity. In short, these women are compounded of excessive egoism."

Bonaparte ordered Germaine to leave France within twenty-four hours. She packed up and, with Benjamin, took the road, not to Switzerland, but to Germany.

Meanwhile, Ouvrard began to find Thérèse more and more of a liability. Ouvrard was hunting big game, in other words Bonaparte, and had a plan in his mind whereby this uncomfortable fellow might be brought to heel. He meant to go to Spain and seek there the help of Cabarras. He did not wish to take Cabarras' daughter with him.

On the other hand he did not wish to quarrel with Cabarras' daughter. He urged her, therefore, to accept at once an offer of marriage which had just been made to her by the son of the Prince de Chimay. Chimay was so violently in love that he cared nothing about Thérèse's past life except to forgive and forget it. A kind, brave man, simple and unsuspecting. She hesitated. Finally she accepted.

Ouvrard left for Spain, where he obtained the right to handle all the gold shipped to that country from South America. Thérèse and her husband went to Italy. In Paris Bonaparte received from the hands of the Pope the Crown of France, and became the Emperor Napoleon I. Josephine was crowned at the same moment, Empress of the French.

Germaine left behind her in Paris seeds of opposition to Napoleon and to his system about the danger of which he was very well aware. Her *salon*, in its last days, had retained something of its old brilliance.

" We used to see there," wrote Chenelle, " Chateaubriand in all the *éclat* of his first glory, Mme Récamier in the delicate flower of her grace and her youth, Mme Visconti with her majestic Roman beauty, the Chevalier de Boufflers in the *négligé* of a country vicar but with all the exquisite air and all the arts of a courtier . . . and among the politicians, Benjamin Constant, tall, erect, good-looking, his long hair falling in curls on his neck. He had an extraordinary expression of mockery and malice in his smile, and especially in his eyes. Nothing could be wittier than his conversation. Always epigrammatic, he discussed the deepest political questions with lucid, concise and forcible logic, his argument tinged with sarcasm."

Benjamin had begun to take some pride in his personal appearance.

" I like," he wrote, " to find in novels heroes with red hair who inspire great passions. Red hair, in my opinion, ought to be an indispensable attribute of such heroes ; it is, I feel sure, a great mark of *esprit* and sensibility. I've been wearing a blonde wig this winter, but I have given it up."

" I am condemned," he wrote to a friend, " to live in Society . . . and of all the many hells of Dante, I believe that one to be the most painful in the long run."

Musée de Louvre

JOSEPHINE

Napoleon's progress towards Christianity and monarchy exasperated Germaine and Benjamin beyond belief, because they recognized in this movement the undoing of all that they had laboured to accomplish.

" He (Napoleon)," Germaine wrote, " commanded a great ceremony in Notre-Dame. There he was, himself, with all the trappings of Royalty. And who, can it be guessed, was told off to preach the sermon ? No other than the Archbishop of Aix, the same who had preached at the Coronation of Louis XVI in the Cathedral of Rheims. . . .

" Bonaparte and his suite went to the cathedral in the King's old carriages which were driven by the former coachmen and surrounded by the footmen who had attended them at Versailles. . . . Nothing, I confess it, has ever caused me such acute exasperation. I shut myself up in my house so as not to see the odious spectacle, but I couldn't help hearing the firing of the guns which announced the passing of the French people into slavery."

So she and her father had killed Louis XVI to make Napoleon King. In spite of all their plottings they had not succeeded in delivering France, wholly, into the money-lenders' hands. (Napoleon refused to pay Necker the £100,000 which the banker asserted was still owing to him by the French Treasury). A new clash between Finance, in its London lair, and Nationalism under the Corsican's leadership, was evidently about to convulse the world.

These distresses had been complicated, for a day or two, by the last illness of Eric Magnus, who was living in a cheap lodging in Paris. With Napoleon's eye on her, Germaine had not dared to leave him to die uncomforted. She offered to take him to Switzerland on condition that, if he recovered, he would go home, for good, to Sweden. The poor man accepted, supposing no doubt that she proposed to pay for the expenses of the journey. But no, he possessed a library of first editions which was his dearest possession. In spite of his most pitiful pleas she sent this off to an auction room in order to reimburse herself. Eric Magnus died at an inn at Poligny. She buried him in the parish cemetery at Coppet.

This short visit to Switzerland had enabled her to help her father with his autobiography and also to insert in the book criticisms of Napoleon. Necker, as has been said, had lately ennobled himself by assuming the title of " Baron de Coppet." But this honour did not fully satisfy him, and he added to it, in consequence, the name " Magistrate of the Truth." Baron de Coppet, Magistrate of the Truth, had some hard things to say about the Corsican and the Corsican's system.

The book caused a good deal of exasperation in Paris, where an inspired writer sneered :

" Happy man, who has contributed powerfully to so many calamities without himself suffering any of them. Happy man, who has never shed a tear except with a pen in his hand."

Germaine read and rejoiced.

" He (Napoleon) fears me," she wrote to Lacretelle. " There's my delight, my pride; and there is my terror. I confess it, I sink at the thought of a proscription, and I'm ill-fitted to endure even the boredom of a long exile. My courage fails; but not my will. I suffer; but I want no humiliating remedies. I have a woman's fears. But they can't make a hypocrite or a slave of me."

She made haste to publish the novel on which she had been at work during several months. It was called *Delphine* and it attacked Napoleon in many different ways. Among other rights the right to love was asserted boldly.

" Women," it was declared, " have no life outside of love. The histories of their lives begin and end with love."

Napoleon expressed the view that the book ought to have been banned before publication. Here was a *salon* which he could not close. As thousand after thousand copies were sold, he opened a new offensive.

" The French," one of his friends wrote, " have nothing to

thank her for. Her whole love has been given to the English. Don't let us wonder at it. Those minds which soar above our sordid world have no motherland. Moreover, in Mme de Staël's case, the right of universal genius is supplemented by a personal right. Born in a land which no longer enjoys a separate existence, married to a Swede, become French by accident, never having possessed a native land except in her imagination, she cannot, probably, conceive of anybody else as the possessor of a native land."

Delphine contained a portrait of Talleyrand—as a woman.

" I hear," that statesman exclaimed, " that Mme de Staël has presented both of us—herself and me—as females."

But the retort lacked the sting of the attack. Very soon Germaine began to wish that she had not written *Delphine*, or, at least, that she had not used it to replace her newspapers. She was told to quit France. She went into hiding, and wrote to Napoleon, who was still at that moment First Consul :

" I was living peacefully at Mafliers," she pleaded, " relying on your assurance that I might stay there, when I learned that *gendarmes* were on the way to arrest me and my two children. Citizen-Consul, I cannot believe it. If you do this a cruel fame will be mine, and I shall have a line or two to myself in your history.

" You will break my good old father's heart. He longs, I know it, to come to you in spite of his age, and to ask you what crime I have committed—what crime my family has committed —to deserve such barbarous treatment. If you're determined to drive me out of France, at least grant me a passport for Germany and allow me to spend eight days in Paris to obtain money for my journey and to take my daughter to a doctor. The long journey has worn her out.

" In no country on earth would such a respite be refused.

" Citizen-Consul, the impulse to persecute a woman and her two children never arose within your breast. It is impossible that a hero can be other than the protector of weakness. I implore you, once again, forgive me. Let me dwell in peace in my father's house at Saint-Ouen. That house is near enough to Paris to allow my girl, when the time comes, to study in the *École polytechnique* and far enough away to prevent me keeping open house to visitors. I'll go there in spring, when the weather makes travelling safe for my children.

" Citizen-Consul, let me beg you finally to pause a moment before bringing a heavy grief on a defenceless soul. You have it in your power, by an act of simple justice, to fill my heart with gratitude truer and more lasting than could perhaps be awakened by many favours."

A few days later a mounted *gendarme* came to conduct her out of France. She persuaded him to allow her to visit Juliette Récamier, because Junot, Napoleon's old companion in arms, was Juliette's lover. Junot was sent off to plead with the tyrant. He returned empty-handed. She turned to Joseph Bonaparte and actually went to stay in his house " Mortfontaine," to gain time. But, as has been said, her enemy was not to be moved even by the solicitations of his brother. He was about to wage war with all Europe for the principles in defence of which Louis XVI had laid down his life. He did not propose that the daughter of the money-lender who had been the chief architect of ruin should remain in France to sap the foundations of his strength.

CHAPTER XXV

ESTHER

THE War Cloud which had been threatening so long broke, suddenly, on the Rhine. Napoleon rushed to Strasburg and drove the Austrians before him all the way to the gates of Vienna. He followed them, after they had effected a union with the Russians, under the Emperor Alexander I, and engaged the allied army on the field of Austerlitz. He destroyed it.

He had taken Josephine with him as far as Strasburg, ostensibly for the pleasure of her company, really because he did not trust her. The battle between her and his own family had grown more and more bitter with the passage of time, nor had the marriage of his brother Louis to Hortense, Josephine's daughter, done anything to help matters. Josephine had made that match in order to supply her husband with the heir which she herself had not given to him. Scandalous tongues, inspired by Josephine, whispered the suggestion that, when the child was born, its real father would be Napoleon.

Hortense did not want to marry Louis, and appealed to her mother. Josephine told her :

" Only your marriage can tighten and strengthen those bonds on which depends my happiness."

That was enough. She consented. A few days later Napoleon remarked :

" Well, so Louis is courting you, is he ? That ought to suit you and your mother, too."

The marriage was a failure from the first, because Louis had heard Josephine's scandalous report about his wife's relations with his brother, though he knew they were untrue, and he could not rid his mind of the idea that they made him ridiculous.

"It's on account of what people will say," he kept on declaring.

When his son was born, this spirit of exasperation became active resentment. He refused to allow Napoleon to adopt the baby and threatened to take it away out of France. Naturally, his mother and brothers and sisters took his side. A series of violent family quarrels began, and this fire of hate discovered fresh fuel in Lucien's marriage to his mistress, Mme Jouberthou, in Pauline's marriage to Prince Borghese, and in the decision to have Josephine crowned Empress of the French. Josephine played her cards very cleverly, contriving usually to pose as the injured party. On the great day of the Coronation in Notre Dame, she gave a worthy and even notable performance.

"I have had the honour," wrote Mme de Rémusat, "to be presented to many ' real princesses '—to use the phrase of the Faubourg Saint-Germain—but I never saw one who, to my eyes, presented so perfect a personification of elegance and majesty. In Napoleon's face I could see the conviction of it. He looked at the Empress with approval ; and when she knelt down, when the tears which she could not repress fell on her clasped hands as they were raised to Heaven—or rather to Napoleon—both then appeared to enjoy one of those fleeting moments of pure happiness which are unique in a lifetime and serve to fill up the lustrum of years.

"His manner of crowning Josephine was most remarkable. After receiving the small crown, surmounted by the cross, he had first to place it on his own head and then to transfer it to her head. When the moment came for crowning the woman whom the people looked upon as his good genius, his manner was almost playful. He took great pains to arrange the little crown, which was placed over Josephine's tiara of diamonds ; he then put it on, took it off, and finally put it on again, as if to promise her that she should wear it gracefully and lightly."

During the whole " campaign of Austerlitz " he wrote to Josephine every day or two. But these letters were bulletins ; the passion of his first love was dead. Thus :

" LOUISBOURG,
" *October* 4, 1805.

" No news. My whole army is on the march. The weather is splendid. I am well. I hope, in a few days, to have something to tell you. Keep well and believe in my entire affection. There is a brilliant court here ; a new bride who is very beautiful, and, on the whole, some very pleasant people—even the Electress, who appears to be extremely kind, though a daughter of the King of England."

" LOUISBOURG,
" *October* 5.

" I shall resume my march immediately. You will, my dear, be five or six days without hearing from me. Don't worry, the reason is the operations now taking place. All goes well, according to my wishes.

" Adieu, dear. I love you and embrace you."

After his bloodless victory at Ulm he wrote :

" *October* 19.

" I have tired myself more than I ought to have done. Soaked clothes and damp feet every day for a week have made me rather ill ; but I've spent the whole of to-day indoors, which has rested me. My plan is accomplished. I have destroyed the Austrian army by marches alone. I have some 60,000 prisoners, 120 cannon, more than 90 flags and more than 30 generals. I am about to fling myself on the Russians. They are lost. I'm satisfied with my army. My losses are only 1500, of whom two-thirds are only slightly wounded.

" When I can give my thoughts to Italy I will make Eugène (who, as Viceroy of Italy, was campaigning in support of his stepfather) win a battle. Very best wishes to Hortense.

" Adieu, my Josephine ; kindest regards to everyone."

From the field of Austerlitz he wrote :

> " AUSTERLITZ,
>
> " *December* 3.

" I have sent Lebrun to you from the field of battle. I have beaten the Russian and Austrian armies commanded by the two Emperors. I'm rather fagged. I have bivouacked eight days in the open air, through rather keen nights . . . The Russian army is not only beaten, but also destroyed. I embrace you."

> " AUSTERLITZ,
>
> " *December* 5.

" I have made a truce. The Russians have vanished. The battle of Austerlitz is the grandest I have ever fought. Forty-five flags, more than 150 cannon, the Standards of the Russian Imperial Guard, 20 generals, 30,000 prisoners, more than 20,000 killed—a horrible spectacle. The Emperor Alexander is fleeing in despair back to Russia. Yesterday, at my bivouac, I received the German Emperor (Francis I of Austria). We talked for two hours ; we have agreed to make peace quickly. The weather is not very bad.

" At last behold peace restored to the Continent ; I hope peace may be restored to the world also. The English won't know how to face us. I look forward with much pleasure to the moment when I can once more be near you . . ."

He had already given her precise instructions about how she was to behave when visiting the Courts of Bavaria and Wurtemburg, which had allied themselves to his cause, thus :

" Take money with you for presents to the ladies and officers who will attend you. They owe everything to you and you owe nothing except politeness. The Electress of Wurtemburg is a daughter of the King of England. She's an excellent woman ; you should be very gracious to her, but without affectation."

Victory came only just in time, because Ouvrard, with the help of Cabarras and others, had organized and carried out a run on the Bank of France during Napoleon's absence. In other words he had put about the suggestion that Napoleon's bank was not safe and had got all Paris to believe him. Paris had begun to clamour for gold. The bank, which possessed very little gold, had been forced to close its doors. Napoleon's reign would have come to a speedy end had he not become possessed, in Vienna, of the millions of gold which London had sent to that city to finance the war.

" I wish," he cried, when he heard of Ouvrard's action, " that I had a gallows to hang that man upon, so high that all France might see him."

Ouvrard was arrested and flung into Vicennes. Thérèse, now princesse de Chimay, was told that neither she nor her husband would ever be received at the French Court.

Meanwhile Josephine had acquitted herself very well among the Kings and Queens. She was doing all she could to please her husband, because she knew that the idea of divorce remained in his mind. She had been unfaithful to him and he was a Corsican. She was bribeable and his secrets affected the lives of millions. She was ruinously extravagant and he had need of all his resources. Knowledge of the weakness of her position had caused her, on the eve of the Coronation, to go to the Pope, secretly, and beg him to insist that Napoleon should be married to her a second time, in Church. A civil marriage might so easily be set aside.

Marriage and Coronation, added to the fact that Napoleon, by his execution of the young duc d'Enghien, had made himself the best hated ruler in Europe, had for a while given her a sense of security. If he did dare to divorce her, who, among the daughters of kings, was going to marry him ? But his resounding conquests had changed everything. The victor of Austerlitz could marry whom he chose. When he joined her, however, her fears grew less. He was eager to marry her son, Eugène, to Augusta, daughter of the King of Bavaria. She supported all his plans and by her tact managed to marry her own kinswoman, Stephanie de Beauharnais, to the hereditary Prince of Baden, who had formally been engaged to Augusta and was very angry with Napoleon. This was a good service, because the Prince of Baden was brother-in-law to both the Emperor Alexander of Russia and the King of Sweden.

Josephine's success enraged Napoleon's own womenfolk, so that they could not contain themselves. His youngest sister, Caroline, who had married General Murat, asked him when he proposed to do something for his own flesh and blood, and when he did not reply, exclaimed :

" Why don't you divorce Josephine and marry Augusta yourself ? "

He saw a family quarrel in prospect, and to save himself gave Elisa, his eldest sister, the Principality of Lucca and bestowed on Caroline and her husband the Grand Duchy of Berg and Cleves. But these gifts lost all their value when it became known that Josephine's daughter, Hortense, who had married Louis Bonaparte, the Emperor's brother, was to be Queen of Holland.

Battle was now joined again between Josephine and the whole Bonaparte family, every member of which hated her with all his or her heart. The Empress's past was mercilessly raked up on every possible occasion. Had not her first husband, Alexandre de Beauharnais, divorced her ? Had he not denied the paternity of Hortense ? Again, Josephine had been Barras' mistress before her marriage to Bonaparte and the mistress of Hippolyte Charles after her marriage ? Why punish Thérèse and let this woman sit upon a throne ? Napoleon knew it all ; but Josephine was his own creation, the woman he had made her, his wife.

All her faults could not quench in his heart the attachment he felt for her. The more his mother and sisters abused, the stronger became their enemy's position.

Nevertheless, he had Josephine watched now as if she was a dangerous foe, and turned over, continually, in his mind the project of a divorce. He knew that so long as he refused to be drawn into the financial schemes of London, his throne would remain unstable in the sense that attacks upon him would continue. He was implacably determined never to accept a loan and never, if possible, to allow the money-lenders to re-establish themselves in Paris. The need to strengthen his position by every possible means was, therefore, urgent. ' Marriage to a King's daughter who might bear him a son would be the strongest support imaginable.

But was his childless condition his own fault or Josephine's fault ? After all, Josephine had borne Alexandre de Beauharnais two children. He wanted to be sure that he was capable of fatherhood. His sister Caroline fastened upon this desire and proposed that he should place himself in her hands. She presented to him a young married woman, named Eléanore la Plaigne, whose husband had deserted her.

Eléanore became pregnant.

The affair was kept a profound secret, but Josephine heard about it almost as soon as it began. Instantly, that skilful and intrepid campaigner took steps to protect herself. With a fine sense of poetic justice, she induced Murat, Caroline's husband, to conduct an affair with the girl. When Napoleon left Paris to open the campaign against Prussia, he took Josephine with him. As they drove out across France, behind his great team of Normandy horses, she managed to drop a hint about Murat's flirtation.

The Prussians had been supplied with much gold from London. Napoleon took it all at the battle of Jena where he destroyed the " Army of Frederick the Great " as completely as, the year before, he had destroyed the Austrian and Russian armies. Josephine, who had remained at Mayence, heard that the whole of Germany had fallen into his hands. Would he divorce her now? The need of someone in whom she could confide became so overwhelming that she wrote to him asking to be allowed to receive Thérèse, who was staying in Mayence. Napoleon replied in terms which drove the blood from her cheeks :

"BERLIN, *Monday, Noon.*

"My dear, I have received your letter . . . I forbid you to see Madame Tallien under any pretext whatever. I will admit of no excuse. If you desire a continuance of my esteem, if you wish to please me, never transgress the present order. She may possibly come to your apartments in the hope of entering them by night. Forbid your porter to admit her. A miserable fellow has married her—with eight (*sic*) bastards. I despise her more than ever I did before. She, who was once a sweet and gentle girl, is now branded as a woman of horror and infamy."

Josephine's fears about divorce now quickened to terror, and she wrote begging to be allowed to follow the Army to Poland where it had marched in order to engage a Russian army that was coming to the help of the Prussians. Napoleon consented, provisionally. She packed up in readiness for his summons. But on December 31, 1806, he heard from Paris that Eléanore had borne a son and on the following day, January 1, 1807, he met Marie Walewska, the twenty-year-old wife of a Polish nobleman who was seventy years old. He fell suddenly and violently in love with this girl at the very moment when Josephine, by her cunning, had snatched away from him the certainty that Eléanore's son was his own. He wrote to Josephine :

"*January* 3.

"I am inclined to think that you ought to return to Paris where your presence is needed."

" January 7.

" Return to Paris to spend the winter there. Go to the Tuileries, receive, and lead the same life as you are accustomed to do when I am there. That is my wish."

" January 8.

" I received your letter. . . . The season is too inclement, the roads unsafe and abominable ; the distances far too great for me to permit you to come hither, where my affairs detain me. It would take you at least a month to come. You would arrive ill ; by that time it might be necessary to start back again ; it would, therefore, be folly. Your stay at Mayence is too dull ; Paris reclaims you ; go there, it is my wish."

Napoleon described himself on one occasion as " entirely a political being." He was in love with Marie Walewska, but this did not blind him to the importance of the part she might be induced to play in his statesmanship. She was a Pole and he wished to win the Poles to his side. She had borne her elderly husband a son and he wished to know whether or not she could bear him a son. Her husband belonged to the party in Poland which was most bitterly hostile to the Russians and he was about to fight the Russians. He let it be known that he had fallen in love.

But he reckoned without his Marie, who refused to see him or have anything to do with him. Marie had worshipped him as the hero who was coming to free Poland from the Russians ; the idea of becoming his mistress filled her with terror and shame, because she was devout and virtuous. But her fellow-country-men shared none of her feelings at a moment when all their hopes were set upon Napoleon.

In fact, she had been indiscreet enough to go with a friend to the post-house outside of Warsaw to meet the hero when he came first to the city. She had recited a welcome and been rewarded with a few gracious words and a bouquet of flowers from the

Imperial carriage. Napoleon did not discover her name, but neither did he forget her face. He knew that she belonged to the nobility and he assumed that, since she had come to meet him, she was anxious to be his mistress. His experience of women had not suggested that many of them were burdened with scruples. He had anticipated no difficulty, therefore, in finding her again.

But he searched in vain the faces of the women who came to his receptions and that vain search whetted his curiosity. All the nobles of Poland were crowding to honour him and all the noble women of Poland were coming day after day to the feasts and entertainments which Poniatowski had provided. Why was this noble girl absent from them all ? He began to make discreet enquiries. He was unaware that inquiries, which were much less discreet, were being made by his Polish hosts about himself. These good Poles had observed with astonishment that the conqueror had brought no women with him. They had made haste to supply the deficiency and experienced a new shock of surprise when their offers were rebuffed. The news that Napoleon was interested, already, in one of their womenfolk filled them with the liveliest satisfaction.

Duroc, who conveyed the news, warned them not to mention the matter to the Emperor who, he said, was exceedingly fastidious and would certainly resent such an intrusion into his private life. But he supplied some details which his master had given him. The lady was young, very young indeed. She had golden hair and a peculiarly angelic expression. Her voice was charming. She was of noble family.

Poniatowski, who was thorough in his methods, caused a search to be made. Napoleon, in the next day or two, saw all the golden-haired girls of noble family in Poland. But he did not see the girl of the post-house. When one of the bevy tried to thrust herself upon his notice, she received a sharp rebuff.

Poniatowski was in despair. He consulted constantly with Duroc who assured him that the Emperor retained a perfectly clear picture of the lady and that the apparent impossibility of finding her was increasing his determination to have nothing to do with anybody else. It was worse than useless, therefore, to attempt to foist other girls upon him. If the lady of the post-house was not available, let them abandon the idea of supplying any lady.

The fate of Poland depended, at that moment, upon Napoleon. Ever since Mme de Pompadour's seven years' war the Poles had been slaves of Russians and Prussians and Austrians. By France they had fallen; by France, as they believed, salvation must come to them. What tragedy in such circumstances, if the only personal wish of the French Emperor should remain unfulfilled ! Must the cause of the fatherland founder upon a pretty face ?

Again Poniatowski sent out his sleuths. Warsaw was "combed" for girls with corn-coloured heads, girls of the people, girls of the stage; any kind of girls so long as they possessed the indispensable *tête d'ange*. Duroc inspected great numbers. He declared, sadly, that his Princess Cinderella was not among them.

This search, like the search with the glass slipper, caused a prodigious stir and set many tongues wagging. In consequence, the girl who had accompanied Marie Walewska to the post-house got news of what was afoot. She had been sworn to secrecy, but her resolution began to waver. She knew that her kinswoman, after the adventure, had gone into hiding in the big house which her husband had rented for the season—a matter of small difficulty seeing that Count Walewski, at his mature age, disliked social gatherings and disliked even more the admiration which his wife's beauty was apt to excite. Marie had been kept hidden away so that very few people knew her even by sight. The fact that she expressed reluctance to take part in the junketings gave rise, therefore, to no regrets.

She had kept Napoleon's bouquet, however, hidden in a veil of lace. That action, perhaps, decided her friend to betray her—for women are unbelievers in love-at-a-distance. In any case the name he was so anxious to hear came, at long last, to Poniatowski's ears. He could scarcely believe it. He knew old Count Anastase Colonna Walewski, a ramrod of a man who had outlived humanity, and he had heard that the old fellow had married as his third wife some young girl of the provincial squirearchy. But he had never seen the lady. He made haste, bellowing with excitement and resolution, to repair the omission. Prince Poniatowski, the " Saviour of Poland," was big, courageous, handsome, a great eater, a ladies' man full of gallantries. The idea of squeamishness in women was foreign to his mind. He invited Marie to a ball in tones which covered her with embarrassment. When she refused, he told her about the search for Cinderella. When that information brought her to the edge of tears, he changed his tune and uttered an eloquent plea for Poland. Napoleon, he urged, held the future of their country in his hands. Let her be sure that Almighty God had not chosen her as the means of softening the conqueror's heart.

Marie wept bitterly now but persisted in her refusal. Poniatowski went away. An hour later a deputation of the great officers of State arrived at the house. They repeated Poniatowski's arguments. Men, they said, gave their lives for their country ; ought women to withhold anything ? Marie choked in the presence of these men. She refused. Her husband, Count Anastase, was told, merely, that his wife would not consent to come to the ball at which all the great nobles and their wives were expected to be present. He was a vain and stupid old man, with an overweening sense of his own and his family's importance. He assumed that the invitation was addressed, really, to the noble house of Colonna Walewski. His anger against this chit of a girl, who was insensible of the honour he had done her by marriage, flamed out. He stormed into Marie's apartments and ordered her, as her husband, to accept the invitation.

Marie resisted no longer. But she demanded that, if she went to the ball, she should not be formally presented to Napoleon. The excuse she gave was fear of being made conspicuous—for

THE COUNTESS WALEWSKA
From the portrait by Gérard.

the formal presentations had already been made. Count Anastase yielded on this point and then sent for dressmakers and abandoned himself to the delight of choosing his wife's frock. He demanded the utmost degree of splendour; Marie disappointingly chose white satin, with a handful of green leaves among her golden curls.

Napoleon was not in the ballroom when they entered it. She tried to efface herself, sitting between two women. But Poniatowski spied her immediately. He came and stood behind her chair. He told her that he had been in agonies lest she should not come. His anxiety and excitement and the terrible hints, which he kept dropping, made her panic-stricken. When he referred to Count Anastase as " *malheureuse victime* " she covered her eyes with her hands.

" I can't dance," she pleaded. " And I don't want to try."

" It is the Emperor's order."

Sentence of death could not have fallen more hideously. She glanced about the room. Everyone was looking at her. Smiling. Bowing. Poniatowski left her. French Staff Officers came and asked her to dance. While she was refusing there was a blare of trumpets. The great doors at the end of the ballroom were opened by liveried ushers. A loud voice announced :

" *L'Empereur.*"

Napoleon walked briskly into the room. He was dressed in the uniform which, already, was legendary—the faded green coat, the white waistcoat. He found her instantly and their eyes met. She ceased to breathe. He began to make the round of the room, asking questions as was his wont without waiting for the answers. Marie had sunk back into her chair, overcome with fear. She was told to stand up. She could not look at him. She heard his voice saying to her loudly :

" White cheeks don't go well with a white dress, Madame."

He added in low tones :

" This isn't the sort of welcome I have the right to expect after . . ."

He did not finish his sentence. He stood gazing at her with his hands behind his back. Then he turned away. She had not spoken a word. A moment later he had left the ballroom. She was mobbed by men and women, envious of her luck. She begged her husband to take her home. He told her on the way that he had accepted an invitation to dine with the Emperor— for her as well as for himself. She had resolved to confess about her visit to the post-house, but this news terrified her to silence. She rushed off to her bedroom. A letter awaited her. It ran :

" I saw nobody but you ; I admired nobody but you ; I want nobody but you. Please answer at once to calm the anxious eagerness of,

" N."

She told her maid that there was no reply. That message was carried at once to Poniatowski, who was acting as intermediary, and was waiting in person in the street. When he heard it he dashed into the house and sprang up the stairs to Marie's bedroom. She heard him coming and managed to shut and bolt the door in his face.

" There is no reply," she told him through the door.

Poniatowski exploded. He kicked the door and cursed her as a traitress to Poland. He made so much noise that it seemed impossible that her husband could fail to hear him. But Count Anastase was old and deaf and weary and had already fallen asleep. She waited until she heard the heavy steps of the Prince Patriot descending the stairs. Then she flung herself down.

Napoleon's bouquet was still in her bedroom, in its veil of lace. She hid his letter also. Conscience and inclination tore her asunder, revealing to her, at last, the true reason of her escapade at the post-house.

But if it was true that she loved Napoleon, was not that a final reason for rejecting him ? She slept and woke to find another letter in the same indecipherable hand. She pinned the first note to it and, without breaking the seal, sent it back to the messenger who was waiting for a reply. She was told that her drawing-room was already full of people and that her visitors included Duroc, the Emperor's aide-de-camp, and members of the Polish Government. She told her maid to excuse her on the ground of a headache.

Count Anastase, meanwhile, had risen and was gazing in stupefaction at his distinguished visitors. Poniatowski told him that the explanation lay in the admiration conceived for his wife by Napoleon. The old man choked but declared that he was not jealous. He disproved that assertion by rushing to Marie's bedroom. Poniatowski accompanied him. The door was locked. Count Anastase demanded that it should be opened. She refused to open it. The two men smashed the door.

Marie was lying on a sofa. Her husband ordered her to get up and show herself in the drawing-room. She did not move. An old man who had ascended the stair and come to the door thereupon addressed her :

" You ought, Madame," he exclaimed, " to yield in view of the great, even the overwhelming, importance to the nation of your behaviour in this matter. We venture to hope, therefore, that your illness will not hinder you from accompanying your husband to the dinner-party. Absence from that dinner would proclaim you, I fear, a bad citizen of Poland."

Marie rose at these words. She said she was ready to obey her husband. Count Anastase had been told, already, by Poniatowski that his, Poniatowski's mistress, Mme de Vauban, was prepared to give some instruction in the etiquette of Courts, she having lived at Versailles in the days of Louis XVI. Marie was sent to Mme de Vauban, who received her with rapture and immediately handed her over to a young girl, a friend of her own, who was equally well-versed in the ways of the great world.

This girl was a singularly happy choice because she possessed the faculty of understanding. Whereas most women would have acted on the assumption that the Conqueror of the World must be an agreeable substitute for a seventy-year-old nonentity, she

marked Marie's swollen eyes and pale cheeks and addressed
herself to the patriot instead of to the woman. They became
friends. Marie began to see herself as the necessary sacrifice for
Poland.

The Polish Government made haste to confirm that impression.
A document was sent to her, officially ; she read :

" MADAME.—Great effects spring often from small causes. At
every period of human existence women have exerted a decisive
influence on the world's policy—ancient history no less than
modern assures us of this. So long as their feelings dominate
men, you will remain, ladies, one of the most formidable of all
powers.

" Are you a man ? You ought to sacrifice your life, if need
be, to the worthy and just cause of the fatherland. Are you a
woman ? You cannot defend the fatherland with your body ;
Nature forbids it. But Nature, by way of compensation, has
given you other means of serving. There are sacrifices which
it may be your duty to make and which you ought not to
withhold, however much the making of them may cost you.

" Do you suppose that it was love which drove Esther to give
herself to Ahasuerus ? Was not the terror which he inspired in
her a terror which caused her almost to faint when he looked at
her, proof that no tender feeling animated her heart ? She gave
herself for the salvation of her people ! For that reason her
sacrifice was glorious.

" Shall we be able, for your glory and our happiness, to say
the same of you ?

" Are you not, whether as daughter, mother or sister, bound
up with the Polish patriots ? With ourselves, they compose a
nation whose greatness of soul can be increased only in respect
of the numbers contributing to it. Remember, Madame, what
Fénelon, a man famed alike for his ability and his holiness, a
pious priest of God, has said :

" ' The most powerful of public men cannot compass the

advantage of their fellows—that advantage which their enlightenment suggests—unless they have the help and support of
women.'

"Listen to that voice. Let it be joined to our voices in
pleading for the happiness of twenty million men."

Meanwhile Napoleon awaited replies to his two letters.
Poniatowski had retained them; on his instructions they were
delivered once more to Marie. She opened the second letter
and read:

"Have I displeased you, Madame? I think that I possess the
right to hope to the contrary. But do I deceive myself? Your
eagerness seems to be cooling at the same rate as mine is
increasing. You're robbing me of my peace of mind. Oh,
please give a little joy, a little happiness, to a poor heart longing
to adore you. Is a reply so very difficult to send? You owe
me two replies.

                                              "N."

Thanks to her new companion's instruction, Marie was able,
now, to see these letters from the world's point of view. A
married woman who acted as she had acted at the post-house
was presumed to be offering herself. And the presumption
became certainty when she was very young and her husband
was very old. Napoleon, therefore, supposed merely that she
was playing a game of hide and seek with him in order to wring
from him better terms for Poland and for herself. Nevertheless
she could not bring herself to answer his letter.

She accompanied her husband, however, to the dinner-party.
Napoleon displayed a charming courtesy.

"Madame," he inquired, "was not very well, I am told? I
hope she has completely recovered."

She had Duroc for partner. The Emperor sat immediately
opposite to her. He did not embarrass her by staring at her, but
she observed, after a few minutes, that he was exchanging

signals with Duroc by means of small movements of his hands.
Suddenly Duroc asked her :

" What has happened to the bouquet of flowers which the
Emperor gave you at the post-house at Bronie ? "

She told him that she was keeping them as an heirloom for
her small son.

" Do please allow His Majesty to make you a gift more
worthy of you."

" I want nothing but the flowers."

" Ah, well," Duroc declared.   " We shall gather laurels for
you on your native soil."

The meal ended.   Napoleon came to Marie.   He took her
hands and gazed into her eyes.

" No, no," he exclaimed.   " With such sweet and tender eyes,
with that look of kindness, one gives oneself ; one does not
enjoy being a torturer.   Or else one is the most abominable of
flirts, the most cruel of women."

Mme Vauban carried Marie off to her house.   It was full of
patriots who surrounded her and urged upon her the necessity
of her country.   Duroc entered and came to her side.

" Can you refuse him," he demanded, " whom nobody ever
refused ?   Oh, his glory is full of sadness.   Only you can give
him those moments of happiness which he deserves."

He handed her a letter.   She read :

" There are moments when too great a height above one's
fellows is a heavy burden.   I am experiencing such a moment.
For how can I fulfil the needs of a heart in love, I who long to
cast myself at your feet, when I am held by the weight of considerations of policy that paralyse the noblest feelings ?   If only
you would. . . . You alone can remove the obstacles which
circumstances have placed between us.   My friend Duroc
will show you the way. . . .

" Oh, come, come—all your wishes shall be gratified.   Your
native land will be dearer to me when you have taken pity on
my poor heart."

She refused to answer the letter. She went home. But next night, in her bedroom, she put on the cloak and veil she had worn at the post-house. At half-past ten there was a knock at the door of her room. Her woman companion entered and inspected her toilet. They went out together to a place where a carriage was waiting. A man wearing a long cloak and with his hat pulled down over his face opened the door. He got in beside her. It was Duroc. They drove to the palace. Duroc conducted her up a staircase, to a door which opened at her coming. She saw Napoleon.

"While waiting for her," wrote Constant, the Emperor's valet, "the Emperor strode up and down and displayed as much emotion as impatience. Every minute he kept asking me what time it was. Madame V (Walewska) at last arrived. But in what a state! Pale, speechless, and with her eyes full of tears."

Napoleon received her as he might have received a foreign diplomatist. He was cold and suspicious. He invited her to sit down and immediately began to question her. Why had she married Count Anastase? Was it possible that a girl of her age was in love with such a man? Was it not, merely, his rank and wealth she had married? Again, why had she come to the post-house. She must have realized the kind of construction which ordinary people would put on such an action carried out in such a way? Marie answered simply that she had married Count Anastase because her mother wished her to do so. She had gone to the post-house because, as a woman of Poland, she had become a hero-worshipper of the man who was expected to deliver her native land.

Napoleon's chief contacts with women had been made through Josephine. So it was difficult to believe what this girl told him. The facts were against her. Her own conduct was against her. No doubt she was bidding high because he had allowed her to see his infatuation. He continued to question her, mercilessly, during several hours, until two o'clock in the morning. He did not make love to her.

At two o'clock Constant came into the room and was told to take Marie back to her carriage. Constant noticed that she was weeping and decided that it was unlikely that she would come back.

Duroc took her home. When he left her, a storm of tears occurred because, after all, there had been nothing to fear. Napoleon had asked for nothing except explanations. The sense of holy martyrdom, with which she had been supporting herself for days, evaporated. He had not forced her to be a martyr. He had not ordered her to come back. So far as he was concerned, there was no need to have any further dealings with him. She realized, suddenly, that the man had read her heart and her secret. He knew now that she loved him.

Her anger with herself and him was still quick when, next morning, her maid brought a letter and two parcels. She refused to open any of them. Her woman friend arrived and displayed more curiosity. One of the parcels contained a diamond necklace of superb beauty. Marie snatched the jewels out of her friend's hands and flung them across the room. She threw the second parcel after them. But when she was alone she opened the letter. She read :

" MARIE, MY SWEET MARIE,

" My first waking thought is of you ; my first wish is to see you again. You will come back, won't you ? You've promised me that you will. If you don't, the eagle will fly to you. Shall I see you at dinner ? Our friend (Duroc) says that I shall. Do please accept this posy. Do please let it serve as a mysterious link, joining us in a secret association among the crowds who will jostle us. Under the eyes of all these people we shall listen to one another. When I put my hand on my heart you will know that my heart beats for you ; and you will answer my sign, will you not, by touching your posy ? Love me, my charming Marie. Don't let your hand stray from your posy.

" N."

Marie went to the dinner party. But she wore neither posy nor diamonds. The Emperor saw and frowned. He strode towards her. Her hand moved, swiftly, to the place where she was to have worn his flowers. A shadow of a smile flickered on his lips. He put his hand on his heart. She told him that it was the gift of the diamonds which had upset her. He did not ask her to return to the palace and she did not return for several days. In this interval she came to a clearer knowledge of her heart. She announced to Duroc that she was ready to return to Napoleon.

" So you've come at last. I had made up my mind that I would never see you again," was how he greeted her.

Later, she told Constant, his valet :

" All my thoughts, all my inspirations spring from and are centred in him ; he is my one joy, my future, my life."

She had a ring made with a lock of her hair in it. Inside of the ring was written :

" When you have ceased to love me, forget not that I love you still."

Marie was conquered. All Poland acclaimed her as the good angel of the Fatherland.

Later, when Napoleon, having failed to break the Russian Army, at a blow, as he had broken the army of Prussia, went into winter quarters at the Castle of Finckenstein in Poland, she joined him and became his constant companion.

CHAPTER XXVI

DIVORCE

IT was the first occasion in his life when Napoleon had known the love of a good woman, and the experience extinguished the last of his tender feelings towards Josephine. But Marie did not fulfil his hopes of her. He made up his mind, finally, that Eléanore's son was Murat's child and that Nature had denied him the power of fatherhood. In these circumstances a divorce from Josephine was not worth the trouble and ill-feeling which it was bound to cause.

Josephine had gone back to Paris, where reports about Napoleon's affair with " the Polish charmer " had reached her. Her anxieties quickened from hour to hour and she began to look about for means of saving herself from the social extinction which, if Marie bore a child, she believed must be her lot. She began to receive German princes, who were prisoners in Paris, and she courted the Ambassadors of Austria and other States as well as the agents of the money-lenders who were the unofficial ambassadors of London. Thérèse returned with her husband to Paris and Germaine de Staël with Fouché's connivance came to stay in the capital. The Emperor's prolonged absence in Poland and his apparent failure to destroy the Russian Army were warming the hopes of his enemies. A fresh financial crisis in Paris became certain unless the tide turned quickly.

Napoleon saw all the danger. His lines of communication extended across Europe. If his credit at home was destroyed military action on the great scale would be seriously endangered.

He addressed bitter protests to Josephine, whose behaviour had been unfavourably reported upon :

March 13, 1807.

" I learn that the vexatious tittle-tattle that filled your drawing-room at Mayence has begun again ; make people hold their tongues."

March 25.

" If you really wish to please me you must live exactly as you live when I am in Paris. Then you were not in the habit of visiting the second-rate theatres and other places. You ought always to go into the Royal box. As for your home life, hold receptions and have your fixed circle of friends ; that, my dear, is the only way to deserve my approval. Greatness has its inconveniences ; an Empress cannot go where a private person may."

May 10.

" I wish you to have only those persons to dinner who have dined with me ; that your list be the same for your assemblies ; that you never make intimates at Malmaison of ambassadors and foreigners. If you should do the contrary you would displease me. Finally, do not allow yourself to be duped too much by persons whom I do not know, and who would not come to the house if I were there."

At the same time Fouché was receiving angry letters about Germaine de Staël.

March, 1807.

" Please obey my orders and see to it that Mme de Staël does not approach nearer than a hundred and twenty miles from Paris. That wicked intriguer had better take care."

April, 1807.

" This woman (Mme de Staël) is a carrion crow ; she thinks

disaster is at hand and is getting ready to profit by it by means of intrigues and mischiefs. Send her back to her lake. Have not these Genevese done us harm enough ? "

April, 1807.

" My decision is that she (Mme de Staël) is never to leave Geneva. . . . She's a whore and an ugly one at that. I won't trouble you with the plans her absurd coterie has made in case, by a lucky chance, I get killed ; a Minister of Police ought to know them. All I hear of this contemptible woman makes it obvious that I must leave her in her Coppet among her Genevese and her Necker relations."

April 20.

" Every day I obtain fresh proofs of the criminal behaviour of this woman (Mme de Staël) who is not only the enemy of the Government but also of France—that France from which she cannot keep away."

May 7.

" I see from your (police) bulletin that Mme de Staël left Paris for Geneva on April 21st. I am very much annoyed that you should be so badly informed. Mme de Staël was in Paris on the 24th, 25th, 26th and 27th and is probably still there. She's been dining out a great deal with literary people."

Germaine was in close touch with Metternich, the Austrian Ambassador, who had become one of Josephine's special friends. Had Austria, at this time, dared to attack Napoleon's lines of communication, a major disaster might have occurred. All the bankers in Europe were prepared to pay for Austrian soldiers to undertake the enterprise, but the fear of Napoleon was too lively. To the question " What protects your line of communication from the Austrians ? " he replied, proudly :

" My name."

The plot withered, suddenly, in June, when it became known

that the Russian army had been destroyed and that Napoleon, there and then, had made friends with the young Emperor Alexander of Russia. Josephine mended her ways and Germaine de Staël fled to Geneva, to the big empty house from which, the year before, Necker's body had been carried to its last resting-place, a huge bath of spirits-of-wine, in which already, Suzanne's body reposed. All the kites and vultures of finance disappeared out of Paris.

A great new anxiety was come to these kites and vultures— namely, the fear that the biggest of the international money-lenders might even be brought to ruin by this unexpected alliance between Napoleon and Alexander. Napoleon's plan was to force the money-lenders to part with their gold. He knew that their chief business, each year, was to buy up the Baltic wheat crop—that is, the wheat from Poland and Russia— and sell it in London. Payment was made in the form of English colonial produce and English manufactured goods. But if English goods could be shut out from Russia and Poland— and all Europe—payment would have to be made in gold. That would break the London bankers and with them the whole Debt system which those who had cornered the world's supply of gold had built up. All the people of Europe, including the English people, would escape at last from that tyranny of Money which was the real, if underlying, cause of the French Revolution. Napoleon's gold mine, unlike Mirabeau's, was to be filled with real gold.

Unhappily it could be filled only if English goods could be excluded absolutely from all the ports of Europe, including those of the Baltic and the Mediterranean. And since Trafalgar, England was mistress of the seas. The plan, therefore, was a desperate one, allowing even for the co-operation of the Emperor Alexander and for the fact that Napoleon, in two years, had destroyed all the great armies in Europe and become, in consequence, master of the whole continent. He had to remain master for an indefinite period if he was to succeed. In other words, he had to exert domination over every land and especially over those lands which possessed coast lines, notably Sweden, Denmark, Holland, Portugal and Spain—the gates of the Baltic and the gates of the Mediterranean.

The plan went wrong almost from the beginning. Canning seized the Danish fleet and bombarded Copenhagen—without a declaration of War—into submission. Soon afterwards the Spaniards rose in opposition to Joseph Bonaparte, who had been raised by his brother to the throne of Spain. Alexander of Russia, in these circumstances, began to feel that his new ally was unequal to the task he had undertaken.

The triumph of the Polish campaign began, thus, to wear a tarnished look. Napoleon invited Alexander to meet him in Germany so that the young man's flagging enthusiasm might be revived. But the meeting was not very cordial. The French Emperor rushed away from it to reconquer Spain and was soon, once more, at Madrid.

The swiftness and immediate success of these moves dazzled many eyes. But clearer observers saw the underlying weakness. Napoleon was not drawing away enough gold from London seriously to embarrass his enemies in that city. Smuggling operations, organized and carried out on the largest possible scale, were bringing English goods into Italy (by way of the Papal States), into Holland (with the connivance of Louis Bonaparte), and into the Baltic. The Russians were growing tired, meanwhile, of the severe restrictions imposed upon them.

In these circumstances fresh pressure was brought to bear upon Austria to attack Napoleon, most of whose best troops were now in Spain. At the same time, the money-lenders in Paris organized a plot against the Imperial Government and began a whispering campaign to the effect that the Emperor was bound to be assassinated in Spain. Josephine joined the plotters. Metternich, the Austrian Ambassador, and his wife, became her dearest friends, and both Fouché and Talleyrand, who were deeply involved, came nightly to her drawing-room. A great deal of money was available for the purpose of buying important people.

The plan was to announce the assassination of Napoleon and then to seize the Government. The Austrian Army was to invade France so as to bring support to the plotters, who, meanwhile, would have declared for a restoration of the old Monarchy in the person of " Louis XVIII." It was calculated that if success attended the stroke, Napoleon's Marshals would turn against him and prevent him from fighting.

But Napoleon had friends in Paris—notably his mother and Marie Walewska, who had followed him from Poland. They kept him informed about what was going on. One day a report reached him that Josephine had received some members of his Parliament and told them, in a short speech, that they represented the nation. Since it had been laid down in the constitution that the nation was represented only by the Emperor, the meaning was clear. Josephine was saying, in effect, that the Parliament could take away the crown from her husband and give it to anyone it might choose. A paragraph was sent at once from Spain for insertion in the newspapers which had published reports of the Empress' speech, declaring :

" The Empress never said that."

Shortly afterwards Napoleon himself arrived in Paris, having driven at full gallop, day and night. He sprang upon the plotters and scattered them. Metternich was placed under arrest, Talleyrand was disgraced after a terrible scene, Fouché was threatened with immediate ruin. At the same time Josephine learned that so far as her husband was concerned, she had ceased to be an object of the slightest respect.

When the war with Austria duly began, Napoleon's suspicions of his wife were made plain. He took her with him to Strasburg and ordered her, sharply, to remain in that city. A few weeks later he was again in Vienna. Marie Walewska was told to join him. He fought the battle of Aspern-Ersling, where he narrowly escaped defeat, and then, after a short lapse of time, the battle of Wagram, which gave him victory. Josephine was ordered to return to Paris; Marie resumed her place by the Emperor's side.

" I used," wrote Constant, " mysteriously to fetch her every evening in a closed carriage without any armorial bearings, driven by a coachman who did not wear livery. I introduced her into the palace by a secret door and conducted her to the Emperor's apartments. The road, though short, was not without danger, especially in rainy weather, because of the ruts and holes everywhere. The Emperor used to say to me every evening :

" ' Be careful to-night, Constant, as it rained to-day and the road must be bad. Are you sure the coachman can be trusted ? Is the carriage in sound condition ? '

" These and similar questions showed how sincerely attached he was to Mme. V. (Walewska). The Emperor, though, was not wrong in urging me to be careful, for one evening, on leaving Mme. V.'s house rather later than usual, the coachman upset us. In trying to avoid a rut he overturned the carriage on the side of the road. I was sitting to the right of Madame V ; the carriage turned over on its right side so that I alone suffered from the shock, whild Mme. V., falling on top of me, was not at all hurt. I was glad that I had been able to protect her from injury. I told her so and she expressed her gratitude with a grace such as she alone possessed. I soon got over my shaking and was the first to laugh at our unlucky spill. Mme. V. laughed also while she was telling His Majesty about the accident."

Josephine knew about these secret visits, because her daughter Hortense recounts that :

" A young Polish Countess whom the Emperor had met in Poland came to Vienna during the armistice. My mother knew that she was hidden in the palace of Schoenbrunn, unseen by anyone, and the infidelity of a husband to whom she was still tenderly devoted, filled her with despair."

Hortense deserves credit for this filial interpretation.

MARIE LOUISE

Josephine's despair was real enough, but it had nothing to do
with Marie Walewska. The victory of Wagram, as she knew,
had brought all her plottings to nothing. She foresaw lean days
ahead, a divorce without, perhaps, substantial compensation.
When the news reached her that Marie was about to bear
Napoleon a child she gave herself up, immediately, for lost.

But the innate courage and fighting spirit of the woman were
not quenched. When he sent for her, on his return to France, to
meet him at Fontainebleau, she came to him with every weapon
in her considerable armoury sharpened for use. A glance at her
haggard, tear-stained face warned Napoleon that he was about
to pass into the valley of tribulation. He was not mistaken.
Josephine had brought hysterical outburst to a fine art. At sight
of her husband she swooned or screamed, so that he was glad to
escape from her presence. After the passage of a fortnight no
word of his intention had crossed his lips. He began to understand that the price of the fulfilment of his wishes would be
high.

The Court came to Paris. There, on a November night, after
dinner, he summoned courage to speak his mind. The Baron de
Bausset, who was waiting in the ante-room, heard Josephine
shriek :

" I shall not survive it. I shall not survive it."

A moment later the door opened. Napoleon came out and
asked :

" Are you strong enough, Bausset, to lift Her Majesty and
carry her to her apartments by the private staircase . . . ? "

Bausset entered the room and saw Josephine lying on the floor.
He lifted her. Napoleon took a candlestick and led the way to
the head of the staircase. Bausset pointed out that the narrow-
ness of the stair made descent dangerous. Napoleon then called
a servant, gave him the candlestick and himself took Josephine's
legs. They scrambled down a few steps. Then Bausset heard a
whisper :

" You're holding me too tightly."

He ceased to feel anxiety. But Napoleon had not heard the whisper :

" The Emperor's agitation and anxiety," he wrote, " were extreme. In his trouble he told me the cause of what had occurred. His words came with difficulty, inconsequently ; his voice was choked and his eyes were full of tears."

The strain, in short, had shattered his nerves. He was ready to offer all that Josephine might ask. He gave her the title of Empress for life and an allowance of £120,000 yearly.

" We were won over," wrote Hortense, " by the Emperor's solicitude for his wife's reputation."

The final scene took place in the presence of most of the Bonaparte family, who did not try to hide their pleasure. Napoleon, who was weeping from sheer mental exhaustion, read a speech in which he assured his mother and sisters that Josephine had adorned fifteen years of his life. Josephine's reply was read for her.

CHAPTER XXVII

AND now for a King's daughter as a means of supporting the plan for drawing gold out of London. Napoleon's choice was made already. Alexander of Russia could be held to his promises about keeping out the English goods only by an Austrian marriage.

Russia was afraid of Austria because Austria had designs on Russian Poland. If Napoleon married an Austrian Archduchess Alexander would hesitate to yield to the blandishments of London, especially in view of the good relations between the Poles and the French Emperor which the liaison with Marie Walewska had done so much to establish. Josephine, who had retired to Malmaison, was told to get into touch with the Metternichs once more and to hint that her former husband might consider a marriage with the Archduchess Marie Louise.

Thus were three women, of three different nationalities, brought into the service of the plan to break the London gold-owners. Josephine, the Frenchwoman, posing as martyr to her patriotism, was to call the new wife; Marie, the Pole, about to become a mother, was to hold her fellow countrymen faithful to the French; Marie Louise, the German, was to unite Austria with France in an alliance which none would dare to challenge.

Napoleon, nevertheless, remained very uneasy while the negotiations with Austria were going on. He was aware that the Emperor Francis was disposed to give his consent only because he believed that, if he refused, a Russian marriage would at once take place. In fact there was no chance of a Russian marriage because the Dowager Empress of Russia would not hear of it. It was essential, therefore, to complete all the plans before the truth about the Russian refusal became known in Vienna.

An almost indecent haste was shown. Marie Louise was married in Vienna, by proxy, before she set out for France. Napoleon treated her as his wife from their first meeting, though further marriage ceremonies were in prospect. And he took care, at once, to inform his father-in-law about this behaviour.

In fact his haste was justified. For religious objections to the marriage were being raised in Rome and might, had there been any delay, have resulted in postponement. In that case news of the Russian refusal would certainly have been communicated to Vienna. As things were, on the contrary, the Austrians believed that they had won a notable diplomatic victory over the Russians, who, for their part, became profoundly uneasy and full of regret that they had not, after all, bestowed their young princess on the French Emperor.

Marie Louise, in other words, gave the policy of breaking the gold monopoly a new lease of life. She was a dull, German girl of simple mind and inexpensive tastes—a refreshing contrast to Josephine. Her husband exerted himself to the utmost to make her happy—in the brief intervals he could snatch from his life and death struggle with London. The struggle was now entering upon a new phase because since the victory of Wagram and the marriage to Marie Louise the great London banking houses were becoming seriously alarmed. Napoleon had deposed his brother Louis from the throne of Holland and had put a stop to the smuggling of English goods into that country. He had seized the Papal States and closed all the Italian ports. The Emperor Alexander continued to support him if only in a half-hearted way. Prussia was crushed, Austria mollified.

In these circumstances the birth of a son to Marie Walewska came as welcome news. No Pole but saw in the child a possible

King of Poland when Napoleon should be strong enough to raise that stricken country once again to independent sovereignty. Marie Louise's pregnancy added a fresh support. The Imperial system, it seemed, was to have heirs after all—heirs too, who would carry on, if needs be, the battle against the bankers.

But history had proved already that the monopolists of gold are never so dangerous as when they are fighting in the last ditch. Their beloved metal was flowing out of London, now, in a strong tide. They girded themselves for a supreme effort.

It took the form of a tentative approach to the people in France who might be supposed to exert influence with Napoleon. Josephine was gone and Talleyrand remained in disgrace but Fouché was still the Minister of Police. To the ex-butcher of Lyons, therefore, the great houses of London addressed themselves. Fouché lent a willing ear, partly because his thirst for wealth was insatiable, partly because his keen vision detected the flaws in Napoleon's strength. Fouché managed to get Ouvrard released from prison. Between them they established relations with the Hopes in Amsterdam and the Barings in London, using as a go-between Sir Francis Baring's son-in-law, Labouchere. At the same time James Rothschild in Paris and his brother Nathan in London were associated with the plan.

This consisted in compromising Napoleon's relations with the Russian Emperor. It had been agreed that, in the matter of peace with England, France and Russia should act together. The object of the London money-lenders was to create, throughout Europe, the impression that Napoleon was trying to make peace on his own account and so to gain advantage over his ally. It was believed, correctly as it turned out, that the Emperor's preoccupation with his new Empress would make him less watchful than usual.

The plan succeeded. Napoleon remained completely in the dark until, by chance, he heard that Ouvrard was in Holland. He acted then with all his strength, dismissing Fouché and flinging Ouvrard back into prison. But the mischief was done.

The gloomy and suspicious Alexander was convinced that his ally had betrayed him, and no protests could shake that conviction. Russia began to arm; she opened her ports to English goods. The drain of gold out of London was staunched.

The tables, in short, had been turned on Napoleon because, without Alexander's co-operation, he was helpless. Nor would it avail him to invade and conquer Russia unless by so doing he could restore the lost friendship—an improbable outcome of conquest. He could not, with Frenchmen, police all the coasts of the Baltic.

He began, therefore, just after the birth of his son by Marie Louise, to woo Alexander anew. But his children and their mothers now had become a handicap rather than a help, because Alexander feared them so greatly. Marie Walewska's son might become King of Poland. Marie Louise's son might help Austria to weaken Russia. The coalition of enemies which, a few years earlier, had been grouped round Josephine began to form again, secretly, with the help of money from London. The divorced Empress, to her exceeding joy, found herself once more an important person whose help the statesmen of Europe were anxious to enlist.

The reason is obvious. Josephine was a Frenchwoman, whereas Marie Louise was German and Marie Walewska, Polish. It began to be whispered in Paris that Austrian Archduchesses brought no luck to French rulers and the name of Marie Antoinette was spoken dismally. What a pity the great alliance, Napoleon–Josephine, had been broken! A vigorous propaganda in Josephine's favour began. She was depicted as the loving and broken-hearted wife who, as a good Frenchwoman, had sacrificed all for France. But was the sacrifice justified? True, Napoleon had an heir. But the boy was a German. Better, surely, if Josephine's grand-son, Louis Bonaparte's boy, had been appointed to the succession. Napoleon was presented as a hard-hearted man who had driven away a good wife in order to gratify his vanity by marrying a daughter of the Cæsars. He was a snob. Worse still, he was no Frenchman. Would a Frenchman have sacrificed a woman of his own race for a German woman, however high born? And so on. With the prospect of a new war—this time in Russia—before their eyes, the French took Josephine back to their hearts.

As a result, angry protests against a war with Russia began to be heard, and Alexander was encouraged, by London, to believe that on this occasion Napoleon would not be able to take the field. The result was a further opening of Russia to English goods. Josephine seized the occasion to demand more money from her former husband. She was told:

August 25, 1811.

" Put some order into your affairs. Spend only £60,000 a year and save as much again every year. This will give you a reserve of £600,000 in ten years for your grandchildren. It is pleasant to be able to give them something and to be helpful to them. Instead of that I hear you have debts which would, really, be too bad. Look after your affairs and don't give to everyone who wants to help himself. If you wish to please me, let me hear that you have accumulated a large fortune. Consider how ill I must think of you, if I know that you, with £120,000 a year, are in debt."

Josephine did not want to please him and she knew that she could make him pay. A few days later he wrote:

" Don't worry any more about the present embarrassment."

But if he paid, he kept close watch. Josephine was growing more dangerous every day because her popularity was continually rising. She returned from the country house of Navarre, to which he had sent her, and took up her abode at Malmaison. " People," in Hortense's words, " flocked to see her."

The number of these visitors increased as the wooing of Alexander more and more failed of its purpose. Napoleon turned from blandishments to threats in his treatment of the Russian and once again his sons and their mothers became politically important. He talked about making Poland into a separate Kingdom and he demanded assurances of help from Austria if he was forced to attack Russia. Josephine was told to leave Paris and go to Milan where her son Eugene's wife was expecting another child. Soon after the Emperor and Marie Louise had left for Dresden, *en route,* in his case, for Poland, she crossed the Alps into Italy. After the confinement she went to Aix where two old acquaintances were waiting for her— namely the sisters Desirée and Julie Clary.

As has been said, they had begun life, these two, as the daughters of a Marseilles silk merchant. But Julie, who had married Joseph Bonaparte, was now Queen of Spain, while Desirée, as Bernadotte's wife, was Princess Royal of Sweden. That stroke of fortune had come to Bernadotte because long ago Desirée had been jilted in favour of Josephine. Napoleon knew that this man was his enemy, the friend of Germaine de Staël and of London. Nevertheless, he had helped him to become the heir of the King of Sweden.

That weakness for his old love was proving now a severe embarrassment because Bernadotte, in Stockholm, was making overtures to Alexander and to the English, and was doing his best to help English trade in the Baltic.

Napoleon, meanwhile, continued to exert his utmost endeavours, by cajolery and threats, to re-establish friendly relations with Alexander. At Dresden, his father-in-law, the Emperor Francis of Austria, had welcomed him with his whole Court and the town was full of German princelings. A French and Allied army of half a million men was already on the march towards Poland, where a national welcome awaited it. The greatest Captain of modern time was to lead this, the greatest host ever before assembled for battle.

Nevertheless, couriers rode out ahead of the troops with letters to Alexander urging him to return, even yet, to his former friendship. Courier succeeded to courier on the long, long road. Then special envoys were sent—among them

Louis de Narbonne, Germaine de Staël's old friend, who had espoused the Emperor's cause. Alexander received the couriers and the envoys with courtesy. But he refused to commit himself. The armies marched on and on. . . .

While they marched Germaine de Staël resolved to arrive in Russia before them. Since the death of Eric Magnus she had stormed her way from liaison to liaison. The reason was that her beloved Benjamin Constant had grown tired of her, in much the same way as Napoleon had grown tired of Josephine. He was exhausted, played out, flogged, so that capacity for feeling anything had been lost. The woman, with her iron will, her iron assertiveness, her personality, her greed, her vanity, her courage, her ability, her noisy and insatiable passions, her jealousy, her theatrical and hysterical emotions, above all, her sheer physical strength, had beaten him. He had one object only in life—to escape. But she gripped him as a poulterer grips a rabbit. Her father's death, which occurred while she was in Germany, afforded a serviceable way of bringing Benjamin back to heel. He had gone to meet her with the sad news. She tore herself and him to pieces in the excess of her affliction. A letter which she wrote from Weimar to her cousin contains the postscript from Benjamin :

" I'll add only a word. I can't conceive of anything more touching, more angelic. How can I console her ? For, except for the unjust reproaches which she heaps on herself, I share all her feelings about the great spirit whom she has lost. Adieu, I dare not torture my eyes any more . . ."

Germaine composed a prayer which set Necker in High Heaven. From the lawn of Coppet she saw, on Mt. Blanc :

" A cloud like a man's face which disappeared towards evening."

" There was nobody like him," she wrote to Gouverneur Morris in America, " there never will be anybody like him. I've lost, not my father only, but my friend, my brother, the best part of me, the only noble part of me . . ."

Napoleon heard the news and remarked :

" She may well regret her father. Poor divinity. Never was a more commonplace man, with his *flon flon*, his self-importance and his columns of figures."

Necker left his daughter a quarter of a million pounds, part of which, however, was in France, in Napoleon's keeping. She was, therefore, one of the richest women in Europe. But wealth no longer attracted Benjamin. When the hurricane of grief blew by he began, once more, to gnaw at the door of his prison. He refused to go to Italy with her. When she returned (having lost her heart simultaneously to Monti, the poet, and a young Austrian officer called Maurice O'Donnell), Benjamin was whipped back to his duty.

" There's going to be an explosion," he wrote in his diary. " The news from Paris is bad ; the Master (Napoleon) is inexorable. I've had to take the kicks. This evening a scene, incredible, horrible, senseless, vile abuse. She's mad or I'm mad. How will it end ? "

A little later he wrote :

" Alas, if I could only get away from these unceasing lamentations about unreal troubles, about the laws of Nature, about old age. Truth to tell I've no stomach for this job of being the butt of the complaints of a woman whom youth is forsaking. If only she wouldn't demand love of me—after a liaison ten years old, when we're both nearly forty, and when I've told her, a hundred times, that I haven't got any love left. I've never gone back on that plain statement ; except temporarily, to soothe her convulsions of grief and rage which frighten me. Since my feelings have no correspondence with my actions, I do wish that these actions, so feeble in any case, were no longer required of me. I must rescue my life from her either by becoming merely her friend or by running away. . . . It's too bad, not to have the pleasure to which one sacrifices dignity nor yet the dignity to which one sacrifices pleasure."

In fact he had met again his former mistress, Charlotte von Hardenberg (who had been divorced by her husband and had married a certain M. Dutertre), and had lived with her once more.

" Mad day, but delicious by reason of love," he had noted in his diary at the time. " During twelve long years I've not known such enjoyment. It's too wildly absurd. This woman whom I've rejected a hundred times, who has never ceased to love me, whom I've thrust away and left without a qualm during the past eighteen months, from whom, only last Monday, I took back my letters—this woman to-day has completely captured my heart.

" I believe that the reason lies in the contrast between her and Mme de Staël—between Mme de Staël's impetuousness, egoism and constant preoccupation with herself and Charlotte's sweetness, calmness and humility. These last qualities have made Charlotte a hundred times dearer to me than the other. I'm weary to death of the man-woman whose iron hand has gripped me for ten years and especially so now when I have another woman who seduces and charms me."

But Charlotte lacked fire.

" Spent the evening with Charlotte," he noted later. " Is the fever passing ? And boredom beginning ? I'm devilishly afraid of it. She has much charm, truly ; but little variety, and her feelings are dreadfully disturbing."

Back in Germaine's clutches, Charlotte began to look to him more like an angel than ever. At last, in despair, he told Germaine about his affair.

" Ungrateful scoundrel, deceiver, liar," she screamed.

She rang for the servants and when they came flung herself, yelling, on the floor. The whole household rushed to her help and Benjamin was defeated.

" Horrible scene," he noted, " which lasts till five o'clock in the morning. I am violent ; I glory in my fault. The best thing will be to slip away without previous warning."

He did go—to Lausanne. Then he changed his mind and rushed back. He asked Germaine to marry him. Instantly the house resounded once more with summoning bells. The *salon* filled up. Germaine pointed to Benjamin and addressed her children, one of whom was his own daughter.

" Look at this fellow," she shrieked, " he gives me the choice between your ruin and my death. If I marry him, as he suggests, you'll lose everything ; if he leaves me, as he wants to do, the deceiver, I shall die."

Down she went on to the floor, screaming and kicking, with a handkerchief twisted round her sturdy neck. Benjamin went to bed. At dawn he rose and saddled his horse. He rode at full gallop back to Lausanne, to his cousin Rosalie. He went up, at once, to bed. He had only just fallen asleep when a carriage dashed up to the door. Rosalie sprang upstairs and locked Benjamin's door on the outside. Then she admitted Germaine. On being told that Benjamin was not available, Germaine flung herself down, tore her hair and her clothing and uttered terrible screams.

" Where is Benjamin ? " she shrieked. " I must see Benjamin."

She tried to ascend the stair. Rosalie barred the way.

" Wretched hypocrite," cried Germaine in threatening tones, " it's you who is taking him from me. He's here. I knew it. And I shall see him."

Benjamin awoke. He trembled. Then he began to knock on the door of his room, asking for release. Rosalie abandoned the field. When Benjamin emerged Germaine threw herself at his feet.

" She came," the diary recounts, " she threw herself at my feet. Fearful shrieks, full of anguish and desolation, broke from her lips. A heart of iron could not have resisted her. Here I am back with her at Coppet. I've promised to stay six weeks. And Charlotte expects me. What am I to do ? Good God, I'm trampling future and happiness under my feet. . . .

" People who accuse me of weakness cannot judge me truly.

To know what they'd do in my position, they must be in my position and (I say it with deep conviction) I believe that to do better than I am doing one would have to be a less decent fellow."

Suddenly Germaine decided to go to Vienna to hunt up Maurice O'Donnell and also, if possible, take a hand with the financiers of Germany and Austria, against Napoleon. Benjamin was allowed to slip away. She drove in great state into the Austrian capital and immediately began to give theatrical performances. Another diarist noted of one of these—the presentation of *Hagar and Ishmael* which she had herself written :

" Mme de Staël was in sandals in her part of Hagar ; you could see all her toes. Her big toe was in convulsions when her body was in action. . . . It's much to be wished that one could avoid seeing her fat, heavy, masculine face which is so terribly badly matched to her part.

" She was dressed in the skins of animals, with dishevelled hair."

The methods which had been perfected in the case of Benjamin were now brought to bear on Maurice. But this young man was in love with his cousin, Flore de Ligne, and responded coldly, saying that he was ill. She demanded, on hearing this, that he should accept her as his nurse and wanted to come and live in his house. But he excused himself.

" What's the use," she wrote violently, " of this sort of life which fame allows me, if I can't do here what would be simplicity itself in France ? Dear Maurice, do you suppose that a world writhing under a tyrant's heel, is concerned that you and I should sacrifice the sweetest affections of our hearts."

To no purpose. She began to think, once more, about Benjamin and wrote to him :

" When I receive a kind letter from you, it helps me during two or three days. But then I tell myself that your liking for me is a thing of the past and that I deceive myself in allowing my soul to lean upon yours. God disposes of us all. I come back with the same attachment to you, an attachment which no neglect can weaken, an attachment which does not permit that you be compared with anyone else on earth. My heart, my life, all are yours if you wish them, in whatever way you wish them. Think about that. . . . The only thing that does my soul any good is tender treatment from you. I want nothing but that. . . . Love me but one hundredth part as much as I love you."

A few days later, on leaving Vienna, she wrote to Maurice from the second post-house.

" Ah, give me, all my life, the joy of loving you. . . . Noble friend of my heart, helper who cannot fail, I give you all the powers of my soul. . . . I took ill at this second post-house and they had to lay me on the grass by the roadside. I thought of the protecting goodness of my friend. I asked myself if all the care that was being taken of me possessed any value at all as compared with the words ' Dear Child ' which your ravishing voice has so often spoken. Ah, never, never forget that I cannot live without you. Your soul is a treasure of heaven. . . . I'll make you more religious and you'll make me more worthy to be religious. . . . We will lead, I hope, our common life with a noble object in view. And when, as must happen, I precede you into the next world, I will go to wait for you beside my father, to whom I will say that, for the first time since his leaving me, hope of strength in another was given me by you."

Maurice did not greatly relish the prospect of eternity spent in Jacques' company. He did not hurry his reply. Meanwhile Germaine busied herself in plotting with German money-lenders against Napoleon. He heard about it and wrote to Fouché from Bayonne :

" I enclose some letters which have passed between Mme de Staël and the man named Gentz. Mme de Staël has become mixed up with the clique of German plotters and with the financiers in London (who are egging them on). Please place this woman under police supervision at Coppet and give orders accordingly to the Prefect of Geneva and the Commander of the Gendarmerie. Her relations with Gentz cannot but do France harm. Until now I've looked on her as a mere fool ; now, as I want you to understand, I place her among those who are trying to disturb the public peace. I've instructed my Foreign Minister to inform all my agents at foreign Courts about this change of attitude and to tell them to keep a sharp eye on her wherever she goes."

Napoleon had penetrated the political design which, as usual in Germaine's case, underlay the amorous adventure. Austria was preparing for the war which, as has been recounted, was to end at Wagram. Money was needed. The money-lender's daughter had business to transact other than the business of giving theatrical performances and making offers of marriage to boys. Indeed, her letter to Benjamin suggests that the O'Donnell affair may have been " staged " for Napoleon's benefit— though that is doubtful in the case of so Gargantuan an appetite for love. In any case, she sent Maurice O'Donnell sums of money with the assurance that she had an income of £5000 a year, without a penny of debt.

Benjamin, meanwhile, was spending his time burning old love-letters.

" I gaze on all these letters," he wrote to a friend, " written by hands which are now dust, on those letters which can no longer be answered, to which, when I did answer them, I opposed so many arguments based on life and circumstance and the future—all those arguments, all those uncertainties, all that future, are buried in graves which have, themselves, disappeared."

He was wondering whether or not he should marry Charlotte before " my harpy " returned from Vienna. He consulted his old father, who urged that, since Charlotte's second husband had now divorced her, the marriage ought to take place at once. A secret wedding, accordingly, was solemnized, though, strangely enough, in an illegal form which made it invalid. Benjamin took his bride to Lausanne and introduced her to Rosalie. Then he set out for Coppet to tell Germaine.

But his nerve was not equal to that task. When, once more, he found himself in the shattering presence, he began to lie. He proposed, so he confessed, to marry Charlotte in the autumn.

" I've had it out with Benjamin," wrote Germaine to Maurice.

Maurice answered that letter by a note to the effect that he was finished with her—a note which set her screaming vocally and on paper during several weeks, for example :

" I swear before God that I have loved you and do love you with all my soul. . . . I call God and one of His Saints, my father, to witness again that I have loved you and do love you. . . . The only real things in life are religion and the capacity to love. . . . When I try to rise up I have to cling to things, and I tremble frequently. . . . If you never wish to hear again that voice which has told you that it loves with such abandon and enthusiasm, my decision is taken. I shall go to America. . . . You exile me with a force equal to Bonaparte's."

But her broken heart did not interfere with her plottings. Since she could not now go to Paris herself, she kept in touch with her friends there through Juliette Récamier, the banker's wife, who received every night the Austrian Ambassador, Metternich, and his wife. Thus there was constant going and coming of messages between Paris and Coppet and Coppet and Vienna—while Austria armed to attack Napoleon, who was still far away in Spain.

" I regard as my personal enemy," wrote The Emperor, " every foreigner who shows himself in Madame Récamier's *salon*."

Meanwhile Benjamin had remained separated from his wife to

whom he did not dare to return. In his abject humiliation, however, he continued to talk about his " marriage in the autumn." A guest at Coppet, a woman, wrote :

" Mme de Staël is frightfully upset just now because of the forthcoming marriage of Benjamin, fixed for this autumn. She's refused, during the past six years, to marry him herself, but she can't endure the idea of his marrying somebody else. This contradiction no doubt looks absurd enough, but for those who know the human heart, it's easy to understand. It's our thwarted wills and the contrasts in our natures which add the touch of reality.

" Mme de Staël has forbidden all those who surround her and all who come to see her to utter a word about the event which occupies and devours her mind. She wishes to find the means of resigning herself in her own spirit and she has turned upon one or two people who have tried to discuss the matter. They have complained to me of the treatment suffered by them.

" Benjamin leaves here in September or October to go and get married and establish himself in Paris with his wife, where his house awaits him."

Napoleon's victory over the Austrians came as a cruel blow. Germaine resolved to go once more to England and then, suddenly, changed her mind and wrote to the Emperor, asking leave to come to Paris to study art. This request, as it happened, came at the time when Fouché was plotting to cause a quarrel between his master and the Emperor Alexander of Russia. Nor is it, certainly, without significance that Metternich, who had returned to Paris as Austrian Ambassador, pleaded Germaine's cause. They had been associated already, these two, in the plottings which preceded the Wagram campaign.

" I don't want Mme de Staël back here in Paris," Napoleon told Metternich. " And I've got the best possible reasons for my decision. It's no concern of mine if Mme de Staël is a Royalist or a Republican, and I should have nothing against her on these counts ; but she's an agitator who excites the *salons*. It's only in France that a woman of that kind is dangerous. I don't want her to come back."

He suppressed her book *On Germany*. A great bitterness descended upon her which the absence of Benjamin did nothing to alleviate. Benjamin had gone away. Would he really dare to get married ? Would he ever come back ? One day she received a message from him asking her to come to the hotel at Séchéron, between Geneva and Lausanne. Charlotte received her at the hotel :

" I am Mme Constant," said Charlotte, " and my husband . . ."

" Mme Constant ! My husband ! What do you mean ? "

" We were married a year ago."

At this frightful piece of news Germaine unloosed all her passions. Charlotte, terrified, whimpered that Benjamin was a " good man."

" Good ! He ! Good !" screamed Germaine. " He's the biggest blackguard on earth. The vainest, the most unfeeling that any woman could meet for her undoing. Good . . . ! Listen to me, Mme, I've loaded this fellow with benefits. If he counts for anything to-day he owes his distinction wholly to me. I lifted him out of obscurity, out of total darkness. I've given him everything, everything. Madame, do you hear ? And the only thanks I've had are ingratitude and betrayal."

Charlotte continued to whimper.

" Where is he ? " shouted Germaine. " Where is the coward skulking ? I insist on seeing him."

Benjamin was behind the door with his knees giving way under him. He came crouching in. Germaine lashed him to helplessness in a few seconds. He begged forgiveness. Charlotte, too. Both promised to obey any orders which might be given them. Germaine ordered that the marriage should be kept secret and that Benjamin should come back with her, at once, to Coppet. They accepted, pleading for a few minutes to bid one another farewell. When they were alone Charlotte wept bitterly. She left at once, nevertheless, for Benjamin's father's house.   He returned to Germaine.

But only for punishment.   She was done with him.   He had to witness a number of passing affairs.   Then, when " John " Rocca appeared, he was allowed to slink away.   But he came back again—to see the pretty Italian boy, about whom Germaine was now raving, established in his stead.   It was the strangest of all Germaine's love affairs, for Rocca was twenty-two and she forty-five, and he loved her.   Even she had boggled, protesting her motherhood to give him chance of escape.   But no, that overpowering nature, in all its ugliness, had captured his imagination.

" I'll love her so much," vowed the gallant lad, who had been sorely wounded, as a second-lieutenant of Huzzars, in one of Napoleon's campaigns, " that she'll end by marrying me."

He taught his horse to kneel to her and that won her heart. They were married secretly at Coppet in the year 1811.   Benjamin did not know that it was a husband this time and not a lover with whom he had to deal.   A jealous husband, too.   Benjamin indulged his wit ; he found himself challenged instantly to a duel.   Terror seized upon him and he made his will.   But Germaine saved him by calling off her " young barbarian."

The secrecy of the marriage was due to the fact that, by it, she had made herself a subject of Napoleon, and lost at the same time the right to her illustrious name.   Unhappily she became pregnant and had to pretend that she was suffering from dropsy. The truth leaked out and a Parisian wit wrote :

> " Even her dropsy as we see,
> Is destined for posterity."

The journey to Russia began as soon as the child—a boy— had been boarded out with Dr. Juvine of Longerod in the Jura. That great *berline*, which had borne its mistress all over Europe, to Prussia and Austria and Rome and Naples, as well as to Paris, was made ready once more and sent away empty from Coppet.

On May 23, 1812, while Napoleon was still junketing with the Kings at Dresden and despatching his couriers to Alexander :

"At two o'clock in the afternoon I entered my carriage, remarking that I would be back for dinner. I took no luggage of any sort with me. I carried my fan in my hand. My daughter had hers also. My son and M. Rocca had stuffed their pockets with such articles as were indispensable for a journey of a few days."

She travelled day and night at the utmost speed of which her horses were capable. The *berline* was waiting near Berne. In that huge carriage she drove into Vienna on June 6. A hitch occurred, but on July 14, the anniversary, as she duly noted, of the taking of the Bastille, she crossed the Russian frontier, vowing, as she did so, never again to set foot in any country under Napoleon's rule. On that same day, away to the North, he was advancing through Russian territory at the head of his Grand Army. She was racing him, chasing him, to Moscow.

Orders had been sent out from Petersburg to receive her with honour. But the Russian squires needed no prompting. Was she not, now, by reason of her quarrel with Napoleon and her stubborn resistance to him, the most famous woman in Europe ? The resounding success of her novels, her reputation as the Corsican's martyr, her close associations with the London money-lenders and the *réclame* which always surrounded her, had made of her almost a figure of legend. Everywhere, by Russians, Swedes, Englishmen, Germans, Spaniards, Frenchmen, Italians, she was called the high priestess of Liberty. A world weary to death of Napoleon and his wars, the object of which was hidden from all, called her blessed and made of her the Mother-Superior of the Sisterhood of Europe.

So quickly did she travel that she had to change her route in order to avoid the French Army. She gazed, day after day, on the wide, sad spaces of the steppes through which her carriage rolled and noted the long horizons, the puny villages and the sense of immobility. Life, she thought, found its complete expression, here, in the silhouette, seen now and again, of a Cossack on his lean nag, with his long lance trailing across the sky. The people who crowded to see her :

" Saw a big fat woman of fifty dressed in a fashion very little suited to her age."

She dashed through Moscow and drove on to Petersburg. The first sight which greeted her in this latter city was the Union Jack flying at the mast-head of an English ship.

" I felt," she wrote, " that in confiding myself to the ocean, I should be passing into the powerful keeping of God."

A few days later she met Alexander, the liberal ruler of whom it had been said " He wants men to be free so that they may be able to do what he tells them." They agreed wonderfully together, especially when she promised to bring Bernadotte over, solidly, to the Russian side.

" Sire," I said to him (she wrote), " your character is a Constitution for your Empire and your conscience is its guarantee."

She left immediately for Stockholm, was nearly wrecked on the island of Aland, and did not reach her destination until September 24, 1812. Not a moment too soon, because Napoleon's victory over the Russians at the Borodino had so terrified Bernadotte that he was thinking of attacking Alexander after all. She spent days and nights with this timid man, strengthening his resolve and curbing his fears. Had she not done so he would, almost certainly, have attacked Russia through Finland. And if he had done that Alexander, on unimpeachable showing, would have made peace with Napoleon.

As it was the Emperor of the French sat, amid the smoking ruins of Moscow, awaiting the offer of friendship which never came. Winter was at hand. The French Revolution had marched to its appointed end—the destruction of the old system of Europe and the victory, complete and overwhelming, of the owners of gold.

CONCLUSION

CHAPTER XXVIII

CURTAIN

A YEAR and a half later, Germaine de Staël travelled down from the Channel to Paris to salute the new dispensation which Napoleon's fall and banishment, to Elba, had inaugurated. She had just crossed from England, from which country Louis XVIII, with a loan of £20,000 in his pocket, supplied, thoughtfully, by Nathan Rothschild, had gone also to France. In Paris, Josephine was receiving the Emperor Alexander and all the Allied sovereigns, Napoleon's conquerors, as though they were her best friends. Marie Louise, with Napoleon's little son, had already made surrender to her father, the Emperor Francis, and was on her way with her boy back to Vienna.

At Fontainebleau, Napoleon alone and deserted prepared to bid good-bye to his Guard—all that was left of half a million men. One night a carriage drove into the great courtyard of the *Cheval blanc* and a woman descended. It was Marie Walewska. She was told that the Emperor was sleeping. She forbade his servants to disturb him. But she left a letter. His reply was despatched on the following day. It ran :

" Marie, I got your letter of the 15th April. The feelings you cherish for me touch me to the quick. They are worthy of your loving soul and of the goodness of your heart."

Josephine contracted diphtheria a month later, on May 26, 1814. She had been expecting Alexander of Russia to dinner, in order to discuss with him her plan for obtaining pensions for herself and her son and daughter from Louis XVIII.   Though ill, she dressed herself in pink satin.   The disease advanced with terrible swiftness, and the party was postponed.   But she remained in her pink satin until she died.   Three years later, while Napoleon wearied and grew old at Longwood on St. Helena, Germaine de Staël had a stroke at a reception in Paris.   Her death took place at five o'clock in the morning of July 14, of glorious memory.

INDEX

A

Alexander I, Emperor of Russia, 233, 236, 238, 257, 258, 263, 266, 267, 268, 280, 281
American War of Independence, 53
Arcole, Battle of, 199
Artois, Comte d', 221
Aspern-Essling, battle of, 259
Assembly, the Legislative, 108 et seq.
Assembly, the National, 81, 83, 107
Assignats, the, 93 et seq.

B

Baden, Prince of, 238
Baring, House of, 204, 225
Barras, Comte de, 131 et seq., 155 et seq.
Bastile, taking of the, 83
Bavaria, the Princess Augusta of, 238
Beauharnais, Alexandre de, 100 et seq., 152, 153, 238, 239
Beauharnais, Hortense de. See Hortense, Queen
Beauharnais, Eugène de, 199, 210, 211, 238
Beauharnais, Marquis de, 100
Beauharnais, Mme. See Josephine.
Beauharnais, Stephanie de, 238
Bernadotte, Marshal, 215, 268
Berthier, Marshal, 200
Berwick, Duke of, 35
Besenval, General, 82, 84, 85
Billaud-Varennes, 126
Bonaparte, Caroline, 238, 239
Bonaparte, Joseph, 191, 198, 206, 219, 226
Bonaparte, Louis, 233, 234, 238, 258
Bonaparte, Lucien, 211, 225, 226, 234
Bonaparte, Madame. See Josephine
Bonaparte, Napoleon. See Napoleon.
Bonaparte, Pauline, 202, 234
Borghese, Prince, 234
Borodino, battle of the, 281
Boufflers, Chevalier de, 228
Bourrienne, 119, 205, 206

Brienne, Lomenie de, 70, 74
Brissot, 108
Buonaparte, Mère, 191, 201 et seq., 210, 225, 259

C

Cabarras, 105, 155, 204, 205, 225, 227, 237
Cabarras, Thérèse. See Tallien, Mme
Calonne, 63, 64, 70
Cambon, 146
Campan, Mme, 210
Canning, 258
Carnot, 145
Carrier, 155
Castellane, 119
Catherine, Empress of Russia, 33
Charles II, 19
Charles, Hippolyte, 198, 199, 204 et seq., 238
Chateaubriand, 228
Châteauroux, Mme de, 21 et seq., 26
Chimay, Prince de, 227
Choiseul, duc de, 36, 38, 39
Churchill, John, 20
Clary, Desirée, 215, 268
Clary, Julie, 268
Collot d'Herbois, 126, 155
Committee of Public Security, 145
Commune, the Revolutionary, 118, 125
Condorcet, 108, 125
Constant, Benjamin, 175 et seq., 202 et seq., 213 et seq., 226 et seq., 269 et seq.
Constant, Rosalie, 183, 272
Constant, Napoleon's valet, 251, 252, 260
Corday, Charlotte, 140
Custine, 113

D

Danton, 86, 88, 110 et seq. ; execution of, 159
Danton, Antoinette, 120
Danton, Louise, 145, 147, 159
Desmoulins, Camille, 120

285

Diamond Necklace, the, 57, 60, 61
Diderot, 49
Dubarry, Mme, 35 *et seq.*, 47, 61, 80 ; execution of, 154
Dubarry, Jean, 35
Dubarry, William, 35
Duclos, 26
Dumonceaux, 35
Dumouriez, General, 35, 114
Duplay, 158
Duroc, 242 *et seq.*

E

Elizabeth, Mme, 124
Emperor, the, 113, 198
Enghien, duc d', 237

F

Fersen, Count, 47, 70, 99, 111
Feuillants, the, 108 *et seq.*
Fontenay, Mme de. *See* Tallien, Mme
Fontenoy, battle of, 22
Foquier-Tinville, 142, 151, 154
Fouché, Joseph, 131 *et seq.*, 155 *et seq.*, 216, 217, 222, 225, 226, 254 *et seq.*, 258, 259, 264, 265, 274
Francis, Emperor of Austria, 236
Frederick the Great, 21, 30, 31, 32, 33, 239
Fréron, Stanislas, 131 *et seq.*, 155 *et seq.*, 202

G

Gentz, 274, 275
Gerando, 220
Gibbon, 49, 137
Girondists, the, 108 *et seq.*
Gohir, 205
Gouvernet, 119
Gustavus III of Sweden, 114, 238

H

Hardenburg, Charlotte von, 271 *et seq.*, 278 *et seq.*
Hébert, 151
Hope, the House of, 204, 213, 225
Hortense, Queen, 187, 192, 199, 210, 211, 233, 238, 260, 262, 267

J

Jacobins, the, 108 *et seq.*
Jena, battle of, 239
Josephine, the Empress, 100 *et seq.*, 152 *et seq.*, 171 *et seq.* and thereafter continuously
Jouberthou, Mme, 234
Joucourt, 104, 124 *et seq.*, 149
Junot, 205, 206, 232

L

Lafayette, 63, 83, 90 *et seq.*, 104, 113, 121
Lally-Tolendal, 104, 119, 124, 125
Lamballe, Mme de, 126, 131
Lameths, the, 104
Laurangais, Mme de, 21
Ligne, duc de, 35
Louis XIV, 19, 20, 33, 39, 225
Louis XV, 20 *et seq.*, 61, 68, 154, 225
Louis XVI, 35, 41 *et seq.*, ; execution of, 134, 215, 224, 225
Louis XVII, 180
Louis XVIII, 180, 184, 221, 259, 282, 283

M

Mailly, Mme de, 20, 21, 26
Manuel, 125, 126, 128, 129
Marat, 110 *et seq.*
Marengo, Battle of, 220, 223
Marie Antoinette, 35, 41 *et seq.* ; execution of, 151, 152, 215
Marie Louise, 263 *et seq.*
Maria Theresa, 31, 32, 33, 40, 41, 43, 72
Mary, Queen of England, 19
Maupeou, 38, 39
Metternich, 254, 258, 259, 277
Mirabeau, 77 *et seq.*, 108, 125, 224, 225
Monarchy, fall of the French, 118
Monnier, Sophie de, 78 *et seq.*, 87, 101
Monti, the poet, 270
Montmorency, Mathieu de, 85, 104, 119, 136, 149, 174 *et seq.*, 221
Montmorency-Laval, Mme de, 221
Morris, Gouverneur, 86, 87, 269
Murat, 238, 239, 245

N

Napoleon, 119, 146, 173, 181 *et seq.*
Narbonne, Louis de, 67, 85, 104, 111 *et seq.*, 119, 121 *et seq.*, 137, 149, 150, 174, 221, 269

National Guard, the, 83, 85, 91
Necker, Jacques, 48 *et seq.*, 136, 174, 177, 182, 183, 209, 212, 219, 220, 221, 225, 230, 257, 269
Necker, Mme, 48 *et seq.*, 74, 94, 137, 174
Necker, Germaine. *See* Staël, Mme de
Nile, Battle of the, 204
Normant, le, de Journheim, 24
Normant, le, d'Étoiles, 24

O

O'Donnell, Maurice, 270, 273 *et seq.*
Orleans, Regent, 20
Orléans, duc d', 93
Ouvrard, 174, 204 *et seq.*, 211, 212, 213, 225, 227, 228, 237, 265

P

Pasquier, Chancellor, 186
Pétion, 108
Plaigne, Eléanore la, 239, 240, 254
Poland, partition of, 33, 243 *et seq.*
Polignac, Mme de, 48
Pompadour, Mme de, 24 *et seq.*, 36, 37, 38, 39, 41, 56, 243
Poniatowski, Prince, 242 *et seq.*
Pope, the, crowns Napoleon, 228, 234, 237

R

Récamier, Mme, 215, 220, 228, 232, 275
Reign of Terror, the, 160 *et seq.*
Rémusat, Mme de, 234
Renaudin, Mme, 100, 198
Ribbing, Count de, 174
Richelieu, duc de, 35
Robespierre, 86, 88, 107, 109 *et seq.*; execution of, 164, 165
Rocca, John, 279 *et seq.*
Roland, 109, 114 *et seq.*, 143
Roland, Mme, 109 *et seq.*; execution of, 147, 148
Rothschild, James, 265
Rothschild, Nathan, 265, 282
Rousseau, Jean Jacques, 51, 52, 74

S

St. Just, 163
Sanson, 135, 159

Santerre, 119, 128
Saxe, Marshal, 22
Ségur, 112
September Massacres, 129 *et seq.*
Seven Years' War, 32, 33, 34, 35, 39
Sieyès, the Abbé, 213, 214
Staël, Baron de, 64, 65, 83, 114, 122, 174, 177, 182, 218, 219, 229, 230, 269
Staël, Mme de, 60 *et seq.*, 202 *et seq.*, 254 *et seq.*, 269 *et seq.*
States General, the, 77, 80
Suard, 49
Swiss Guard, Massacre of, 118 *et seq.*

T

Talleyrand, 67, 85, 88, 104, 136, 149, 150, 202, 212, 216, 217, 221, 231, 258, 259, 264
Tallien, 122, 129, 131 *et seq.*, 152 *et seq.*
Tallien, Mme, 86, 88, 105, 133 *et seq.*, 138 *et seq.*, 155 *et seq.*, 197, 222, 225, 227, 237, 238, 240
Tascher, Baron, 100
Tascher-la-Pagerie, Mme, 185 *et seq.*
Tascher-la-Pagerie, Rose. *See* Josephine
Tour de Pin, 119
Tournelle, Mme de, 21
Turgot, 47, 50, 52, 53, 72

U

Ulm, battle of, 236

V

Valmy, battle of, 132
Varennes, flight to, 99, 100
Vauban, Mme de, 247, 250
Vergennes, 60
Vintimille, Mme de, 21
Visconti, 228
Voltaire, 28, 39

W

Wagram, battle of, 261
Walewska, Marie, 240 *et seq.*, 259, 260, 264, 282
Walewski, Count, 240 *et seq.*
William III, 19
Women, March of the, 90 *et seq.*